THE MONARCH OF WIT

BY THE SAME AUTHOR

The Metaphysical Poets: Donne, Herbert, Vaughan, Traherne
The Three Parnassus Plays (1598–1601)
Translating Horace
Themes and Variations in Shakespeare's Sonnets
The Art of Marvell's Poetry

TRANSLATIONS FROM RAINER MARIA RILKE
Requiem and Other Poems
Duino Elegies
Sonnets to Orpheus
From the Remains of Count C. W.
Poems (1906–1926)
Selected Works: Poetry
New Poems

TRANSLATIONS FROM HÖLDERLIN
Selected Poems

DONNE AS A YOUNG MAN

THE MONARCH OF WIT

AN ANALYTICAL AND COMPARATIVE
STUDY OF THE POETRY OF JOHN DONNE

J. B. Leishman
late Senior Lecturer in English Literature in the
University of Oxford and Fellow of St John's College

*Here lies a King, that rul'd as hee thought fit
The universall Monarchy of wit.*
THOMAS CAREW

HUTCHINSON UNIVERSITY LIBRARY
LONDON

HUTCHINSON & CO *(Publishers)* LTD
178–202 *Great Portland Street, London, W*1

London Melbourne Sydney
Auckland Bombay Toronto
Johannesburg New York

★

First published 1951
Second edition 1955
Third edition 1957
Fourth edition 1959
Fifth edition 1962
Sixth edition 1962
Reprinted 1965, 1967

This book has been set in Bembo, printed in Great Britain
by Balding & Mansell of London and Wisbech and
bound by Wm. Brendon of Tiptree, Essex

CONTENTS

ACKNOWLEDGEMENT

The portrait of John Donne as a young man which appears as the frontispiece to the hardcover edition of this book and on the cover of the paperback edition is reproduced by kind permission of the Trustees of the Marquis of Lothian. Painted *c.* 1595 by an unknown artist, it represents Donne as a victim of 'Lover's Melancholy', the Latin inscription ('Lighten our darkness, Mistress') being an irreverent parody of the prayer 'Lighten our darkness, we beseech thee, O Lord'. It was bequeathed by Donne to his friend Sir Robert Ker, ancestor of the present Marquis of Lothian, and was identified at Newbattle Abbey by Mr John Bryson, who described it in an article in *The Times* of 13 October 1959.

PREFACE TO THE FIFTH EDITION

IT IS now ten years since this book was first published, and, although I still think that it will be found useful, there are various things in Donne's poetry to which my attitude has changed, and about which I should now express myself differently.

It was what I originally wrote about 'Jest and Earnest' in the *Songs and Sonets* of which, as I re-read the book, I found myself making the most 'agonizing re-appraisal'. To re-write the whole section was impossible, but, by altering certain passages, I have perhaps been able to make it a less distorting mirror of the complex relationship between fact and fiction, actual and imagined situation, in these poems.

The re-setting has, though, at least enabled me to re-write my discussion (pages 66 to 70) of *The Expostulation* and the other more or less Donne-like elegies in Jonson's *Underwoods*, for the inadequacy of which I apologized in my Preface to the Second Edition. It is true that, since I no longer believe that Donne wrote *The Expostulation*, this discussion is not, in its place, strictly relevant. Had I been writing the book to-day, I might perhaps have found room for a general discussion of the resemblances and differences between Donne and his imitators in this kind of poetry; for *The Expostulation* is not the only elegy that has been wrongly ascribed to him: *Iulia* (XIII), *A Tale of a Citizen and his Wife* (XIV), and *Variety* (XVII) ought almost certainly to be excluded from the canon.

J. B. L.

Oxford
April 1961

PREFACE TO THE THIRD EDITION

I HAVE again taken the opportunity to make a few small corrections and alterations and to add one or two foot-notes.

J. B. L.

Oxford
February 1957

PREFACE TO THE SECOND EDITION

I HAVE taken the opportunity afforded by the call for a second edition to correct various misprints and to make such a minimum of small alterations in the text as is compatible with the present high cost of printing. There is indeed much more that I should have liked to alter, although even then I should still have been unable to persuade myself that I had written the last word, which, whether on Donne or any other subject, would seem to belong to the last man. I have little sympathy with that kind of criticism which seems to assume that there is some finally ascertainable 'truth', or 'point', about each author, and that, when this has once been stated, the blackboard may be wiped and the class dismissed. It was nearly always because they were so well expressed, so good in their kind, that I quoted, often in order to disagree with them or to suggest modifications of them, the views of other writers. If they had not existed, it would have been necessary to invent them—as speakers in a dialogue; for it is only, it seems to me, in writing that has some approximation to dialogue or discussion that such 'truth' as we may hope to reach in these matters can become apparent.

I purposely limited my discussion of the *Divine Poems* because I knew that the subject would be treated so much more fully and satis-factorily in the edition of them upon which my colleague Miss Helen Gardner was then engaged. This fine piece of scholarship has now been published, and it has led me, as I hope it will lead others, to modify many of my views. Some of the results of my reflections upon it I have been able to incorporate in the last pages of my book, from which I have removed what seemed to me, when 'to-morrow' came, some 'considerable residuum of nonsense'.

Had it been possible, I should have liked to rewrite the pages (65 to 67)[1] in which I have discussed *The Expostulation* and what some have regarded as the un-Jonsonian elegies in Jonson's *Underwoods*. I am now convinced that *The Expostulation* was not written by Donne and that it should be rejected from the canon: partly because it contains an amount of deliberate and detailed (as distinct from merely general) imitation of passages in Latin authors which, although thoroughly Jonsonian, is without parallel in Donne's other poems; and partly because it is a kind of poetry which, although Donne seems to have initiated it, soon came to find many imitators.

Finally, while describing (page 77)[2] various seventeenth-century collections of prose paradoxes, I unaccountably forgot to mention Donne's own *Paradoxes and Problems*, most (though not all) of which were written, as his son said in the preface to the 1652 edition of them, as 'the entertainment of the Author's Youth'.

J. B. L.

Oxford
September 1954

PREFACE TO THE FIRST EDITION

PUTTING first things first, I will begin by expressing my deep gratitude to the Delegates of the Clarendon Press for kindly allowing me to quote so liberally from Sir Herbert Grierson's great edition of *The Poems of John Donne* (1912); also to Sir Herbert Grierson himself for having laid so well and truly the foundations on which all serious study of Donne's poetry must rest.

Next, I must gratefully acknowledge the help received from my friends Professor John Butt, of King's College, Newcastle, and Professor Bernard Wright, of University College, Southampton, who read my proofs and enabled me to make some very important corrections and improvements.

In the course of this book I have often had occasion to criticize the views of other scholars and critics, all of whom I respect and from many of whom I have learnt much: I will therefore take this opportunity of publicly admitting that I have myself in past years both talked and written on the subject of John Donne as much (or almost

[1] Pp. 66 to 70 in the Fifth Edition.
[2] Pp. 79–80 in the Fifth Edition.

as much) of what now seems to me erroneous, or even nonsensical, as any of them. Since, as A. E. Housman once observed, great literary critics would seem to be a good deal rarer than great poets, it is but natural that most of us who meddle with the art should talk a great deal of nonsense. Perhaps the best we can hope for is that we should gradually come to perceive that it *was* nonsense, and that we should contrive to talk less nonsense as we grow older. There may, for all I know, still be some considerable residuum of nonsense in the pages that follow: I shall at least not be offended with any who may think so,

>For by to-morrow, I may thinke so too.

J. B. L.

St. John's College
Oxford

DONNE AND SEVENTEENTH-CENTURY
POETRY

IN the historical consideration of literature there are three dangers
against which we should be continually on our guard: the danger
that we may lose sight of the larger differences and distinctions
through concentrating too much attention upon the subsidiary
ones; the danger that we may pervert these subsidiary distinctions
into antitheses; the danger that within these subsidiary distinctions
we may insist too much upon identity and too little upon difference.
In the present field of study we have, on the one hand, heard
perhaps too much of a School of Jonson and a School of Donne,
of the classical and the so-called metaphysical strains in seventeenth-
century poetry, and not enough of those larger differences between
the characteristic non-dramatic poetry of the Age of Elizabeth
and that of the Jacobean and Caroline periods, differences in which
both Jonson and Donne equally share; while, on the other hand,
we have had, perhaps, too many generalizations about the so-called
metaphysical poets and not enough insistence on the very important
differences between them. It is, indeed, easier to perceive certain
obvious differences between the poetry of Donne and Jonson than
to perceive certain important resemblances, just as it is easier to
perceive certain superficial resemblances between, say, Donne and
Crashaw than to become aware of their fundamental differences.
The ultimate purpose of such generalizations, classifications and
distinctions is to increase awareness, to enable us, by analysis and
comparison, to achieve a clearer recognition, a more intense appre-
ciation, of the peculiar virtue, the essential *thisness*, of whatever
literature we may be studying; this, though, is a strenuous task,
and most of us, I fear, tend unconsciously to manipulate these
generalizations, classifications and distinctions, disregarding here,
over-emphasizing there, until we have spread over everything a
veil of custom and a film of familiarity which shall save us as much

as possible from the insupportable fatigue of thought. Donne has been too often considered as a so-called metaphysical poet and too little as a seventeenth-century poet (many characteristic seventeenth-century poets began to write during the reign of Elizabeth); let us begin, then, by trying to reach some not too inadequate conception of the characteristics of seventeenth-century poetry in general and of the principal differences and varieties within that fundamental identity.

That such a conception is both real and necessary is proved by the fact that the poetry of those two very individual and very different poets, Ben Jonson and John Donne, who are commonly regarded as the founders of two different schools, has many important characteristics in common. They were—to begin with an important fact which has received too little attention—they were both, in a sense, coterie-poets, poets who made their initial impact not upon the common reader but upon comparatively small circles of intellectuals and literary amateurs. Apart from his contributions to the facetious commendations of Thomas Coryat in the latter's *Crudities* (1611) and to the elegies on Prince Henry in *Lachrymae Lachrymarum* (1613), the only poems Donne printed during his lifetime were the two *Anniversaries* upon the religious death of Mistris Elizabeth Drury, in 1611 and 1612. The first collected edition of his poems was not published until 1633, two years after his death, and his great reputation as a poet during his life-time was gained entirely through the circulation of his poems in manuscript. Jonson, it is true, was a much more public poet than Donne: he wrote plays, which were not only acted, but published, under very careful supervision, by himself. Nevertheless, although, like his master Horace, he regarded poetry as his profession and did not shrink from publication, he too, though less exclusively and remotely than Donne, was the master, the *arbiter elegantiarum*, of a circle, of a coterie, of various young Templars and Courtiers who gathered round him in taverns, hung upon his words, begged copies of his verses, and were proud to be known as his sons.

When we speak, as we often do, of Jonson and Donne as the two great influences on the non-dramatic poetry of the first half of the seventeenth century, and when we think, as we often do, of that poetry chiefly in its relation to either or both of them, we should not forget that we are speaking and thinking only of that

portion of seventeenth-century poetry which we now chiefly read
and remember, and that much even of this poetry, easy, familiar,
harmlos (to borrow a German word) as it now seems to us, may
well have seemed quite exceptionally choice and sophisticated to
its writers and first readers. There are many seventeenth-century
poems which may seem to us only very superficially like Donne's,
but which at the time may well have seemed astonishingly *dernier
cri* and quite beyond the reach of simple-minded admirers of Forests
of Arden and Bowers of Bliss. Both Jonson and Donne were
superior persons, and both seem to have been well aware of their
superiority, but Donne, though far more urbane, was a much more
superior person than Jonson, and, except superficially, much less
imitable. Contemporary allusions to his poetry are few and far
between, and even quite advanced men seem to have remained
ignorant of it for an incredibly long time.[1] In the various miscel-

[1] All hitherto known contemporary allusions to Donne's poetry have recently
been collected (together with many discoveries of his own) by Mr. W. Milgate in
a series of articles in *Notes and Queries* (27th May, 10th June, 8th July, 2nd September,
1950). Perhaps the most remarkable result of these investigations is their revelation
of the extreme scarcity and comparative lateness of any definite allusions to Donne's
lyrics. Round about 1606 or 1608 Francis Davison, editor of the *Poetical Rapsody*
(1602), was compiling a list of 'Manuscripts to gett', and he noted, among other
things, 'Satyres, Elegies, Epigrams etc. by John Don. q^{re}· some from Eleaz. Hodgson,
and Ben: Johnson'. Thus as late as 1606 or 1608 even so enthusiastic a poetry-lover
as Francis Davison does not seem to have known (except, possibly, as an 'etc.')
that Donne had written lyrics. The first certainly dateable evidence that Donne's
lyrics were in circulation is a setting of *The Expiration* in Alfonso Ferrabosco's
Book of Ayres, 1609; the first reference to a (manuscript) 'book' of 'Jhone Dones
lyriques' occurs in a list made by William Drummond of Hawthornden of books
read by him during the year 1613. It was, as might be expected, for his Satires and
Epigrams, those of his poems least unlike what many of his contemporaries were
doing, and, to a lesser extent, for his Elegies (for which, it may be suggested,
Marlowe's translation of Ovid's *Amores* had prepared the ground) that Donne was
first admired. No surviving manuscript collection of his poetry bears an earlier date
than 1620. Indeed, it was during the late 1620s and the 1630s that most of the
surviving seventeenth-century manuscript commonplace-books (private anthologies,
one might call them), which in various ways owe so much to Donne, were put
together. It would seem to have been during those years that the change of taste
rather splenetically alluded to by Drayton in the Preface to the first part of his
Poly-olbion (1612) became really widely diffused, at any rate among courtiers and
university men, and that Ben Jonson was being in some sort its spokesman when, in
1619, he told Drummond that his poems were 'not after the fancie of the tyme'.
It would seem to have been during these years that, among what one may call the
literary amateurs, Donne's reputation and influence were at their height. Nevertheless, in discussing seventeenth-century poetic taste and the history of poetic reputations during that period, it seems necessary to make some distinction between what
I have called literary amateurs and common readers. In a very important letter to
the *Review of English Studies* (January, 1946), occasioned by Dr. Percy Simpson's
review of Professor G. E. Bentley's *Shakespeare and Jonson. Their Reputations in the*

lanies published between 1640 and 1660, whose contents seem to have
been derived partly from printed texts and partly from manuscript
commonplace-books, and which may be regarded as reflecting
fairly accurately the taste of the average cultivated gentleman of the
time of Charles I, both the number of Donne's poems included and
any obvious traces of his influence are remarkably small. The influence of Jonson, the epigrammatic rather than the moral Jonson, the
Jonson of 'Still to be neat, still to be drest', 'Come my Celia, let us
prove', and 'If I freely may discover', is far more striking. It is in the
wittily, often impudently, argumentative love-poem, and in the in-
decently, sometimes obscenely, witty 'elegy', epigram, or paradox,
that Donne's influence upon the secular poetry of the seventeenth
century is chiefly apparent.[1] Such poems, though, are more frequent
in the published works of particular poets (Carew, Suckling, Love-
lace, Cowley), and in certain manuscript collections, than in the
miscellanies, where the persistence both of the hearty Elizabethan
song and of the Elizabethan pastoral tradition is far more noticeable.
In the main, Donne's dialectic is simplified and his wit coarsened by
his imitators. One wonders what Donne thought of them. (It must
sometimes have been an embarrassment to him that, at the time
when he was preaching in St. Paul's, various obscene epigrams were
being handed about and attributed to 'Dr. Donne'.) Jonson, so often
prickly and dogmatic, was probably a more indulgent parent: when
he declared that 'my son Cartwright writes all like a man', the
modern reader finds it hard to know just what he meant, and will
perhaps reflect that, after all, it's a wise father who knows his own
children.

William Drummond of Hawthornden, a disciple of Spenser
and of the Italians, has recorded that when Ben Jonson visited him
in 1619 he told him that his poems 'were all good . . . save that they

[1] His influence in a narrower and more specialized field, that of eulogy and
funeral elegy (or, as he himself would have called it, 'epicede'), was perhaps still
more immediate and decisive. Poems of this kind, though, are more frequent in the
manuscript commonplace-books than in the miscellanies, except in such essentially
academic miscellanies as *Parnassus Biceps*.

Seventeenth Century Compared, Dr. W. W. Greg suggested that, if the bibliographical
evidence were placed beside that of literary allusion, the conclusion would seem to
be that, while writers praised Jonson, readers read Shakespeare. In these matters it
is very necessary to know, not merely who is speaking, but who he is speaking *for*.
The great admirers of Donne were nearly all men who were accustomed to write a
little poetry themselves, even if no more than an occasional eulogy or elegy.

smelled too much of the Schooles, and were not after the fancie of the tyme'. Jonson, no doubt, was speaking for himself and for those who agreed with him, but it is really impossible to know just how many did agree with him, or to form even a rough estimate of the proportion of then readers of English poetry who shared this 'fancie of the tyme'.[1] In saying that the poetry of Jonson and of Donne was in a sense coterie poetry, I want to insist upon the fact that it is almost impossible to know just how far the coterie extended, whom it included, who, so to speak, were in the inner circle and who were merely on the fringe. Where fashion and mode are active the detection and disintrication of 'influences' become formidably difficult. Milton admired Homer and Virgil and Ovid, Tasso and della Casa, not because anyone had told him to do so, but because he believed that was how great poetry should be written: one often feels, though, that many of his contemporaries admired Donne because to admire Donne was the done thing. Similarly, although to-day one constantly hears it said that contemporary English poets have been greatly influenced by Hopkins, by Mr. Eliot, and even by Rilke, it may well be that future generations will find the business of detecting these 'influences' a most baffling task. Generalizations even about those seventeenth-century poets whose work is available in modern editions can at best be

[1] In an undated letter to the physician and celebrated Latin poet, Dr. Arthur Johnston, published in the folio edition of his *Works* (1711, p. 143), Drummond has expressed his own opinion of a certain 'fancie of the tyme'. Although (as we shall see later) he admired Donne as an 'epigrammatist' and praised his Second Elegy, *The Anagram*, it is almost impossible not to suppose that Drummond is here alluding to Donne and to some of Donne's imitators. The letter begins abruptly with a Sidneian encomium on the antiquity and dignity of poetry, and then proceeds as follows: 'In vain have some Men of late (Transformers of every Thing) consulted upon her Reformation, and endeavoured to abstract her to *Metaphysical* Idea's, and *Scholastical* Quiddities, denuding her of her own Habits, and those Ornaments with which she hath amused the World some Thousand Years. *Poesy* is not a Thing that is yet in the finding and search, or which may be otherwise found out, being already condescended upon by all Nations, and as it were established *jure Gentium*, amongst *Greeks, Romans, Italians, French, Spaniards.* Neither do I think that a good Piece of *Poesy*, which *Homer, Virgil, Ovid, Petrarch, Bartas, Ronsard, Boscan, Garcilasso* (if they were alive, and had that Language) could not understand, and reach the Sense of the Writer. Suppose these Men could find out some other new *Idea* like *Poesy*, it should be held as if Nature should bring forth some new *Animal*, neither Man, Horse, Lyon, Dog, but which had some Members of all, if they had been proportionably and by right Symmetry set together. What is not like the Ancients and conform to those Rules which hath been agreed unto by all Times, may (indeed) be something like unto *Poesy*, but it is no more *Poesy* than a Monster is a Man. Monsters breed Admiration at the First, but have ever some strange Loathsomness in them at last.' Milton would probably have subscribed to every word of this.

tentative. Not even the well-known poets will fit neatly into categories: even in them we encounter all manner of paradoxes and tergiversations. Cowley has related that it was the discovery of a volume of Spenser in his mother's parlour that made him irrecoverably a poet; when, however, he went out into the world he discovered that not Spenser but Donne was the man, and set himself to imitate Donne—'to a fault', as Dryden said, who himself confessed that Cowley had been the darling of his youth. When, though, one turns from the poets whose works are available in modern editions to the miscellanies and manuscript common-place books of the age, the task of generalizing about seventeenth-century poetry, seventeenth-century taste, and seventeenth-century sensibility seems almost impossible. If I am now attempting to generalize myself, it is with an almost overwhelming conviction of the vanity of dogmatizing.

Each of these two very characteristic seventeenth-century poets, Jonson and Donne, was born during the reign of Elizabeth, and each had begun to establish his reputation during the last decade of the sixteenth century. Nevertheless, great as are the differences between them, the poetry of each has more in common with that of the other than it has with the poetry of Spenser, or of the Sonneteers, or with the lyrics in the song-books, or with such poems as *Venus and Adonis* and *The Rape of Lucrece*. On the one hand, neither Jonson nor Donne seems ever to have shared the ambition of Spenser and of several of Spenser's disciples to write a large-scale heroic or narrative poem. On the other hand, they both took the short poem more seriously than the typical Elizabethan poets did. Even if one leaves out of account the great mass of utterly undistinguished Elizabethan lyric, where the same rhymes, phrases, and properties appear over and over again with wearisome iteration, where nymphs and swains on the plains trip at leisure in a measure, view with pleasure Flora's treasure in meadows fresh and gay where fleecy lambs do play, weave in bowers crowns of flowers, or where fountains spring from mountains sigh and languish in their anguish,— even if one forgets what the great majority of the poems (including Spenser's and Sidney's) in, say, *Englands Helicon* are really like,— even if one confines oneself to the long-sifted contents of modern anthologies, one often feels that even the best Elizabethan poets just tossed off their delightful lyrics: partly, perhaps, because they were generally intended to be sung and therefore ought not to be too weighty or condensed. And one's general impression of the Elizabethan sonneteers is that they wrote too many sonnets and wrote them too easily. Jonson's foolish Matheo in *Every Man in His Humour* would, when melancholy, 'write you your halfe score or your dozen of sonnets at a sitting'. Both Jonson and Donne seem to have set a new fashion of writing short but very concentrated poems—Donne's always and Jonson's often intended to be handed round in manuscript and admired by connoisseurs. For it cannot be too strongly insisted that most of what we now chiefly remember of the non-dramatic poetry of the first half of the seventeenth century was poetry that for years had been circulating in manuscript before it finally found its way into print, while most of the non-dramatic poets who were publishing were either belated Elizabethans or pertinacious disciples of Spenser, and were regarded by the young intellectuals of the Court, the Inns of Court, and the Universities as old-fashioned and out of date. (One can go a good way towards 'placing' the younger Milton among his contemporaries by saying that for him neither the *Faerie Queene* nor Ovid's *Metamorphoses* was out of date.) It is significant and almost symbolic that that grand old Elizabethan, Michael Drayton, who was born a year earlier than Shakespeare and who lived and wrote and published until 1631, should have twice rather bitterly and contemptuously protested against this new fashion for short poems circulated in manuscript. In 1612, in the Preface to the first part of his immense *Poly-olbion*, that 'chorographical description of all the tracts, rivers, mountains, forests, and other parts of this renowned isle of Great Britain', he declared that

> in publishing this Essay of my Poeme, there is this great dis-aduantage against me; that it commeth out at this time, when Verses are wholly deduc't to Chambers, and nothing esteem'd in this lunatique Age, but what is kept in Cabinets, and must only passe by Transcription;

and in his *Epistle to Henry Reynolds, Esquire, of Poets and Poesie,* published in 1627, after reaching the end of his description of English poets from Chaucer to the two Beaumonts and William Browne, he added that he was not concerned with those poets who were too proud to publish and who chose to be known only through the circulation of their poems in manuscript.

Jonson, as I have admitted, was a less exclusive, a more public, poet than Donne, but he too wrote what he most valued for an audience fit though few. Spenser, one might almost say, wrote for all who cared for poetry at all; both Jonson and Donne wrote very emphatically for those who knew what was what. There is some analogy, though only a slight one, between the literary situation then and that which exists to-day; there was something, though only something, of the same gulf between 'serious' and 'popular' poetry. The position of Spenser had been in some ways similar to that of Tennyson; the position of Jonson and Donne was in some ways similar to that of Mr. Eliot. The Jacobean intellectuals, or some of them, reacted against the Elizabethans somewhat as the inter-war intellectuals did against the Victorians. This analogy, though, must not be pressed too far:[1] it is sufficient to insist that much of the most memorable non-dramatic poetry of the first half of the seventeenth century, a poetry very greatly influenced by the example of either Jonson or Donne or both, is a more exclusive and

---

[1] The chief danger of such analogies is that they tend to make us forget what I may call the Elizabethan time-scale and the fact that scarcely anything of what now seems to us most memorable in Elizabethan poetry and drama had been published or acted before the last decade of the sixteenth century. So far as we know, with the possible exception of Kyd's *Spanish Tragedy*, Marlowe's *Tamburlaine* (1587) was the first serious blank-verse drama to be acted on a public stage: some ten years later Shakespeare, who, like so many others, had begun by not very successfully attempting to imitate the 'mighty line' and the 'great and thundering speech', was already parodying them through the mouth of Ancient Pistol. When we speak of a 'reaction' against Spenser or against the sonneteers we tend, perhaps, to convey the impression that Jonson and Donne had been brought up on the *Faerie Queene* and on sonnet-sequences, had been cloyed and surfeited with them, whereas in fact it was rather a case of dislike at first sight. The first three books of the *Faerie Queene* were not published until 1590, and the remaining three books not until 1596. The first Elizabethan sonnet-sequence, Thomas Watson's Ἑκατομπαθία, containing a hundred eighteen-line 'sonnets', was published in 1582, but sonnet-sequences did not become the rage or the fashion until the publication of Sidney's *Astrophel and Stella* in 1591; then followed (to mention only the most famous) Daniel's *Delia* and Constable's *Diana* in 1592, Drayton's *Idea* in 1594, Spenser's *Amoretti* in 1595.

One may perhaps describe the situation with some approximation to truth by saying that the poetry of Spenser, of Jonson and of Donne and of their several disciples and imitators was all simultaneously competing for public favour, but that during the first half of the seventeenth century, among the more intellectual and sophisticated, the examples of Jonson and of Donne on the whole prevailed.

When we speak of nineteenth- or twentieth-century literary 'movements' or 'reactions', we are generally thinking in terms of generations; if we transfer these phrases to the Elizabethan literary scene we must learn to think in terms of a few years, or even, sometimes, of a few months.

critical and intellectual kind of poetry than that which is typically
Elizabethan. The phrase 'strong-lined' is often used by seventeenth-
century writers to describe the new qualities which they admired
in the poetry both of Jonson and of Donne: something close-packed
and strenuous, requiring some effort and connoisseurship to appreciate it, as distinguished from the easily appreciated, 'the soft,
melting and diffuse style of the Spenserians'.[1] The facts, not merely
that no one[2] has ever thought of calling Jonson a metaphysical poet,
but that his poetry shares many typical seventeenth-century characteristics with Donne's, should suggest to us that it is worth while
to try to consider Donne more as a typical seventeenth-century or
'strong-lined' poet, and less as a so-called metaphysical one.

Jonson addressed two very encomiastic epigrams to Donne
(xxiii and xcvi), as well as one (xciv) commending a manuscript of
his Satires to the Countess of Bedford, and Donne, who never condescended to praise any other contemporary poet, contributed some
very flattering Latin verses to the quarto edition of Jonson's Vol-
pone. They had, indeed, much in common. Both, one might almost
say, wrote as though Spenser had never lived: Spenser's national
and patriotic strain, his Platonic idealism, his elaborate description,
his amplification and ornamentation—all these find no place in their
verse. They rejected too what one may call the Petrarchan tradition,
the too often merely extravagant and conventional adoration of the
sonneteers, and they rejected the elaborate and mainly frigid
decoration of such poems as Venus and Adonis and The Rape of
Lucrece. Both insisted on what Jonson called 'language such as men
do use', and would have disagreed with Gray and agreed with
Wordsworth (in theory, though not always in practice) that there
should be no essential difference between the diction of poetry and
that of conversation. Both wrote much poetry that was satirical
and realistic. Both—a very notable characteristic of the typical
seventeenth-century as distinguished from the typical Elizabethan
lyrist—stamped an image of themselves upon nearly all they wrote;
for, while one of the chief characteristics of the Elizabethan lyric is
a certain anonymousness, the song rather than the singer, seven-

---

[1] See an article by G. Williamson, 'Strong Lines', in *English Studies*, 1936, 152 ff.;
reprinted in *Seventeenth-Century Contexts*, 1960.

[2] Except perhaps (by implication) Johnson in his *Life* of Cowley: 'This kind of
writing . . . had been recommended by the example of Donne . . . and by Johnson'
(*Lives of the Poets*, ed. Birckbeck Hill, I, 22).

teenth-century lyrists, as Moorman has observed, lyrists otherwise so
different as Crashaw, Vaughan, Suckling or Herrick, 'whether their
poetry be intense or not, stand revealed to us in what they write'
Finally, both Jonson and Donne wrote poems more sequacious,
organic and untransposable than their predecessors, although with
Donne this new sense of structure seems to have been stimulated by
scholastic logic, with Jonson by the example of the classical lyric.

Much of seventeenth-century poetry, then, is colloquial in
diction, undecorative and untraditional in imagery, dispensing with
what Carew, in his elegy on Donne, called

> the goodly exil'd traine
> Of gods and goddesses, which in thy just raigne
> Were banish'd nobler Poems,

personal in tone and logical in structure. In these respects both
Jonson and Donne are characteristic seventeenth-century poets.
'But,' some readers may be inclined to ask at this point, 'what about
Donne's metaphysics, what about his famous metaphysical wit?'
In the pages that follow I shall hope to demonstrate, among other
things, first, that Donne is certainly not a metaphysical poet in the
wider sense of being a philosophic one; secondly, that although,
in the narrower sense which Dryden had in mind when he declared
that Donne 'affected the metaphysics', he does indeed occasionally
draw illustrations and analogies from the realms of philosophy,
theology, and popular science, what, probably, most readers have
in mind when they call him a metaphysical poet is an often syllogistic
argumentation and argumentativeness which might, however, be
more appropriately called scholastic or dialectical than metaphysical;
thirdly, that in almost all Donne's best poetry there is a dramatic
element, an element of personal drama, which is no less characteristic
than the argumentative, scholastic or dialectical strain; and fourthly,
closely connected with this element of drama, that there is in many
of his poems a very strong element of sheer wit and paradox. Now
if one regards Donne's poetry chiefly in this way, as what I have
called the dialectical expression of personal drama, one will, I think,
perceive more clearly what are the really important resemblances
and differences, on the one hand, between his poetry and that of
other so-called metaphysical poets, and, on the other hand, between
his poetry and that of Jonson and of poets who are commonly

regarded as belonging to the School of Jonson. What, looked at in one way, seem differences in kind appear, when looked at in another way, to be rather differences in degree. The important thing, perhaps, is to decide which is the right way of looking, which is the viewpoint that will enable us to distinguish rightly between differences in degree and differences in kind, and to decide precisely at what point differences which at first seem merely differences in degree pass into differences in kind.

Consider, for example, the stylistic relationship between Herbert and Donne: the best poetry of both might equally well be described as the dialectical expression of personal drama. Herbert, like Donne, can make the purest poetry out of almost bare argument, and Herbert's expression of his relationship to God is no less dramatic than Donne's expression of various imaginary relationships with women and, perhaps, of his relationship with his wife; true though it be that Donne's dialectic is more ingenious than Herbert's and his analogies more various and, as it often seems to us, more far-fetched, and although in much of Donne's poetry there is an element of sheer invention, sheer wit and sheer paradox which we do not find in Herbert's. How much of the poetry of other so-called metaphysical poets may be appropriately described as the dialectical expression of personal drama? Certainly Marvell's *To his Coy Mistress* and *The Definition of Love*, although in most of Marvell's poetry the dialectical element is more apparent than the dramatic, and although the *Horatian Ode* is nearer to Jonson's kind of poetry than to Donne's. Crashaw's poetry is personal and often dramatic, but is it dialectical? Vaughan's poetry is personal, but less intimately so than Herbert's; dialectical, but less tightly and consistently so than Herbert's; occasionally, but not pervasively, dramatic, and with a strong element of vision and visual imagery that is found neither in Herbert's poetry nor in Donne's.

Now, on the other hand, between Donne's kind of poetry and Jonson's, which are the differences in degree and which are the differences in kind? Although the differences between Donne's kind of poetry and Jonson's are greater than those between Donne's kind of poetry and Herbert's, although very little, if any, of Jonson's poetry could be described as the dialectical expression of personal drama, and although the element of sheer wit is as absent from Jonson's poetry (though Jonson could admire it in Donne's) as it is from Herbert's, there still remain many differences which may perhaps be profitably regarded as differences within a fundamental identity, that, namely, of seventeenth-century poetry in general, differences in degree rather than in kind. Both Donne's language and Jonson's language is colloquial, 'language such as men do use', but Donne's is more defiantly and resolutely colloquial. Jonson's poetry, in comparison with the typical Elizabethan lyric or with Spenser or with the sonneteers, is free from decoration, but Jonson does not exile the gods and goddesses so rigorously or reject the whole apparatus of classical mythology and allusion so utterly and consistently as Donne. Jonson's lyrics, in comparison with typical Elizabethan lyrics, are organic and untransposable, but they are seldom so rigorously logical, so capable of prose-analysis, as Donne's, Donne's dialectical method here introducing what almost amounts to a difference in kind. And although, in comparison with the anonymity of the typical Elizabethan lyric, Jonson's lyrics are personal and individual, they are so rather in the way in which Horace's Odes are so than in the way in which Donne's poems are. The style and tone are individual, but, as with Horace, never, or very seldom, eccentrically and unclassically individual, and the matter, as with Horace, is essentially public, 'what oft was thought, but ne'er so well expressed'.

Indeed, the idea or ideal of the kind of poetry that Jonson most wanted to write and was continually trying to write, a poetry memorably expressing that 'high and noble matter' of which he spoke in his Epistle *To Elizabeth Countesse of Rutland*, has been, I cannot but think, most perfectly realized in some of Horace's Odes. Were I limited to the choice of one ode which should represent as completely as possible both the manner and the matter of the graver Horace, I think I should choose the sixteenth of his Second Book, of which I here offer a translation 'according to the Latin measure, as near as the language will permit':

Peace is what one, caught on the open sea, will
beg of heav'n above when the sombre storm clouds
hide the moon, and stars are no longer certain
guides for the sailor.

Peace the savage fighters of Thracia pray for,
peace, the Mede resplendent with broidered quiver,

peace, unbought, dear Grosphus, with proffered gold or
purple or jewels.

Ah, for neither treasure nor lictors bearing
rods before a Consul can check the spirit's
wretched civil strife or the cares that circle
costliest ceilings.

Well can fare on little, his humble table's
brightest piece of plate the ancestral salt-dish,
one of whose light sleep not a fear or sordid
wish has deprived him.

Why, with such short span, do we so contend for
large possessions? Why do we seek for countries
warmed with other suns? Has an exile ever
quitted himself then?

Sickly Care can clamber aboard the brass-bound
galleys, keep abreast of the knightly riders,
swifter far than stags or the cloud-compelling
easterly breezes.

Let the soul, content with the present, scorn to
reck what lies beyond, and with stubborn smiling
sweeten what seems bitter. From ev'ry aspect
nothing is perfect.

Early death removed the renowned Achilles,
age prolonged left little to cheer Tithonus;
me perhaps some blessing denied to you some
hour will have granted.

Flocks in hundreds bleat and Sicilian cattle
low around your folds, in the stables whinny
chariot-racing horses, and doubly-dyed in
African purple

glows the wool you're clad with; to me, with small do-
main, the subtle spirit of Grecian Muses
came as Fate's mixed gift, and a soul aloof from
envious throngers.

It was, I say, towards poetry of this kind, individual indeed, but both
in manner and in matter essentially public and classical, a poetry of
statement and of weighty generalization, that Jonson was continually
striving. I need not multiply examples: consider the concluding lines
of *To the World*: *A farewell for a Gentle-woman, vertuous and noble*:

> My tender, first, and simple yeeres
>   Thou did'st abuse, and then betray;
> Since stird'st vp iealousies and feares,
>   When all the causes were away.
> Then, in a soile hast planted me,
>   Where breathe the basest of thy fooles;
> Where enuious arts professed be,
>   And pride, and ignorance the schooles,
> Where nothing is examin'd, weigh'd,
>   But, as 'tis rumor'd, so beleeu'd:
> Where euery freedome is betray'd,
>   And euery goodnesse tax'd, or grieu'd.
> But, what we'are borne for, we must beare:
>   Our fraile condition it is such,
> That, what to all may happen here,
>   If't chance to me, I must not grutch.
> Else, I my state should much mistake,
>   To harbour a diuided thought
> From all my kinde: that, for my sake,
>   There should a miracle be wrought.
> No, I doe know, that I was borne
>   To age, misfortune, sicknesse, griefe:
> But I will beare these, with that scorne,
>   As shall not need thy false reliefe.
> Nor for my peace will I goe farre,
>   As wandrers doe, that still doe rome,
> But make my strengths, such as they are,
>   Here in my bosome, and at home.

Or consider one of the most Horatian, I might almost say, one of the most Roman, things Jonson ever wrote, the verses *To Sir Robert Wroth*, penetrated with that characteristically Roman reverence for the traditional pursuits and festivals of the countryman which recurs so often, and with equal spontaneity, in the poems of Jonson's disciple Herrick. After describing, in magnificently animated and colourful verse, the varied activities of the estate and the hospitality of its owner, Jonson concludes with a passage which, in part at any rate, is no less Virgilian than Horatian, and which was probably inspired by some famous lines at the end of Virgil's second Georgic:

> Let others watch in guiltie armes, and stand
>   The furie of a rash command,
> Goe enter breaches, meet the cannons rage,
>   That they may sleepe with scarres in age,
> And shew their feathers shot, and cullors torne,
>   And brag, that they were therefore borne.
> Let this man sweat, and wrangle at the barre,
>   For euery price, in euery iarre,
> And change possessions, oftner with his breath,
>   Then either money, warre, or death:
> Let him, then hardest sires, more disinherit,
>   And each where boast it as his merit,
> To blow vp orphanes, widdowes, and their states;
>   And thinke his power doth equall *Fates*.
> Let that goe heape a masse of wretched wealth,
>   Purchas'd by rapine, worse then stealth,
> And brooding o'er it sit, with broadest eyes,
>   Not doing good, scarce when he dyes.
> Let thousands more goe flatter vice, and winne,
>   By being organes to great sinne,
> Get place, and honor, and be glad to keepe
>   The secrets, that shall breake their sleepe:
> And, so they ride in purple, eate in plate,
>   Though poyson, thinke it a great fate.
> But thou, my WROTH, if I can truth apply,
>   Shalt neither that, not this enuy:
> Thy peace is made; and, when man's state is well,
>   'Tis better, if he there can dwell.

> God wisheth, none should wracke on a strange shelfe:
> To him, man's dearer then t'himselfe.
> And, howsoeuer we may thinke things sweet,
> He alwayes giues what he knowes meet;
> Which who can vse is happy: Such be thou.
> Thy morning's and thy euening's vow
> Be thankes to him, and earnest prayer, to finde
> A body sound, with sounder minde;
> To doe thy countrey seruice, thy selfe right;
> That neither want doe thee affright,
> Nor death; but when thy latest sand is spent,
> Thou maist thinke life, a thing but lent.

It is in what may be called, in a wide sense, his moral poetry, that portion of his non-dramatic verse which is still far less widely known than it deserves to be, that Jonson is most fundamentally akin to Horace and, at the same time, most representative of one of the most characteristic strains in seventeenth-century and Augustan verse. From Wotton's

> How happy is he born and taught
> That serveth not another's will

to the youthful Pope's

> Happy the man whose wish and care
> A few paternal acres bound,
> Content to breathe his native air
> In his own ground

how much of the morality, one might almost say how much of the religion, of English poets seems almost indistinguishable from that blend of Stoicism and Epicureanism which has been so perfectly expressed by Horace! How often we find it, the disintrication of the mean from its extremes, the exposure and rebuke of immoderate ambitions and desires and of every kind of too-muchness, the praise of moderate hospitality, of good talk and good wine, of the health-fulness of country life as distinguished from that of the city and the court, the celebration of antique virtue and simplicity—these, together with exhortations not to be too cast down by grief or ill-fortune, but to recognize and accept the conditions of human life.[1]

Although they both share in varying degrees those common characteristics of seventeenth-century poetry in general which I have tried to indicate, there is a very great difference, a difference not merely in degree but in kind, between Donne's exercises in sheer wit, Donne's dialectical expression of personal drama, and that essentially classical and public poetry towards which Jonson was always striving. Jonson's most memorable lines (often adapted from classical authors) are weighty and general:

Men have beene great, but never good by chance.[2]

Man may securely sinne, but safely never.[3]

A good *Poet's* made, as well as borne.[4]

'Tis wisdom, and that high,
For men to use their fortune reverently,
Even in youth.[5]

Donne's most memorable lines are personal and dramatic:

I wonder by my troth, what thou, and I
Did, till we lov'd?[6]

For Godsake hold your tongue, and let me love.[7]

If yet I have not all thy love,
Deare, I shall never have it all.[8]

---

[1] There is, of course, another way of looking at the matter, which may be suggested by the following entry in the Diary of John Manningham, of the Middle Temple, under 12th February, 1602: 'Ben Jonson the poet nowe lives upon one Townesend and scornes the world. (*Tho: Overbury.*)' (ed. Bruce, Camden Society, p. 130.)

[2] *An Epistle to Sir Edward Sacvile,* l. 124.
[3] *Epode,* 'Not to know vice at all'.
[4] *To the Memory of my beloved, the Author Mr. William Shakespeare.*
[5] *An Ode,* 'High-spirited friend'.
[6] *The good-morrow.*
[7] *The Canonization.*
[8] *Lovers infinitenesse.*

Donne's style and manner are not only individual, but, in comparison
with Horace's or Jonson's, eccentrically and unclassically individual.
And as for the matter of his poetry, where he is being mainly witty
and paradoxical, it is public only in the sense that we can imagine
its being publicly recited and enjoyed in companies whose conceptions of wit, whose tastes, in comparison with Horace's or Pope's or
Dr. Johnson's (for Ben Jonson, although his own practice was very
different, could admire Donne's wit), were eccentric and unclassical.
Where, on the other hand, Donne is being serious, or mainly serious,
the matter of his poetry, in comparison with that of Ben Jonson or
Horace, is essentially private, not 'What oft was thought, but
ne'er so well expressed', but something 'seldom thought and seldom
so expressed'. A. N. Whitehead once defined religion as 'What the
individual does with his own solitariness':[1] nearly all Donne's
serious poetry, his love-poetry no less than his religious poetry, and
nearly all Herbert's poetry and Vaughan's, is in this sense essentially,
not merely nominally, religious, is a record of what the poet has
been doing with his solitariness. This solitariness, this privateness,
this self-containedness, this, together with the often dialectical and
dramatic expression of it, is, it seems to me, the most important
difference between the serious poetry of Donne and the so-called
Metaphysical School and that of Jonson and the Classical or Horatian
School.

[1] *Religion in the Making*, 1927, p. 6.

2

DONNE THE MAN

JOHN DONNE was born in 1572, the son of John Donne, a prosperous London ironmonger, who died when the future poet was only three or four years old, and of Elizabeth, daughter of John Heywood, the epigrammatist. Besides the poet, there were four daughters and a younger son. Both parents were Catholics, and many of their relations had made considerable sacrifices for their convictions; indeed, Donne himself, whose younger brother Henry had died of gaol fever in 1593 while in prison for harbouring a seminary priest, was to declare in the Preface to his *Pseudo-Martyr*, 1610, that 'No family (which is not of far larger extent and greater branches) hath endured and suffered more in their persons and fortunes for obeying the teachers of Roman doctrine'. It was therefore to be expected that the widowed mother would bring up the children in her own faith. At the age of twelve or thereabouts John Donne, together with his younger brother Henry, went up to Oxford and matriculated from Hart Hall in October 1584. Walton says that about the age of fourteen he was removed from Oxford to Cambridge and that he remained there until his seventeenth year, but there is no evidence of this, and Sir Richard Baker, who was Donne's contemporary at Hart Hall, speaks only of his having been at Oxford. The first documented fact about him after his matriculation at Oxford is that of his admission, not later than May 1591, as a law-student at Thavies Inn. It is almost impossible, however, to suppose that he resided from 1584 to 1591, that is to say, for nearly seven years, at Oxford. Not only would he, as a Catholic, have been unable, however long he had stayed up, to take a degree, but on reaching the age of sixteen he would have been compelled to take the Oath of Supremacy, a burden upon the conscience which, as Dr. Jessopp has observed, many Catholic parents avoided by sending their sons to the University at a very early age. If, then, Donne left Oxford at the age of sixteen, that is to say, about 1588, how did he spend the time between then and his admission, not later than May 1591, at Thavies Inn, from which he was transferred to Lincoln's Inn in May 1592? Walton knew that as a young man Donne had travelled and that he had stayed 'some years' in Italy and Spain, but, in one of those chronological hazes which sometimes afflict him, he seems to imply that Donne spent 'some years' in Italy and Spain on his way back from the Islands Expedition in 1597, which is impossible, for by 1598 he was Secretary to Sir Thomas Egerton. It is almost certain, I think, that the period of Donne's travels was between his leaving Oxford, probably in 1588, and 1591, when Marshall made the famous engraved and dated portrait of him. This portrait represents him in military dress and bears a Spanish motto. Sir Herbert Grierson, in his article on Donne in the *Cambridge History of English Literature*, long ago argued convincingly, as it seems to me, in favour of an early date for Donne's travels. He observed that in one of the three earlier Satires, dated in one MS. 1593, Donne already describes his library as lined with

> Giddie fantastique poets of each land

and remarked that in those days a young man did not usually possess a large collection of foreign books unless he had bought them while abroad. He also suggested—and this seems to me a very strong argument indeed—that the tone and spirit of Donne's earlier poetry and his general emancipatedness seemed to reveal an early familiarity with the life and literature of Italy.[1]

We may assume that from 1592 until 1596 Donne was in more or less continuous residence at Lincoln's Inn, studying law, studying divinity, associating with the wits of his time at the Mermaid, writing verses, going to plays, falling in and out of love—leading, in fact, a very intense and varied life, and throwing himself with characteristic energy and wholeness into whatever part he had elected to play. In considering Donne's life and poetry we must, if we are to understand them aright, continually try to reconcile various apparent contradictions: during these years, for example, we must reconcile the Donne who wrote so much witty and outrageous poetry, the Donne recollected by his contemporary at Hart

---

[1] I am aware that others (notably, Mr. John Sparrow in *A Garland for John Donne*, 1931) have argued in favour of a later date for Donne's travels.

Hall, the chronicler Sir Richard Baker, 'who leaving *Oxford*, lived at the *Inns of Court*, not dissolute, but very neat, a great visiter of Ladies, a great frequenter of Playes, a great writer of conceited Verses', we must reconcile this Donne with the serious student 'whose bed', says Walton, even in the most unsettled days of his youth, 'was not able to retain him beyond the hour of four in a morning: and it was no common business that drew him out of his chamber till past ten. All which time was employed in study; though he took great liberty after it.'[1] Donne himself, many years later, declared in a letter to his friend Sir Henry Goodyer that although he had only begun the study of law with the intention of preparing himself for some profession where it would be useful, he was 'diverted by the worst voluptuousness, which is an Hydroptique immoderate desire of humane learning and languages: beautiful ornaments to great fortunes; but mine needed an occupation, and a course'.[2] Walton, however, suggests that the study which kept Donne in his room nearly every day from four till ten in the morning was not all merely study for study's sake, for he tells us that

> he, being then unresolv'd what Religion to adhere to, and considering how much it concern'd his soul to choose the most Orthodox, did ... presently lay aside all study of the Law: and, of all other Sciences that might give him a denomination; and begun seriously to survey, and consider the Body of Divinity, as it was then controverted betwixt the *Reformed* and the *Roman Church*.[3]

And Donne himself, in the Preface to his *Pseudo-Martyr*, 1610, declares that he proceeded with 'frequent praier, and equall and indifferent affections', and that he did not come to any decision until he had 'survayed and digested the whole body of Divinity, controverted betweene ours and the Romane Church'. Donne may well have begun this course of study a year after his admission to Lincoln's Inn, after the tragic death of his younger brother in August 1593, who, as I have said, died of gaol fever after he had been arrested for harbouring a seminary priest. No doubt Donne was

[1] *World's Classics* ed., 67.
[2] *Letters*, 1651, 50–2; Gosse, *Life and Letters of John Donne*, I, 191.
[3] *World's Classics* ed., 25.

moved by a sincere desire for truth, 'saving truth', as it would have seemed to him and to his contemporaries—his Third Satire, on the search for true religion, which must have been written at this time, sufficiently reveals that he was; nevertheless, our motives are seldom entirely unmixed, and Donne's were often, as it seems to us, most strangely mixed. Must he not often have asked himself (it is not, I think, a cynical suggestion), whether the differences between the Roman and the Anglican Churches were of such fundamental importance as to make it necessary for him to continue to endure the disabilities imposed upon Catholics, which had already prevented him from taking a University degree and which would deny him all possibility of public employment; and may not these reflections, together with those on the sufferings of his own family, have been, as it were, suddenly galvanized into action by the tragic death of his brother? And may one not, without being cynical, suggest that he reached the conclusion he subconsciously wanted to reach, although Walton expresses it otherwise, saying that 'truth had too much light about her to be hid from so sharp an Inquirer; and, he had too much ingenuity, not to acknowledge he had found her'?[1] We must, I repeat, continually try to reconcile apparent contradictions, and above all we must not (as I shall insist later), interpreting the more impudent and outrageous of his early poems autobiographically, assume that the young man whom Baker described as 'not dissolute, but very neat', and whom Ben Jonson, no careless eulogist, praised for his

language, letters, arts, best life[2]

was ever a mere man of wit and pleasure about town, still less that he was the unprincipled and unpleasant young blackguard whom some modern critics have tried to make us believe in.

In 1596 Donne sailed with the Cadiz expedition under Essex, and then with the less fortunate Islands Expedition in 1597. Among his companions on both these voyages was young Thomas Egerton, son of Sir Thomas Egerton, later Lord Ellesmere, Keeper of the Great Seal and Lord High Chancellor. This was most fortunate for Donne, for soon after the Islands Expedition returned in October

[1] *World's Classics* ed., 25.
[2] Epigram xxiii.

1597 he was appointed Secretary to the Lord Keeper, 'by the favour', as he wrote four years later, 'which your good son's love to me obtained'. Since Donne had now forsaken what he was ready to call 'a corrupt religion', the way to public employment was open. Walton says that Egerton

> taking notice of his Learning, Languages, and other Abilities, and much affecting his Person and Behaviour, took him to be his chief Secretary; supposing and intending it to be an Introduction to some more weighty Employment in the State; for which, his Lordship did often protest, he thought him very fit.
>
> Nor did his Lordship in this time of Master *Donne's* attendance upon him, account him to be so much his Servant, as to forget he was his Friend; and to testifie it, did alwayes use him with much courtesie, appointing him a place at his own Table, to which he esteemed his Company and Discourse to be a great Ornament.[1]

And when, five years later, Egerton was forced to part with Donne, he declared that 'He parted with a Friend; and such a Secretary as was fitter to serve a King then a Subject.'[2] A beginning was actually made with that 'more weighty Employment in the State' to which, according to Walton, Egerton intended Donne's secretaryship to be an introduction; for in October 1601 Donne was elected one of the Members of Parliament for Brackley, a constituency controlled by Egerton. But these brilliant hopes and prospects were not destined to be fulfilled. In 1596 Egerton had married as his second wife the sister of Sir George More, owner of an estate in Surrey, Chancellor of the Garter, and Lieutenant of the Tower of London. This second Lady Egerton seems to have brought with her as a companion her brother's young daughter Ann, who continued to reside at York House after her aunt's death in January 1600. At some time—when exactly we do not know, although there may well be something in Dr. Jessopp's conjecture that after Lady Egerton's death 'the supervision of the domestic arrangements in the Lord Keeper's house was perhaps less vigilant than it had been'—at some time Donne and Ann More, who had been a mere

---

[1] *World's Classics* ed., 26–27.
[2] *op. cit.*, 29.

child when Donne first came there, fell violently in love. Sir George
More, who evidently had other views for his daughter, got wind
of what was going on and carried her off to his home in Surrey;
but she and Donne, during one of her father's unavoidable visits
to London, contrived to meet secretly, and at the end of 1601
were secretly married, Ann being then seventeen and Donne
twenty-nine. Seldom, perhaps, has a single action so completely
altered the course and direction of a life. Had he remained unmarried, or had he made a more prudent marriage, Donne might
well have had a career similar to that of his friend Sir Henry Wotton.
As it was, all his prospects of secular employment collapsed like a
house of cards, collapsed—to borrow a memorable phrase from his
sermons—'irreparably, irrevocably, irrecoverably, irremediably'.
Bacon, who knew something about it, declared that all rising to
great place was by a winding stair, but henceforth the only stair
on which Donne was ever to get a foothold would be one which
led to a pulpit. He was a master of drama and a master of paradox,
and yet, when one considers it, there is perhaps nothing in his poetry
or in his prose quite so dramatic or quite so paradoxical as the fact
that this clandestine marriage should eventually have brought him
to the Deanery of St. Paul's. This, though, is to anticipate. Sir
George More, when the news reached him, was furious. He first
compelled Egerton, much against his will, to dismiss Donne from
his service, and did not feel himself sufficiently revenged until
Donne and the two friends who had, respectively, married him
and given away the bride 'were all committed to three several
prisons'. As soon as he was free Donne exerted himself to obtain
the release of his friends, and he then had to begin a long and
expensive lawsuit to obtain possession of his wife, whom Sir George
More had carried off to his house in Surrey until the Court of High
Commission should adjudicate upon the case. This lawsuit, as
Walton says, 'proved troublesome and sadly-chargeable to him,
whose youth, and travel, and needless bounty, had brought his
estate into a narrow compass'. After a time, moved partly by
Donne's winning behaviour, 'which when it would entice, had a
strange kind of elegant irresistible art', and by the fact that most
people approved of his daughter's choice, Sir George repented of
his harshness and tried to persuade Egerton to readmit Donne into
his service, but the Lord Keeper replied that 'though he was

unfeignedly sorry for what he had done, yet it was inconsistent with his place and credit to discharge and readmit servants at the request of passionate petitioners'. Sir George, if we look at the matter through Walton's eyes, had played the part assigned to him by Providence, and the consequences of his behaviour would be what they would be. In order, apparently, to keep up some show of consistency, he had asked that this request should be kept secret, and he still refused 'to contribute any means that might conduce to their livelihood'.

And now the curtain rises upon the Second Act of Donne's life, upon a more sober, a more melancholy, a more Hamlet-like Donne, who 'lacks advancement' and who, although he is still capable of brilliant wit and intense intellectual exertion, is often afflicted by moods of deep depression, in which his isolatedness seems total and insuperable and his hold on life but slight, this goodly frame the earth but a sterile promontory and that paragon of animals man but a quintessence of dust.

For a time he and his wife resided in the house of her cousin, Sir Francis Woolley, at Pirford, in Surrey, where Donne devoted himself to the study of Canon and Civil Law; then, in order to be near London, they moved first to Camberwell and then, in 1605, to Mitcham, where Donne would often leave his wife and rapidly increasing family for a lodging in the Strand, his purpose being, not merely to enjoy the conversation of his friends, but to be near the Court and to those whose influence, he continually hoped, might at last obtain for him that 'weighty Employment in the State', that secretaryship or ambassadorship, for which his service with Egerton was to have been a preparation. Fate, though, or, as it seemed to Walton, Providence, was against him. For some years, perhaps from about 1604, he seems to have given considerable assistance to one of King James's most favoured Chaplains, Thomas Morton, later Bishop of Durham, in a cause which the King had very much at heart, an attempt, namely, to convert the English Roman Catholics or Recusants, as they were called, 'by weight of reason, and not by rigour of law'. The fact that Donne had been himself brought up as a Catholic and that many years ago he had made an exhaustive study of the points of controversy between the Roman and Anglican Churches, peculiarly fitted him to assist Morton in this task, although he probably entered upon it from very mixed motives:

partly, one may suppose, in order to occupy his mind with some-thing, and partly, or perhaps mainly, in the hope of receiving some desirable reward. When, though, Morton in 1607 became Dean of Gloucester, he tried to persuade Donne to take Orders, and offered to resign in his favour a valuable living in Yorkshire which he had previously been holding. Donne, declares Walton, who gives a very circumstantial account of the matter, declined, giving as his reasons, first, his fear that various irregularities in his past life would bring scandal upon the profession, and secondly, that if, in his present condition of poverty, he were to take Orders, he would find it almost impossible to decide whether his chief motive was, as it should be, the Glory of God, or not rather the desire for a settled and substantial income. The scruples may well have been genuine, but, at the same time, they may well have been con-venient, for it is almost impossible not to suppose that Donne was still hoping for secular preferment. It is also possible—or rather, perhaps, it is probable—that the reason why this secular preferment never came was that Morton had already convinced the King that Donne was needed by the Church.

Although Walton professed to detect the hand of Providence, for a modern reader, perhaps, there is something powerfully ironical in the situation. Donne, while still a student at Lincoln's Inn, moved partly by a sincere desire for truth and partly, as I have suggested, by a strong subconscious desire to escape from the disabilities imposed on him by his religion, made a careful study of the chief doctrinal differences between the Roman and Anglican Churches, forsook what he soon came to call a 'corrupt religion', and seemed to have his feet firmly planted on the ladder of secular preferment. Then, after Sir George More's reaction to his marriage had flung him once more to the ground, anxious to make the best use of such resources as were left to him, and, above all, to gain the attention and favour of the King, he resumed his theological studies in order to help the King's favourite Chaplain in the King's favourite project. With what result? Why, that instead of, as he supposed, advancing himself towards that secretaryship or ambassadorship he wanted, he was putting them forever out of his reach, since the knowledge and qualities he was, from his then point of view, incautiously and imprudently, revealing were convincing Morton and the King that he was a born theologian and had in him the makings of a great divine. In fact, the Muse of Theology (if there be one) would seem to have resolved, from the moment when Donne first meddled with her, to lead her captor captive, and not to become in his hands a mere instrument of secular preferment. One day, Walton tells us, the King, with whom Donne often dined and with whom he had become a great favourite, was so impressed with the arguments he used against Catholic objections to the Oaths of Supremacy and Allegiance, that he commanded Donne to write a book on the subject. The result was the *Pseudo-Martyr*, published in 1610, in which Donne insisted that the recusants were not real martyrs but sham martyrs. This book was another nail in the coffin of Donne's secular ambitions, for Walton tells us that when the King had read and considered it, 'he perswaded Mr. Donne to enter into the Ministry; to which at that time he was, and appeared very unwilling', not so much because, as Walton declares, he apprehended it '(such was his mistaking modesty) to be too weighty for his Abilities', but, we may believe, because he still had other ambitions.[1]

Indeed, it was about this time that he attracted to himself the attention and patronage of the ambitious and wealthy Sir Robert Drury by writing a funeral elegy upon the death of Sir Robert's daughter Elizabeth, who died at the age of fifteen, and whom Donne had never seen. Then, on his return in August 1612 from a long visit to the Continent with Sir Robert, Donne began to attach himself to the reigning favourite Robert Carr, Viscount Rochester as he then was and later Earl of Somerset. The failure of other hopes since his interview with the King after the publication of *Pseudo-Martyr* in 1610 seems to have led Donne, at any rate for a short time, to reconsider his decision not to take Orders, for in his first letter to Carr he declared that he had 'resolved to make my Profession Divinitie', in order, as he said in a covering letter to his friend Lord Hay, 'that I may try, whether my poor Studies, which have profited me nothing, may profit others in that course; in which also a fortune may either be better made, or, at least, better lost, than in any other'.[2] A year later, however, in 1613, we find Donne requesting the Earl of Somerset, as he then was, and on whose bounty, Donne declares,

[1] *World's Classics* ed., 45.
[2] *A Collection of Letters made by Sir Tobie Mathews, Kt.*, 1660, 319–20, 322; Gosse, II, 20, 22.

he has been living for the last year, to get him the vacant ambassadorship at Venice.[1] This 'great instrument of God's providence in this
Kingdom', as Donne calls him, was at this time trying to get the
marriage between the Earl of Essex and Frances Howard, whom he
married at the end of the year, pronounced null and void; and,
although Gosse mistakenly attributed to Donne the legal tractate
in support of the nullity which still exists in manuscript, but which
had been drawn up by Sir Daniel Donne, Dean of Arches, there are
at least two passages in his letters which strongly suggest that Donne,
who had already promised an epithalamium to celebrate the
marriage, had offered the benefit of his knowledge of Canon and
Civil Law in return for Somerset's patronage. In a letter 'To my
worthy friend G. K.', written on 19th January (1613?), he says, after
mentioning 'some treatise concerning this Nullity': 'My poor study
having lyen that way, it may prove possible, that my weak assistance
may be of use in the matter, in a more serious fashion, then an
Epithalamion';[2] and a letter to Somerset begins: 'After I was grown
to be your Lordships, by all the titles that I could thinke upon, it
hath pleased your Lordship to make another title to me, by buying
me'.[3] A year later Donne made his last attempt to obtain secular
preferment, for in 1614, as has been recently discovered,[4] he was
elected a Member of Parliament for Taunton, and sat from 5th
April until the dissolution on 7th June. In the same year Somerset
at last made some attempt to redeem his promises, and invited
Donne to join him at Theobalds, where he was staying with the
King, saying that a Clerkship to the Council was vacant and that
he knew the King would not deny him if he requested it for Donne.
He was mistaken, for the King now said positively what he had
probably long ago decided, although hitherto he had confined
himself to hints and persuasions: 'I know Mr. *Donne* is a learned
man, has the abilities of a learned Divine; and will prove a powerful
Preacher, and my desire is to prefer him that way, and in that way,
I will deny you nothing for him'.[5] All other avenues of preferment

---

[1] Did Donne know that Sir Robert Drury, did he know that Donne, was also
among the unsuccessful applicants for this post? See R. C. Bald, *Donne and the
Drurys*, 1959, pp. 131–2.
[2] *Letters*, 1651, 180; Gosse II, 25.
[3] *op. cit.* 290; Gosse II, 23.
[4] By Mr. I. A. Shapiro, who communicated his discovery in a letter to the *T.L.S.*
10th March, 1932.
[5] Walton, 45–6.

were, apparently, closed, and there seemed no course open to Donne but to take Orders. Nevertheless, while staying at Theobalds he seems to have discovered for the first time that Somerset and Archbishop Abbot were bitter enemies, and, accordingly, in December 1614, he wrote to his father-in-law Sir George More, asking him to try to discover whether the Archbishop knew anything of his relations with Somerset—a fact which suggests that, although he had at last consented to take Orders, he was unwilling to proceed if it should appear that his chances of preferment had been impaired. However, the result of his inquiries seems to have been reassuring, for in January 1615 he was ordained, and preferment followed rapidly until, in 1621, he was made Dean of St. Paul's.

But before proceeding to what we may call the Third Act, Donne the Preacher, let us review for a moment that Second Act which extended from his dismissal from Egerton's service at the beginning of 1602 until his entrance into Holy Orders in January 1615. Even in the brief and almost purely factual chronicle I have given, there are many of those apparent contradictions which I have insisted that we must try to reconcile, and much that should suggest to us that we are in the presence of a mind and character, and also in a world, which are in some respects very strange and remote, and that our inferences from sayings and doings are likely, unless subjected to a kind of necessary historical correction, to lead to very erroneous conclusions.

'The minde of man', wrote Sir Walter Raleigh, in one of those passages which sometimes brighten the vast but rather monotonous expanses of his *History of the World*,

> the minde of man hath two Ports, the one alwaies frequented by the entrance of manifold vanities: the other desolate and over-growne with grasse, by which enter our charitable thoughts and divine contemplations.[1]

We can recognize plenty of contradictions in ourselves and in our friends, and we can often say with Ovid's Medea

Video meliora proboque,
deteriora sequor;

[1] Bk. I, Chap. VII, § ix; ed. 1634, 83.

nevertheless, in Donne, as in some of his contemporaries, though perhaps most surprisingly in him, the manifold vanities and the divine contemplations often seem most strangely mingled. One often detects, or thinks that one has detected, a strange worldliness, a curious scepticism and detachment and fundamental unseriousness in his attitude even to those things to which he seems to be devoting himself most seriously. Much of the worldliness and opportunism, the sycophancy almost, so apparent in Donne's relations with Somerset, whom, shortly before taking Orders, he addressed as 'a great instrument of God's providence in this Kingdom', much of this may, it is true, be attributed to the fact that in that age almost any kind of public or ecclesiastical promotion depended so much on patrons and favourites and that, as Bacon expressed it, all rising to great place was by a winding stair. Nevertheless, a modern student of his life and writings may often be tempted to ask exactly how much any of the various things to which he devoted himself really meant to Donne. How much, for example, before he finally took Orders, did theology really mean to him? His early preoccupation with it was due, partly at least, to worldly motives, to a desire, perhaps never quite consciously admitted, to discover whether he could conscientiously cease to be a Catholic and therewith cease to be excluded from public employment. And yet even in saying this I have found it necessary to use the word 'conscientiously' as well as the word 'worldly', and the Third Satire sufficiently proves that Donne's interest in religion was at the same time what we should describe by those words rather dangerously over-employed in modern criticism, 'genuine' or 'sincere'. Later he seems to have resumed his theological studies mainly from worldly motives, in the hope of pleasing the King and obtaining some public office, and yet, at the same time, shortly after the beginning of his friendship with Mrs. Herbert in about 1606, he began to write religious poems, and about 1608 he wrote the deeply felt and deeply moving *Litanie*, and shortly afterwards the two *Anniversaries*, begun, very probably, from the worldly motive of attracting the attention and favour of a wealthy patron, but where, nevertheless, 'by Occasion of the religious Death of Mistris Elizabeth Drury', he was led to some most impressive meditations on the vanity of all worldly, temporal and visible things in comparison with those which are unseen and eternal. And yet (how often one must use this phrase

in speaking of Donne!), and yet at the same time as he was writing
these genuinely, or sincerely, religious poems (as I suppose we
should call them), he was also, in verse-epistles to various noble
and learned lady friends, using theological conceptions as material
for hyperbolical compliments, for exercises in almost sheer wit.

Again, what exactly was Donne's attitude to his wife and
children? For, mingled with genuine tenderness, there often appears
what seems (although I am not sure whether it really is) a strange
detachment. The letter in which he conveyed to his wife the
melancholy news that Egerton had dismissed him concluded, so
Walton tells us,

John Donne, Anne Donne, Vn-done,

and later Walton declares that Donne's marriage was 'the remarkable error of his life', and that, 'though he had a wit able and very
apt to maintain Paradoxes, yet he was very far from justifying it'.[1]
'Though I dyed at a blow then when my courses were diverted,
yet it wil please me a little to have had a long funerall, and to have
kept my self so long above ground without putrefaction', Donne
wrote to Sir Henry Wotton in 1612;[2] and in many of the letters
from what he sometimes calls 'my Mitcham hospital' or 'my hospital at Mitcham', he often suggests that he regards his life since
1602 as a kind of prolonged dying from which death would be a
merciful release. He loved his wife, but he could not conceal from
himself the fact that she had undone him, and that he, perhaps, had
undone her. In one letter he says that he is writing, not from his
study, but 'from the fire side in my Parler, and in the noise of three
gamesome children; and by the side of her, whom because I have
transplanted into a wretched fortune, I must labour to disguise that
from her by all such honest devices, as giving her my company,
and discourse, therefore I steal from her, all the time which I give
this Letter'.[3] Tenderness, yes, but tenderness, one might be tempted
to think, more dutiful than spontaneous, though just how right or
how wrong one would be I cannot really decide, and I put forward
most of even these only half-suggested inferences very tentatively.

[1] *World's Classics* ed., 60.
[2] *Letters*, 1651, 121–2; Gosse I, 291.
[3] 1651, 137; Gosse, I, 214–15.

Everyone who has read anything of Donne has read *A Valediction*: *forbidding mourning*, that astonishingly witty, and, at the same time, movingly tender poem which, according to Walton, Donne addressed to his wife before setting out with Sir Robert Drury on a long visit to the Continent at the end of 1611.

> Dull sublunary lovers love
> (Whose soule is sense) cannot admit
> Absence, because it doth remove
> Those things which elemented it.
>
> But we by a love so much refin'd,
> That our selves know not what it is,
> Inter-assured of the mind,
> Care lesse, eyes, lips, and hands to misse.

This, surely, is the language of the heart as well as of the intellect, and one remembers Walton's account of how unwillingly Donne was persuaded to leave his wife, who was then expecting another child, and of how, two days after they had reached Paris, Donne said to Sir Robert Drury, who had returned after a brief absence to the room where they had been dining: 'I have seen a dreadful Vision since I saw you: I have seen my dear wife pass twice by me through this room, with her hair hanging about her shoulders, and a dead child in her arms'.[1] And yet the man who could feel so intensely was also capable of writing, about the same time, to a friend in England with a brevity, a detachment, and even a turn of wit which is certainly surprising, and which, if we had no other evidence, we might be tempted to call unfeeling. 'I am yet,' he wrote,

in the same perplexity, which I mentioned before; which is, that I have received no syllable, neither from her self, nor by any other, how my wife hath passed her danger, nor do I know whether I be increased by a childe, or diminished by the losse of a wife. I hear from *England* of many censures of my book, of Mris. *Drury*,

[1] *World's Classics* ed., 40.

and he proceeds to express himself on this topic as though, for the time being, it were the one that chiefly occupied his mind.[1] I mention this, partly as an example of the way in which Donne's mind worked, and partly as an example of the difficulty of drawing just inferences, of the danger of inferring too much, from things that may seem strange to us in his poems and letters; for, had we not had Walton's account of the unwilling parting and of the vision in Paris, we might, perhaps, have been tempted to make more of a paradox out of the co-existence of the *Valediction: forbidding mourning* and of this letter than there really was—might have been tempted, as it were, to under-read the element of tenderness in the poem and to over-read the element of sheer intellect and wit. Nevertheless, the element of detachment, of strange detachment, is there. In a very melancholy letter from his hospital at Mitcham, written probably about 1613, after describing how every member of the family except himself is ill, how his wife has just had a miscarriage, and how one of his children is almost past hope, he continues: 'This meets a fortune so ill provided for physique and such relief, that if God should ease us with burials, I know not well how to performe even that'.[2] 'If God should ease us with burialls'—a revealing phrase, I think, although, as with other phrases, we must resist the temptation to infer too much from it. Again, in a letter to his friend Sir Robert Carr, later Earl of Ancrum, inviting him to attend the christening of one of his daughters, he says:

> Sir, I have so many and so indeleble impressions of your favour to me, as they might serve to spread over all my poor race. But since I see that I stand like a tree, which once a year beares, though no fruit, yet this Mast of children, and so am sure, that one year or other I should afflict you with this request, I had rather be presently under the obligations and the thankfulnesse towards you, then meditate such a trouble to you against another year.[3]

I am not sure, though, whether this passage should be regarded so much as evidence of Donne's detached attitude towards his children as of the fundamental unseriousness of much of his wit.

[1] *Letters*, 1651, 74–5; Gosse, I, 305–6.
[2] *Letters*, 1651, 151–3; Gosse, II, 36.
[3] *Letters*, 1651, 271–2; Gosse, II, 75–6.

Much of his wit, I am inclined to think, like much even of his serious study, was an attempt to escape, through some kind of intellectual activity, from the melancholy and depression that so constantly afflicted him during these years. Indeed, alternation between feverish activity and deep depression seems to have been almost as characteristic of Donne as it was of Hamlet, whom Donne in some ways so much resembles. In one of his letters from Mitcham, speaking of the diseases of the soul and their remedies, he says:

> Therefore sometimes when I finde my self transported with jollity, and love of company, I hang Leads at my heels; and reduce to my thoughts my fortunes, my years, the duties of a man, of a friend, of a husband, of a Father, and all the incumbencies of a family: when sadness dejects me, either I countermine it with another sadnesse, or I kindle squibs about me again, and flie into sportfulnesse and company: and I finde ever after all, that I am like an exorcist, which had long laboured about one, which at last appears to have the Mother[1] that I still mistake my disease.[2]

What was his disease, his 'sore distraction'? He has described the symptoms in many a letter from his 'hospital at Mitcham'. One of these symptoms was a longing, like Hamlet's, to be done with it all, to escape from the whips and scorns of time, to shuffle off this mortal coil. 'Two of the most precious things,' he wrote,

> which God hath afforded us here, for the agony and exercise of our sense and spirit, which are a thirst and inhiation after the next life, and a frequency of prayer and meditation in this, are often envenomed, and putrified, and stray into a corrupt disease. . . . With the first of these I have often suspected my self to be overtaken; which is, with a desire of the next life: which though I know it is not meerly out of a wearinesse of this, because I had the same desires when I went with the tyde, and enjoyed fairer hopes then now: yet I doubt worldly encombrances have encreased it.[3]

[1] *i.e.* hysteria.
[2] *Letters*, 1651, 71; Gosse, I, 184.
[3] *Letters*, 1651, 49–50; Gosse I, 190–1.

A longing like Hamlet's, I said, to escape from the whips and scorns of time—although there is some subtle distinction, for Donne insists that there was no element of rebelliousness or repining in this longing for death, and he was not, like Hamlet, restrained by the fear of what dreams might assail him when he had crossed that bourn from which no traveller returns. His longing was, he insists, rather to experience the next life (about which he seems to have been far less uncertain than Hamlet) than to escape from this one. He admits, indeed, that what he calls 'worldly encombrances' may have increased it, but he insists that he had the same longing in his brilliant and apparently careless youth, and he says much the same in the Preface to his *Biathanatos*, that elaborate, learned and para-doxical defence of the legitimacy, under certain circumstances, of suicide, which he wrote between 1606 and 1608, and which for many years he kept under lock and key and showed to very few even of his closest friends. 'I have often such a sickely inclination,' he there wrote:

> And, whether it be, because I had my first breeding and con-versation with men of a suppressed and afflicted Religion, accus-tomed to the despite of death, and hungry of an imagin'd Martyrdome; Or that the common Enemie find that doore worst locked against him in mee; Or that there bee a perplexitie and flexibility in the doctrine it selfe; Or because my Conscience ever assures me, that no rebellious grudging at Gods gifts, nor other sin-full concurrence accompanies these thoughts in me, or that a brave scorn, or that a faint cowardlinesse beget it, whensoever any affliction assailes me, mee thinks I have the keyes of my prison in mine owne hand, and no remedy presents it selfe so soone to my heart, as mine own sword. Often Meditation of this hath wonne me to a charitable interpretation of their action, who dy so: and provoked me a little to watch and exagitate their reasons, which pronounce so peremptory judgements upon them.[1]

So far as I can see, it is only possible to reconcile Donne's insistence (in which, indeed, there may be some element of exaggeration) that his longing for the next life was free from all rebelliousness or repining—it is only possible to reconcile this insistence with his

[1] 1644, pp. 17–18.

conception of death as a key that would release him from a prison
by supposing that Donne, even in his youth, not merely believed as
a doctrine but felt as an intuition the Catholic and medieval notion
that the world itself was a kind of prison, a place of passage and
pilgrimage, in which we were placed merely in order that we might
come to perceive its vanity, and that, when any particular affliction
assailed him, it increased his longing for the next life, not because he
rebelled against having to endure that particular affliction, but
because that particular affliction reminded him, rekindled his
awareness, of the general afflictedness and vanity of all temporal
life, of man in the world, of the soul imprisoned in the body, and
that when, in fact, in 1611 or 1612, he wrote in *The Second Anniversarie* that impressive passage about the imprisonment of the soul
in the body, which concludes

> But thinke that Death hath now enfranchis'd thee,
> Thou hast thy' expansion now, and libertie;
> Thinke that a rustie Peece, discharg'd, is flowne
> In peeces, and the bullet is his owne,
> And freely flies: This to thy Soule allow,
> Thinke thy shell broke, thinke thy Soule hatch'd but now.[1]

he was expressing a conviction, an attitude, which, although no
doubt it had been strengthened and deepened by long years of
solitary brooding and disappointed hopes, had, if not quite so intensely or continuously, been his from the beginning, even in those
days when his mind had seemed most frequented by the entrance
of manifold vanities, when he had been a great frequenter of plays,
a great visiter of ladies, a great writer of conceited verses, the glass
of fashion and the mould of form, th'admired of all beholders. And
if this supposition be correct, would it not, perhaps, largely explain
that strange detachment on which I have commented and that
difficulty I have mentioned of deciding just how much any of the
things to which Donne devoted himself really meant to him? For
were they not all, not merely the plays and the visits and the verses,
the travels and the expeditions, the talk at the Mermaid, the books
in his study, the Lord Keeper's favour, the prospect of public employment—were they not all, not merely these, but even, in some

[1] 179–84.

degree, the volumes of School divinity and theological controversy ('In heaven thou straight know'st all concerning it, And what concernes it not, shalt straight forget'), even, in some sense, his wife and children, even, in some sense, himself—were they not vanities, shadows, not substantial things? And must it not often have seemed to him, in some moods at any rate, that, where all was vanity, it did not much matter with what particular vanity one occupied oneself, did not much matter whether one was employing one's so limited intellectual powers to demonstrate why grass is green or why our blood is red, or to demonstrate, for the diversion of oneself and one's friends, that it was in every respect better to marry an old and ugly woman than a young and handsome one, or that inconstancy was a virtue, or that his mistress was denying to him what she had permitted to a flea?[1]

This, then, was one of the symptoms of Donne's disease, as he called it: a longing, not so much like Hamlet's, to escape from a sea of troubles into, if it were possible, a dreamless sleep, but a longing to pass from appearance to reality, a detachment from life and from the world. Nevertheless, there was another side of Donne, another self in him, if you will, which wanted to play some part in this unsubstantial pageant, this fair, this pilgrimage, this huge stage, even if it presented nought but shows on which the stars in secret influence comment. And indeed in that very same letter to Sir Henry Goodyer in which we have heard the more unworldly and visionary Donne longing to escape from his prison into the next life, we also hear the more worldly and realistic Donne complaining of his isolatedness and of the fact that he is an actor without a part. 'When I must shipwrack,' he declares,

[1] It may well have been of such an unregenerate thought, or mood, in his earlier self that Donne the preacher—in whose sermons one seems to detect so much autobiography—was thinking when, in the sixty-fifth of his *LXXX Sermons* (1640, p. 657), he found it necessary to explain precisely in what sense the Psalmist was to be understood when he declared that men were altogether lighter than vanity: 'And surely they that pervert and detort such words as these, to such a use, and argue from thence, Man is nothing, no more then a worme or a fly, and therefore what needs this solemne consideration of mans actions, it is all one what he does, for all his actions, and himselfe too are nothing; They doe but to justifie or excuse their own lazinesse in this world, in passing on their time, without taking any Calling, embracing any profession, contributing any thing to the spirituall edification, or temporall sustentation of other men. But take the words, as the Holy Ghost intends them, comparatively, what man compared with God, or what man considered without God, can doe any thing for others, or for himselfe?'

I would do it in a Sea, where mine impotencie might have some excuse; not in a sullen weedy lake, where I could not have so much as exercise for my swimming. Therefore I would fain do something; but that I cannot tell what, is no wonder. For to chuse, is to do: but to be no part of any body, is to be nothing.

And he concludes, after reviewing his previous attempts and failures:

Yet I would try again: for to this hour I am nothing, or so little, that I am scarce subject and argument good enough for one of mine own letters: yet I fear, that doth not ever proceed from a good root, that I am so well content to be lesse, that is dead.[1]

And this isolated and frustrated Donne sometimes expresses himself in language and imagery strangely similar to that of his contemporary Hamlet, the Hamlet who declared that for him this brave o'erhanging firmament was but a pestilent congregation of vapours: 'The pleasantnesse of the season,' he wrote to Goodyer, 'displeases me. Everything refreshes and I wither, and I grow older and not better, my strength diminishes, and my load growes.'[2] Yes, there are many resemblances between Donne and Hamlet: the alternation between intense activity, sometimes occupying itself with trifles, and deep depression; the longing (though with the important differences I have indicated) for death, the detachment, the double vision, the tenderness and the hardness. And yet in some, though only in some, respects, there is an even greater likeness between Donne and that king who played many parts and who delighted to watch himself playing them, knowing that, in a sense, they were only parts, and he himself only a player, appearing in life's unsubstantial pageant now as the deputy anointed by the Lord, now as a mockery king of snow melting before the sun of Bolingbroke. Donne was, I often feel, in the sense in which Shakespeare's Richard was, an actor of parts, sometimes consciously, but almost always, I think, half-consciously, watching himself playing them, and almost always at least half-aware that the stage upon which he played them was but

[1] *Letters*, 1651, 50–2; Gosse I, 191.
[2] *Letters*, 1651, 78; Gosse I, 185.

a stage. Here, I think, it is very difficult but very important to get the emphasis right, and easy to be unjust to Donne, easy to accuse him of egotism and self-centredness, if one neglects what I may call the transcendental aspect and forgets, while directing attention, rather contemptuously perhaps, upon Donne as an actor on a stage, that for Donne the whole world was, in a sense, a mere stage, an unsubstantial pageant, and all the men and women merely players. Professor Crofts, in his brilliant essay on Donne in *Essays and Studies*, seems to me, in an eloquent passage which I will quote, to over-simplify, to leave certain important things unsaid, and, consequently, to present a portrait that is considerably out of focus. 'Throughout his life,' says Professor Crofts,

> he was a man self-haunted, unable to escape from his own drama, unable to find any window that would not give him back the image of himself. Even the mistress of his most passionate love-verses, who must (one supposes) have been a real person, remains for him a mere abstraction of sex: a thing given. He does not see her—does not apparently want to see her; for it is not of her that he writes, but of his relation to her; not of love, but of himself loving. And so, in later life, though the stuff of his meditations changes, this inability to lose himself remains. It is not of God that he thinks so often or so deeply as of his relation to God; of the torturing drama of his sin and its expiation, the sowing and the reaping, the wheat and the tares. The great commonplace of his sermons, it has been said, is death: but in truth it is not death that inspires his frightful eloquence so much as the image of himself dying; and the pre-occupation culminates in that ghastly charade of his last hours, described by Walton, when he lay contemplating the portrait of himself in his winding-sheet like a grim and mortified Narcissus.[1]

There is important truth in this passage, but it seems to me, through the over-emphasis of some aspects and the under-emphasis or omission of others, to be distorted into something like caricature; and, although I admire the brilliance and penetration of his essay, I feel that here, as occasionally elsewhere, Professor Crofts has tended to write of Donne too much as some have written (and in schools

[1] *Essays and Studies by Members of the English Association*, 1936, 133-4.

still write) of that 'weak King', Shakespeare's Richard. To-day, for those, and they are very numerous, who are always looking and asking for what they call 'sincerity' in literature, the presence of any considerable element of self-dramatization in a writer is offensive and, perhaps, only half-intelligible. And yet it was precisely the lack of what he called 'dramatic lyrical expression' in English poetry that was deplored by the greatest English poet of this century, W. B. Yeats, who declared that Villon and Ronsard had made magnificent drama out of their own lives, and who strove, not unsuccessfully, to do the same himself, rather despising the modern cult of sincerity and opposing to it his doctrine of the mask. The dramatic element in Donne's life and in Donne's poetry is most important, and we must have some taste for drama in order to understand and appreciate it. This dramatic element in Donne is, as I have insisted, closely connected with his detachment and his fundamental scepticism. In a sense, he could only lose himself, only escape from his continually recurring awareness of the nothingness of life, by playing a part, and during the thirteen years that followed his dismissal from Egerton's service in 1602 until his ordination in 1615 he was without a part. The part which was at last allotted him, and which at first he entered upon so reluctantly, proved to be peculiarly suited to his temperament and genius, for his very function was now to proclaim that the stage upon which he was mounted was but a stage. Nowhere do we find him exercising it more impressively than in the famous passage from one of his sermons with which I will conclude this chapter, reserving until I come to consider the *Divine Poems* a more detailed study of what I have called his Third Act:

Man is, sayes the Prophet *Esay*, *Quasi stilla situlae*, *As a drop upon the bucket*. Man is not all that, not so much as that, as a drop upon the bucket, but *quasi*, something, some little thing towards it; and what is a drop upon the bucket, to a river, to a sea, to the waters above the firmament? Man to God? *Man is*, sayes the same Prophet in the same place, *Quasi momentum staterae*; we translate it, *As small dust upon the balance*: Man is not all that, not that small graine of dust; but *quasi*, some little thing towards it: And what can a graine of dust work in governing the balance? What is man that God should be mindfull of him? Vanity seemes to be the lightest thing, that the Holy Ghost could name; and when he had named that, he sayes, and sayes, and sayes, often, very, very often, *All is vanity*. But when he comes to waigh man with vanity it selfe, he findes man lighter then vanity: *Take*, sayes he, *great men, and meane men altogether, and altogether they are lighter then vanity.* When that great Apostle sayes of himselfe, that he was in *nothing behinde the very chiefest of the Apostles*, and yet, for all that, sayes he was nothing; who can thinke himselfe any thing, for being a Giant in proportion, a Magistrate in power, a Rabbi in learning, an Oracle in Counsell? Let man be something; how poore, and inconsiderable a ragge of this world, is man? Man, whom *Paracelsus* would have undertaken to have made, in a Limbeck, in a Furnace: Man, who, if they were altogether, all the men, that ever were, and are, and shall be, would not have the power of one Angel in them all, whereas all the Angels, (who, in the Schoole are conceived to be more in number, then, not onely all the Species, but all the individualls of this lower world) have not in them all, the power of one finger of Gods hand: Man, of whom when *David* had said, (as the lowest diminution that he could put upon him) *I am a worme and no man*, He might have gone lower, and said, I am a man and no worm; for man is so much lesse then a worm, as that wormes of his own production, shall feed upon his dead body in the grave, and an immortall worm gnaw his conscience in the torments of hell.[1]

---

[1] *LXXX Sermons*, pp. 64–5.

3

EPIGRAMS, ELEGIES, SATIRES,
VERSE LETTERS

I PROPOSE, for various reasons, to begin this study of Donne's
poetry with his couplet poems, the *Epigrams, Elegies, Satyrs* and
Letters to Severall Personages. A direct comparison between Donne
and Jonson is more possible here, and certain obvious characteristics of Donne's genius and method will emerge more quickly
and clearly than they would from the more complex and concentrated *Songs and Sonets*. Indeed, if we begin with the couplet poems,
I think we shall find ourselves much more able to get the *Songs
and Sonets* into true perspective. In nearly all Donne's poetry what
one may call sheer wit plays a very great part, and this element
of sheer wit is, I think, more immediately apparent in the couplet
poems than in the *Songs and Sonets*, where it has often been mistaken for the expression of actual convictions, attitudes and experiences. It is necessary to insist that it was this element of sheer wit
which seems to have made the greatest impression on Donne's
contemporaries, even when, like Jonson and Drummond, they
were poets whose own achievements and ideals were very different.
'He esteemeth John Donne the first poet in the world in some
things', Drummond reported of Jonson: 'his verses of the Lost
Chaine he heth by heart, and that passage of the Calme, *That dust
and feathers doe not stirr, all was so quiet*. Affirmeth Done to have
written all his best pieces ere he was 25 years old.' Professor F. P.
Wilson, I think, has been the first to insist on the true significance
of this passage, on its evidence as to what, exactly, Jonson considered
to be Donne's 'best pieces', and declared him to have written before
he was twenty-five, that is, by 1597. Most of us, I suppose, think
of certain of the *Songs and Sonets* as Donne's best pieces, and find
it hard to believe that Donne had written them all by 1597; but, as
Professor Wilson insists, Jonson was not thinking of the *Songs and
Sonets*. 'It is significant,' he says,

that he chose for special commendation not the 'Valediction forbidding mourning', not 'The Good Morrow', not one of the lyrics secular and divine which have gone to the head of the twentieth century, but two epistles in decasyllabic couplets.[1]

The 'verses of the Lost Chaine', which Jonson had by heart and which was one of those 'best pieces' for which he esteemed Donne 'the first poet in the world', is the Eleventh Elegy, entitled *The Bracelet. Vpon the losse of his Mistresses Chaine, for which he made satisfaction,* one of the most astonishing of all Donne's exercises in sheer wit, in which he elaborates in something over a hundred lines the conceit that twelve righteous angels, which Heaven appointed to be his providers and guides, must be damned for offences not their own, cast into the furnace, and melted down to replace the lost chain. The other poem, or, rather, passage from a poem, which Jonson especially admired was a couplet from the verse epistle wittily and realistically describing the calm which beset the Island voyagers of 1597:

> No use of lanthornes; and in one place lay
> Feathers and dust, to day and yesterday.

Drummond himself wrote of Donne:

> I think, if he would, he might easily be the best Epigrammatist we have found in *English*, of which I have not yet seen any come near the Ancients.
> Compare Song, *Marry and Love, &c.,* with *Tasso's Stanzas against Beauty*; one shall hardly know who hath the best.[2]

Drummond is here using the word Epigrammatist in a rather wide sense, and the poem he is referring to is the Second Elegy, entitled *The Anagram,* which defends, by a series of ingenious analogies, the preposterous proposition that an old and ugly woman will make a better wife than a young and handsome one. Thus what Drummond too seems to have especially admired in Donne was his sheer wit, a wit displayed in a kind of poetry as far as possible removed

---

[1] *Elizabethan and Jacobean,* 54.
[2] *Critical Essays of the Seventeenth Century,* ed. J. E. Spingarn, I, 216–17

from either the poetry of statement, the poetry of suggestion, the poetry of confession, or even, one might almost say, from the poetry of objective description, since the subject, whatever it happens to be, is almost completely indifferent to the poet—a mere starting-point, a mere trapeze for the performance of intellectual gymnastics, a mere stick for a rocket. Only part of Donne's poetry is wholly of this kind, but a great deal of it is partly of this kind—a fact we must remember when we feel tempted to interpret it autobiographically. We must always be prepared to make very large allowance for the element of sheer wit.

I.   The Epigrams

I need not spend much time over Donne's Epigrams, of which only a tiny handful have survived. They are very much shorter than Jonson's, and the impulse behind them is not (as with the best of Jonson's) moral, but purely intellectual and ingenious. It is worth recording, as one more piece of evidence as to what Jonson especially admired in Donne, that, according to Drummond, the epigram on *Phryne* was among the commonplaces of his repetition:

> Thy flattering picture, *Phryne*, is like thee,
> Onely in this, that you both painted be.

In the epigram on *Hero and Leander* he has ingeniously contrived to introduce the four elements:

> Both rob'd of aire, we both lye in one ground,
> Both whom one fire had burnt, one water drownd.

II.   The Elegies

What is most peculiar and characteristic in Donne's genius and method, the great part played in his poetry by sheer wit, emerges, perhaps, most clearly and rapidly from a careful study of the Elegies. They may be divided into three main groups: (1) witty discourses on a broomstick, where the subject is a mere occasion for displaying wit; (2) apparently serious defences of outrageous propositions; (3) dramatic situations, real or imaginary, in which also considerable elements of sheer wit or sheer paradox may be incidentally present.

Let us begin with the third group, which I have called the dramatic elegies, but before doing so let us glance briefly at a book which had, I think, no inconsiderable influence on the tone and on the situations of several of them, Ovid's *Amores*. Ovid's *Elegies* the Elizabethans called them, and that was the title of the not always very accurate or felicitous translation by the youthful Marlowe, which, together with the *Epigrams* of Sir John Davies, appeared in an undated volume which claimed to have been printed at Middleburgh, and which must certainly have been printed before 1599. The original meaning of *elegia* or *elegeia* was a funeral elegy written in elegiacs (*elegi*), that is to say, in couplets consisting of an hexameter followed by a pentameter, but Ovid and other Roman poets used the word to describe a love-poem written in that metre. The *Amores* was one of Ovid's most youthful works, and most of the poems are either to or about a probably imaginary Corinna, for whose *vir* (*i.e.*, her current 'man') he expresses great contempt. They are distinguished by their impudence, their insolence, and a certain witty depravity. Ovid and his contemporaries, I need hardly say, had never heard of anything like the doctrine of Courtly Love, but, although Ovid's attitude and his wit seemed a good deal less novel, surprising and shocking to the Romans than Donne's did to the Elizabethans, it is probable that some degree of outrageousness and exaggeration was deliberately intended and felt. Indeed, the assumption, or pretended assumption, that his cynical and amoral attitude was normal and natural is one of the chief elements in Ovid's wit.[1] Augustus, at any rate, who seriously set himself to regenerate Roman morals, did not share this attitude, and when, some twenty-five years later, Ovid published his still more outrageous *Ars Amatoria* and it became a best-seller, the Emperor exiled him for the rest of

[1] To those who are inclined to regard works of literature mainly as social documents and to draw from them inferences about the social and moral characteristics of the periods in which they were written, it may be suggested that 'shocking' pieces of writing should perhaps be taken to imply the continued existence of persons capable of being shocked: that, for example, Ovid's *Amores* should be regarded as evidence, not so much of the corruption of Roman society, as of the continued existence of numerous Elder Catos, Portias, Volumnias whose fire mischievous urchins like the young Ovid took a delight in drawing ('It drew the old colonels beautifully', a friend of mine once remarked of a letter to the *New Statesman*). In her essay on *The Italy of the Elizabethan Dramatists* in *Euphorion* Vernon Lee maintained, rather too melodramatically perhaps, the interesting paradox that, while the uncorrupted and therefore horrified children of the North were writing plays full of treachery, poisoning and incest, the black-hearted Italians themselves were writing and enjoying charming pastorals about Phyllis and Chloris.

his life to the shores of the Black Sea and had his book expelled from
the public libraries. Thomas Carew, in his Elegy on Donne, declared
that the lesser poets whom Donne had left behind

> Will repeale the goodly exil'd traine
> Of gods and goddesses, which in thy just raigne
> Were banish'd nobler Poems, now, with these
> The silenc'd tales o' th' Metamorphoses
> Shall stuffe their lines, and swell the windy Page.

Donne's predecessors had exploited classical mythology and classical
legend and had drawn largely on the Ovid of the *Metamorphoses*;
Donne, who despised such mere ornaments and childish fancies,
proceeded to do something much more daring and original, something, too, which was the almost complete antithesis of that Petrarchan adoration and Platonic idealism of which, together with
classical mythology and classical allusions, he and many of his
contemporaries had had more than enough: he proceeded to repro-
duce something of the tone, the situations and the cynical wit of
Ovid's *Amores*. There are, it is true, great differences in style: the
smooth progression, the details seldom in themselves extravagant,
the crackling fire of epigram which distinguish Ovid's *Amores* are
very different from the drama, the extravagance, the vivid realism,
the subtle analogies and syllogistic arguments of Donne. What
Donne has caught are the impudence and insolence and the assumptions about the true nature and end of love and the proper attitude
to husbands.[1] One of the most consistently witty and epigrammatic
of all Ovid's elegies is the nineteenth of the Second Book, where he
contemptuously tells Corinna's complacent keeper to guard her for
her lover's sake if not for his own, since things too easily obtained
lose their attraction. 'If you yourself, you fool,' he begins, 'feel no
need to guard your *puella*, at least guard her for my sake, so that I
may desire her more passionately. What is lawful gives no pleasure,
what is not excites us all the more keenly.' This insolent beginning
is quite in the manner of Donne's Elegies, but the crackling epigrams
that follow are more like Dryden, who translated this elegy, vigor-
ously enough, but, as only too often, with a good deal of coarsening

[1] Ovid probably did not mean that Corinna's *vir* was her husband, but that was
how Donne and his contemporaries understood him.

and blackguardization. Marlowe was not up to it. More like Dryden, I say, or, even, perhaps, like Pope:

> *Pinguis amor nimiumque patens in taedia nobis*
> *Vertitur et, stomacho dulcis ut esca, nocet.*

A full-fed and too easy love becomes tedious and disagrees with me as over-sweet food does with the stomach.

> *Quod licet et facile est, quisquis cupit, arbore frondis*
> *Carpat et a magno flumine potet aquam!*

Let him who craves what is lawful and easy, gather leaves from a tree and drink water from a great river!

> *Ille potest vacuo furari litore harenas,*
> *Uxorem stulti siquis amare potest.*

A man capable of loving a fool's wife[1] is capable of stealing sand from a barren shore.

> *Quid mihi cum facili, quid cum lenone marito?*
> *Corrumpit vitio gaudia nostra suo.*

What use to me is a complaisant, a prostituting husband?[1] His immorality spoils my pleasure.

Another of Ovid's wittiest elegies is the tenth of the Second Book, which concludes with a passage where he even seems to be impudently parodying the sort of thing Virgil and Horace had said about tillers of the soil and lovers of the rustic gods, how much happier they were than soldiers, lawyers and merchants who wore themselves out in the quest of glory or gain.

> *Fortunatus et ille deos qui novit agrestes*

[1] The attitude of Corinna's 'man' towards the infidelities of his 'girl' is like that of a complacent husband towards those of his wife. By putting an *uxor* and a *puella* on the same level, Ovid is making fun of Augustus's purity campaign.

said Virgil;

Felix, quem Veneris certamina mutua rumpunt!

said impudent young Ovid:

> Happy he whom Venus's mutual contests bring to his end. May
> the Gods make that the cause of my decease! Let the soldier
> present his breast to opposing darts and purchase an eternal name
> with his blood; let the miser go in search of riches, and, ship-
> wrecked, drink with his perjured mouth the waves his ploughing
> vessel has left behind; but let me grow old in the service of Venus
> and die in her cause.

Such are the impudent paradoxes and the smooth, elegant,
epigrammatic style of Ovid's *Amores*. The Ovid of the *Metamorphoses*, the mythological Ovid, had already been exploited *ad
nauseam*; Donne seems to have been the first to perceive what novel,
surprising and shocking effects might be produced by exploiting
the more realistic and naturalistic Ovid of the *Amores*. To transfer
some of Ovid's characteristic situations and assumptions to Elizabethan London, and to express them as though they were perfectly
normal, was in itself a daring piece of originality. We must, of
course, resist the temptation to regard such poems as autobiographical, or to infer from them anything about Donne's own conduct,
morals and opinions. The fact that in several of them there appears
the triangular situation of poet, mistress and husband, led Gosse
to infer that round about 1596 Donne was having an intrigue with
some married woman; it is, though, much more probable that he
was simply dramatizing the situation he found in Ovid's *Amores*.
We should remember, too, a remark of the later and graver Donne
about the poetry he had written in youth: 'I did best,' he said, 'when
I had least truth for my subjects.'[1]

Proceeding now to our study of what I have called the dramatic
elegies, let us begin with the First Elegy, entitled *Iealosie*, of which,
since it is not very long, I will quote the whole:

[1] Gosse, II, 215; *Poems*, ed. Grierson, I, 288.

Fond woman, which would'st have thy husband die,
And yet complain'st of his great jealousie;
If swolne with poyson, hee lay in'his last bed,
His body with a sere-barke covered,
Drawing his breath, as thick and short, as can
The nimblest crocheting Musitian,
Ready with loathsome vomiting to spue
His Soule out of one hell, into a new,
Made deafe with his poore kindreds howling cries,
Begging with few feign'd teares, great legacies,
Thou would'st not weepe, but jolly,'and frolicke bee,
As a slave, which to morrow should be free;
Yet weep'st thou, when thou seest him hungerly
Swallow his owne death, hearts-bane jealousie.
O give him many thanks, he'is courteous,
That in suspecting kindly warneth us.
Wee must not, as wee us'd, flout openly,
In scoffing ridles, his deformitie;
Nor at his boord together being satt,
With words, nor touch, scarce lookes adulterate.
Nor when he swolne, and pamper'd with great fare,
Sits downe, and snorts, cag'd in his basket chaire,
Must wee usurpe his owne bed any more,
Nor kisse and play in his house, as before.
Now I see many dangers; for that is
His realme, his castle, and his diocesse.
But if, as envious men, which would revile
Their Prince, or coyne his gold, themselves exile
Into another countrie, 'and doe it there,
Wee play'in another house, what should we feare?
There we will scorne his household policies,
His seely plots, and pensionary spies,
As the inhabitants of Thames right side
Do Londons Major; or Germans, the Popes pride.

The situation, as I have said, comes from Ovid's *Amores*, but, here
as elsewhere, there is much more drama and play of mind than in
Ovid.

> Wee must not, as wee us'd, flout openly,
> In scoffing ridles, his deformitie;
> Nor at his boord together being satt,
> With words, nor touch, scarce lookes adulterate.

These lines were almost certainly suggested by a much longer passage in the fourth elegy of Ovid's First Book, but how different is Donne's rapidity and vivid concentration from the leisurely elaboration of Ovid, who is, as it were, rather coolly, methodically and exhaustively working out a prescribed theme than, like Donne, setting down images and impressions which seem to have occurred to him for the first time in the heat of composition. Here is Ovid in Dryden's translation (Dryden only translated three of the *Amores*):

> Sit next him (that belongs to decency)
> But tread upon my foot in passing by.
> Read in my looks what silently they speak,
> And slily, with your eyes, your answer make.
> My lifted eyebrow shall declare my pain;
> My right hand to his fellow shall complain;
> And on the back a letter shall design;
> Besides a note that shall be writ in wine.
> Whene'er you think upon our last embrace,
> With your fore-finger gently touch your face.
> If any word of mine offend my dear,
> Pull, with your hand, the velvet of your ear.
> If you are pleas'd with what I do or say,
> Handle your rings, or with your fingers play.
> As suppliants use at altars, hold the board,
> Whene'er you wish the devil may take your lord.
> When he fills for you, never touch the cup,
> But bid th'officious cuckold drink it up.
> The waiter on those services employ:
> Drink you, and I will snatch it from the boy;
> Watching the part where your smooth mouth hath been,
> And thence with eager lips will suck it in.

'Nor,' continues Donne,

Nor when he swolne, and pamper'd with great fare,
Sits downe, and snorts, cag'd in his basket chaire,
Must wee usurpe his owne bed any more,
Nor kisse and play in his house, as before.

This, though incomparably more vivid, is much closer to Ovid, from whom, lest there should be any doubt that Donne had this elegy in mind, I will again quote the corresponding passage in Dryden's translation:

Encourage him to tope; but kiss him not,
Nor mix one drop of water in his pot.
If he be fuddled well, and snores apace,
Then we may take advice from time and place.

Donne pretty certainly had in mind this passage from the *Amores* about the secret signs between lover and mistress when he wrote the Seventh Elegy, but again it was but the starting point for something which, except for its impudence and insolence, is quite unlike Ovid—a kind of dramatic monologue in which what one may call the descriptive element is only incidental and in which that indulgence in mere epigram, so characteristic of Ovid, is completely absent. Ovid, one may say in general, is continually describing, and making witty and epigrammatic remarks about, situations which are static or given, is, as it were, contemplating them from the outside, in detachment; Donne, at any rate in the elegies we are now considering, is much more dramatic, continually throwing himself, as it were, into a part, continually imagining new aspects of the triangular situation, and speaking, thinking and feeling vividly and rapidly, as in a play. While Ovid merely describes situations, Donne enacts them: the nature and details of the situation emerge, as it were, incidentally, from an overheard discourse or tirade. Such elegies are essentially dramatic monologues—monologues, that is to say, whose tone is modified by, adapted to, the particular kind of person Donne imagines himself to be addressing. Here he imagines that the mistress-wife was an ignorant and stupid woman until he made her expert in the theory and practice of love, and that now she has begun to get above herself and to talk of her duty to her husband, or even to affect other lovers. Again, since the elegy is short, I will quote the whole of it, but in one passage, where the phrase 'Remember since' is used, rather confusingly, in the sense of 'Remember from the time when', I will, for the sake of immediate comprehensibility, substitute 'when' for 'since'.

> Natures lay[1] Ideot, I taught thee to love,
> And in that sophistrie, Oh, thou dost prove
> Too subtile: Foole, thou didst not understand
> The mystique language of the eye nor hand:
> Nor couldst thou judge the difference of the aire
> Of sighes, and say, this lies, this sounds despaire:
> Nor by the'eyes water call a maladie
> Desperately hot, or changing feaverously.
> I had not taught thee then, the Alphabet
> Of flowers, how they devisefully being set
> And bound up, might with speechlesse secrecie
> Deliver arrands mutely, and mutually.
> Remember when all thy words us'd to bee
> To every suitor: *I, if my friends agree*;
> When household charmes, thy husbands name to teach,
> Were all the love trickes, that thy wit could reach;
> And when an houres discourse could scarce have made
> One answer in thee, and that ill arraid
> In broken proverbs, and torne sentences.
> Thou art not by so many duties his,
> That from the worlds Common having sever'd thee,
> Inlaid thee, neither to be seene, nor see,
> As mine: who have with amorous delicacies
> Refin'd thee'into a blis-full Paradise.
> Thy graces and good words my creatures bee;
> I planted knowledge and lifes tree in thee,
> Which Oh, shall strangers taste? Must I alas
> Frame and enamell Plate, and drinke in Glasse?
> Chafe waxe for others seales? breake a colts force
> And leave him then, beeing made a ready horse?

[1] Ignorant, not a clerk in love's mysteries. It seems possible that in this elegy Donne is magnificently expanding and transforming a mere hint in Tibullus, I, vi, 5–14.

In the Fourth Elegy, entitled *The Perfume*, the mistress is a young unmarried woman, a mere girl. One can still feel Ovid in the background, and the desire to surprise, to shock, by the pretended acceptance of an immoral and cynical code which, I think we may be pretty sure, was never Donne's own; but, although there is more detail than in *Iealosie*, it is entirely unimitative, entirely English, and most brilliantly, vividly and concentratedly imagined. Indeed, the description of the mother's careful examination of her daughter is, in its elaborately but at the same time concentratedly imagined detail, reminiscent of some of the best things in Jonson's comedies. Here are the first forty-two lines, the most brilliant and characteristic passage, I think, in all Donne's dramatic elegies:

> Once, and but once found in thy company,
> All thy suppos'd escapes[1] are laid on mee;
> And as a thiefe at barre, is question'd there
> By all the men, that have beene rob'd that yeare,
> So am I, (by this traiterous meanes surpriz'd)
> By thy Hydroptique father catechiz'd.
> Though he had wont to search with glazed eyes,
> As though he came to kill a Cockatrice,
> Though hee hath oft sworne, that hee would remove
> Thy beauties beautie, and food of our love,
> Hope of his goods, if I with thee were seene,
> Yet close and secret, as our soules, we'have beene.
> Though thy immortall mother which doth lye
> Still buried in her bed, yet will not dye,
> Takes this advantage to sleepe out day-light,
> And watch thy entries, and returnes all night,
> And, when she takes thy hand, and would seeme kind,
> Doth search what rings, and armelets she can finde,
> And kissing notes the colour of thy face,
> And fearing least thou'art swolne, doth thee embrace;
> And to trie if thou long, doth name strange meates,
> And notes thy palenesse, blushing, sighs, and sweats;
> And politiquely will to thee confesse
> The sinnes of her owne youths ranke lustinesse;

[1] Escapades.

Yet love these Sorceries did remove, and move
Thee to gull thine owne mother for my love.
Thy little brethren, which like Faiery Sprights
Oft skipt into our chamber, those sweet nights,
And kist, and ingled on thy fathers knee,
Were brib'd next day, to tell what they did see:[1]
The grim eight-foot-high iron-bound serving-man,
That oft names God in oathes, and onely than,
He that to barre the first gate, doth as wide
As the great Rhodian Colossus stride,
Which, if in hell no other paines there were,
Makes mee feare hell, because he must be there:
Though by thy father he were hir'd to this,
Could never witnesse any touch or kisse.
But Oh, too common ill, I brought with mee
That, which betray'd mee to my enemie:
A loud perfume, which at my entrance cryed
Even at thy fathers nose, so were wee spied.

Together with the other characteristics I have mentioned, the reader will not have failed to notice the element of high-spirited, of almost rollicking, exaggeration. I think only a very impercipient reader would be tempted to regard such writing as autobiographical, and to begin searching among records for evidence that some London household of the time had in its employment a grim eight-foot-high iron-bound serving-man. I doubt whether even Professor Manly would think it worth while.

Though hee hath oft sworne, that hee would remove
Thy beauties beautie, and food of our love,
Hope of his goods.

This piece of gratuitious cynicism is, of course, simply thrown in (as Rymer said of Chaucer's linguistic borrowings) 'like new Stum to raise a Fermentation', to shock, to startle, to give full measure. Jonson, too, though not, like Donne here, irresponsibly and high-

---

[1] The main verb, 'could', is still to come: although next day they were kissed, coaxed ('ingled'), and bribed to tell, the 'little brethren', like the serving-man, had never been able to 'witnesse any touch or kisse'.

spiritedly, was a master of such almost casually and parenthetically delivered satire:

> Drest with an exquisite, and poynant sauce;
> For which, Ile say vnto my cooke, there's gold,
> Goe forth, and be a knight.

We are, as it were, without any warning, suddenly tricked into accepting some proposition, some attitude, we should like to qualify or protest against, but the author gives us no time to do so, and sweeps us along as though we had agreed with him. In fact, he's got away with it again.

In the Twelfth Elegy, *His Parting from her*, the mistress is again a married woman, and again the lines describing the secret signs between them seem to have been written with that passage in Ovid's *Amores*, which I have already quoted, in mind:

> Have we not kept our guards, like spie on spie?
> Had correspondence whilst the foe stood by?
> Stoln (more to sweeten them) our many blisses
> Of meetings, conference, embracements, kisses?
> Shadow'd with negligence our most respects?
> Varied our language, through all dialects,
> Of becks, winks, looks, and often under-boards
> Spoak dialogues with our feet far from our words?[1]

On the other hand, in this poem it is only the husband who is (very briefly and incidentally) a theme for impudent wit:

> Was't not enough, that thou didst hazzard us
> To paths in love so dark, so dangerous:
> And those so ambush'd round with houshold spies,
> And over all, thy husbands towring eyes
> That flam'd with oylie sweat of jealousie.[2]

In Donne's address to the woman and in his description of their love there is real tenderness, although it is impossible (and unnecessary) to decide whether the situation was real or imaginary. Lines

[1] ll. 45–52.
[2] ll. 39–44.

67–82, a defiant apostrophe to Fortune, in which he declares that
his mistress's image will be perpetually present to him during his
absence from her, might almost have occurred in one of Shakespeare's earlier comedies:[1]

> Do thy great worst, my friend and I have armes,
> Though not against thy strokes, against thy harmes.
> Rend us in sunder, thou canst not divide
> Our bodies so, but that our souls are ty'd,
> And we can love by letters still and gifts,
> And thoughts and dreams; Love never wanteth shifts.
> I will not look upon the quickning Sun,
> But straight her beauty to my sense shall run;
> The ayre shall note her soft, the fire most pure;
> Water suggest her clear, and the earth sure.
> Time shall not lose our passages; the Spring
> How fresh our love was in the beginning;
> The Summer how it ripened in the eare;
> And Autumn, what our golden harvests were.
> The Winter I'll not think on to spite thee,
> But count it a lost season, so shall shee.

It is, as I have said, impossible to decide whether the situation was
real or imaginary: why should not Donne, just for the sake of
variety, have attempted now and then what one might call a more
Shakespearean, a less Ovidian, dramatization of himself? Outrageousness, no doubt, was excellent fun, but too much of it was apt to
become tedious. Donne, after all, was never a one-note man: there
was much music, excellent voice, in that little organ.

The Fifteenth Elegy, *The Expostulation*, although included in all
printed editions and in most of the manuscript collections of Donne's
poems, seems to me more likely to have been inspired by him than
written by him. In the first place, it contains an amount of detailed,
as distinct from merely general, imitation of passages in Latin
authors which is without parallel in Donne's other poems—indeed,
few even of Ben Jonson's are such centos as this.[2] In the second

---

[1] A fact which, like some other things in this elegy, may raise doubts as to whether
it has been correctly ascribed to Donne.

[2] See the commentary on the poem by Percy and Evelyn Simpson in the Oxford
Jonson, Vol. XI, pp. 70–1.

place, its four-fold structure is not characteristic of Donne: the poet first accuses his mistress of inconstancy, then suddenly rebukes himself, curses the person in whom she innocently confided and who made them jealous and mistrustful of one another, and insists that everything between them is just as it was before. The mention at line 52 of 'the Kings dogges' is a clear allusion to James I's passion for hunting and proves that the poem must have been written after 1603, later than Donne's other elegies and after the pioneer had begun to find imitators. Nevertheless, there are good things in the poem, things which are often very like Donne and which could scarcely have been written without his example, such as the concluding lines, partly imitated from the second elegy of Ovid's Third Book, describing himself at the circus with Corinna, she watching the races, he watching her, where the English poet has substituted the playhouse for the circus:

> Now have I curst, let us our love revive;
>   In mee the flame was never more alive;
> I could beginne againe to court and praise,
>   And in that pleasure lengthen the short dayes
> Of my lifes lease; like Painters that do take
>   Delight, not in made worke, but whiles they make;
> I could renew those times, when first I saw
>   Love in your eyes, that gave my tongue the law
> To like what you lik'd; and at maskes and playes
>   Commend the selfe same Actors, the same wayes;
> Aske how you did, and often with intent
>   Of being officious, be impertinent;
> All which were such soft pastimes, as in these
>   Love was as subtilly catch'd, as a disease;
> But being got it is a treasure sweet,
>   Which to defend is harder then to get:
> And ought not be prophan'd on either part,
>   For though'tis got by *chance*, 'tis kept by *art*.

In the second volume of the folio edition of Ben Jonson's works, which the poet had been preparing at the time of his death and which was completed by his friend Sir Kenelm Digby and published by him in 1640, there is a collection of some hundred miscellaneous poems entitled *Underwoods* or *The Under-Wood*. It contains this elegy, *The Expostulation*, preceded by one and followed by two other elegies which are so much nearer to Donne's habitual manner than to Jonson's that, among those who have assumed that *The Expostulation* was by Donne, there has long been dispute as to whether Jonson was here deliberately trying to imitate Donne, or whether, like *The Expostulation*, they were erroneously attributed to Jonson by Digby, who had perhaps found among Jonson's papers copies which Donne had given him, or which Jonson himself had transcribed. My own view is that, like *The Expostulation*, they are superficially, often brilliantly, but not really like Donne, and that no sound reasons can be produced for assigning them to anyone but Jonson; although I should not be surprised if evidence eventually appeared that one or other of them were by some member of the Donne-Jonson circle such as Sir John Roe. In the first of them, *xxxviii*, ' 'Tis true, I'm broke!', the poet begs his mistress to forgive him for having in some way betrayed her confidence when he was drunk, and to remember that she is a divinity and that divinities are merciful. The semi-serious theological argument (some may think it rather too 'profane and full of blasphemies' for Jonson) is quite often in Donne's manner, but it is surely impossible to suppose that the elegant and fastidious Donne would ever have represented himself, even fictitiously, as having been drunk and as confessing this to a woman: one is reminded of Grierson's remark, in discussing certain other poems erroneously ascribed to Donne, about the contrast between the witty, Italianate depravity in which Donne sometimes indulged and that 'coarseness of the tavern and the camp' which we often find in Jonson.[1] The second of these elegies, *xl*, is a witty defence of the poet's apparent gaiety during absence from his mistress, and the manner, sustained throughout, of its opening lines is certainly more suggestive of Donne than of Jonson:

> That Love's a bitter sweet, I ne're conceive
>   Till the sower Minute comes of taking leave,
> And then I taste it. But as men drinke up
>   In haste the bottome of a med'cin'd Cup,
> And take some sirrup after; so doe I,
>   To put all relish from my memorie

[1] *The Poems of John Donne*, Vol. II, p. cxxxii.

Of parting, drowne it in the hope to meet
    Shortly againe: and make our absence sweet.
This makes me, M$^{rs.}$ that sometime by stealth,
    Under another Name, I take your health;
And turne the Ceremonies of those Nights
    I give, or owe my friends, into your Rites.

Here, though, as in both *xxxviii* and *xli*, the poet addresses the woman as 'Mistris' and calls himself her 'servant', and, as Dr and Mrs Simpson have observed in their commentary on these poems, Donne never uses the word 'mistress' as a term of address. The last of these elegies, *xli*, 'Since you must go', is a witty description of what absence from her is like, and concludes with a subtle and dramatic variation, quite in Donne's manner, on the common theme of the exchange of hearts:

My health will leave me; and when you depart,
    How shall I doe, sweet Mistris, for my heart?
You would restore it? No, that's worth a feare,
    As if it were not worthy to be there:
O, keepe it still; for it had rather be
    Your sacrifice, then here remaine with me.
And so I spare it. Come what can become
    Of me, I'll softly tread unto my Tombe;
Or like a Ghost walke silent amongst men,
    Till I may see both it and you agen.

Earlier in *Underwoods* there are two short elegies, *xviii*, 'Can Beautie that did prompt me first to write', and *xix*, 'By those bright eyes, at whose immortall fires', which are also near enough to Donne's manner to stand out rather exceptionally among Jonson's poems. The fact that the second of these contains several similarities with passages in Jonson's poems and plays, including, as Mr John Carey has shown in an unpublished dissertation, a refashioning of Wittipol's wooing of Mistress Fitzdottrel in *The Devil is an Ass* (I, vi, 127ff. and II, vi, 63ff.), seems to remove any difficulty in believing that Jonson was the author of the other Donne-like elegies in *Underwoods*, and that even this sturdiest and most independent of neo–classicists, whose admiration for the wittier Donne has been sufficiently attested by Drummond, had been temporarily magnetized into imitating the Monarch of Wit.

Returning to those elegies which have never been attributed to any poet but Donne, and continuing our examination of those which I have described as 'dramatic', we come to the famous Sixteenth, *On his Mistris*, dissuading her from her wish to accompany him on a foreign journey disguised as a page, which in one manuscript alone, the Bridgewater, has the title *His wife would have gone as his page*. For various reasons I agree with Grierson that this poem was almost certainly not addressed by Donne to his wife. In the first place, so far as we know, the first time that Donne travelled abroad after his marriage was when he went to Paris with Sir Robert Drury in 1611. Before leaving her, he gave his wife, as Walton tells us, the *Valediction: forbidding mourning*, and it seems to me almost certain that it was knowledge of the circumstances under which this poem had been written which led the writer of the Bridgewater MS. to assume, rather superficially, that the Sixteenth Elegy had been written at the same time. In the second place, it is perfectly clear from internal evidence that the real or imaginary addressee of this elegy was neither in reality nor in imagination Donne's wife: he calls her his 'Mistris', and she is still a mere girl and has a nurse. Some might object that the writer of the Bridgewater MS. meant no more than that the elegy had been addressed by Donne to his *future* wife, that is to say, to Ann More, on some occasion before their marriage, but the fact that at line 7 all the manuscripts except one, and that a late one, read 'by thy parents wrath', suggests that the reading of the printed texts 'by thy fathers wrath', was introduced later by someone who believed, like the writer of the Bridgewater MS., that the poem had been addressed, either before or after marriage, to Donne's wife, and who knew that, as a matter of fact, not both her parents but only her father was alive at the time of their first acquaintance. It is, of course, possible that at some time before their marriage Donne had imagined a situation in which Ann, who was only seventeen when he married her in 1601, had wished to accompany him on a foreign journey disguised as a page; but is it really more necessary to posit a real existence for the young girl of this elegy than for the young daughter of the 'Hydroptique father' and 'immortall mother', guarded by

The grim eight-foot-high iron-bound serving-man

in *The Perfume*? I ask the question, because it seems to be so generally assumed that whenever Donne is writing tenderly rather than merely wittily, cynically and impudently, whenever he is expressing himself, as one might say, Shakespeareanly rather than Ovidianly, he must have been writing out of actual experience, not just out of his imagination. Even Grierson groups together the present elegy, *His Parting from her*, *The Expostulation*, and *His Picture*, which we still have to consider, as bearing what he calls 'the imprint of some actual experience'.[1] But why, as I have asked before, should not Donne, if only for the sake of variety, have now and then dramatized other moods of his very diverse and volatile self besides that of mere outrageousness? Whether, though, the experience behind this elegy was real or imaginary, it is a superb piece of drama. Here are the opening lines:

> By our first strange and fatall interview,
> By all desires which thereof did ensue,
> By our long starving hopes, by that remorse
> Which my words masculine perswasive force
> Begot in thee, and by the memory
> Of hurts, which spies and rivals threatned me,
> I calmly beg: But by thy fathers wrath,
> By all paines, which want and divorcement hath,
> I conjure thee, and all the oathes which I
> And thou have sworne to seale joynt constancy,
> Here I unsweare, and overswear them thus,
> Thou shalt not love by wayes so dangerous.
> Temper, ô faire Love, loves impetuous rage,
> Be my true Mistris still, not my faign'd Page.

And here is the conclusion:

> When I am gone, dreame me some happinesse,
> Nor let thy lookes our long hid love confesse,
> Nor praise, nor dispraise me, nor blesse nor curse
> Openly loves force, nor in bed fright thy Nurse

[1] II, cxxxvii.

With midnights startings, crying out, oh, oh
Nurse, ô my love is slaine, I saw him goe
O'r the white Alpes alone;[1] I saw him I,
Assail'd, fight, taken, stabb'd, bleed, fall, and die.
Augure me better chance, except dread *Iove*
Thinke it enough for me to'have had thy love.

The last elegy I would classify as primarily dramatic is the Fifth, *His Picture*, which some may like to think of as having been written before his departure with the Cadiz expedition in June 1596.

Here take my Picture; though I bid farewell,
Thine, in my heart, where my soule dwels, shall dwell.
'Tis like me now, but I dead, 'twill be more
When wee are shadowes both, then 'twas before.
When weather-beaten I come backe; my hand,
Perhaps with rude oares torne, or Sun beams tann'd,
My face and brest of hairecloth, and my head
With cares harsh sodaine horinesse o'rspread,[2]
My body'a sack of bones, broken within,
And powders blew staines scatter'd on my skinne;
If rivall fooles taxe thee to'have lov'd a man,
So foule, and course, as, Oh, I may seeme than,
This shall say what I was: and thou shalt say,
Doe his hurts reach mee? doth my worth decay?
Or doe they reach his judging minde, that hee
Should now love lesse, what hee did love to see?
That which in him was faire and delicate,
Was but the milke, which in loves childish state
Did nurse it: who now is growne strong enough
To feed on that, which to disus'd[3] tasts seemes tough.

From this elegy we can infer absolutely nothing about the woman to whom it is addressed, whether she was married or single, whether, even, she was real or imaginary. She may well have been composite.

[1] Cf. Virgil, *Eclogues*, X, 46–9.
[2] The reading of the editions 1635–69.
[3] Unpractised, unaccustomed.

Even if Donne had not happened to have one, or a particular one, in mind, or, perhaps I should rather say, in heart, at the time, to write a farewell to his mistress would have been dramatically appropriate to the situation of one departing on a military expedition, and Donne, like Shakespeare's Richard II, was a born self-dramatizer.

When Ben Jonson told Donne that the two *Anniversaries* he had written in 1611 and 1612 to commemorate the daughter of his patron Sir Robert Drury, who had died at the age of fifteen, 'were profane and full of blasphemies', and that 'if it had been written of the Virgin Mary it had been something', Donne replied that 'he described the Idea of a woman, and not as she was'. So, too, in these dramatic elegies Donne, it seems to me, is playing with, dramatizing, various ideas of women, various ideas of himself, in various imaginary situations, and not describing either them or himself 'as they were'. To conclude with a brief review of the elegies we have been considering, in *Ielosie* we have a cynical, in 'Natures lay Ideot' a contemptuous, and in *His parting from her* a tender address to a married woman; in *The Perfume* we have a high-spirited but rather cynical, and in *On his Mistris* a tender and impassioned, address to a young girl; in *The Expostulation* a mis-understanding is cleared up and renewed affection protested to a woman whom what we may call the hero presumably regards with honourable intentions, while in *His Picture* the hero takes a witty but not untender farewell of some indeterminate mistress before departing on an expedition. Much in these elegies is witty and outrageous and cynical and satirical and realistic, and much is tender and impassioned, but, if one wanted to describe their author in one appropriate word, one would have to call him, I think, an essentially *dramatic* poet. About the last thing one would think of calling him, if one knew him from these poems alone, would be a 'metaphysical' poet. That, indeed, is the question we must always keep before us: what are the really essential characteristics of Donne's poetry, and how much of it may appropriately be called metaphysical? The affixing of the label 'metaphysical' to Donne has, I fear, saved far too many people the trouble and deprived them of the fascination of trying to discover what his poetry is really like.

Let us now turn to those elegies which are primarily 'witty' rather than dramatic. In three of them the wit may perhaps best be described as Ovidian, while in the rest it is of a more scholastic kind than we have yet encountered. Although in several of them some kind of situation is indeed implied, I have classified them as 'witty' rather than 'dramatic', because what we are primarily aware of is not, as in the elegies we have been considering, the situation, the characters (real or imaginary) and their emotions and attitudes, but simply the writer's wit, his ingenious comparisons, analogies and arguments, his power, as it were, to keep going for so long on subjects one might have supposed very rapidly exhaustible. His attitude to his subject is much more external than in the dramatic elegies—is often, indeed, almost indifferent. The subject does not matter—the important thing is what Donne can find to say about it.

Let us first consider the three Ovidian elegies. The Twentieth, *Loves Warre*, which begins

Till I have peace with thee, warr other men

has affinities with at least three of Ovid's *Amores*: with the ninth of the First Book, which begins

Militat omnis amans, et habet sua castra Cupido

and in which Ovid very wittily and antithetically insists on the similarity between the qualities of a good lover and a good soldier, such as capacity to endure night watches, to sleep on the ground, not to fear the face of an enemy, to besiege and take by storm, to surprise the enemy while he is asleep, to elude watchmen and sentries: although it is true that Donne, unlike Ovid, is concerned not with the similarities but with the differences. Then there is that impudent elegy which I have already referred to, the tenth of the Second Book, with that passage beginning

Felix quem Veneris certamina mutua rumpunt,

which almost seems to parody what Virgil and Horace had written in praise of the simple life; and the twelfth elegy of the Second Book, in which Ovid celebrates his bloodless victory over Corinna, declaring that by his own generalship alone he has overcome countless enemies without shedding a drop of blood and without causing a new war:

> *Haec est praecipuo victoria digna triumpho,*
> *In qua, quaecumque est, sanguine praeda caret.*

The victory which above all deserves a triumph is that in which the prize, whatever it be, is got without bloodshed.

> *Me quoque, qui multos, sed me sine caede, Cupido*
> *Iussit militiae signa mouere suae.*

Me too, after so many others, Cupid commanded to raise his standard, but without shedding blood.

Donne has not imitated any of the verbal detail of these elegies, but some of his epigrammatic lines are quite in Ovid's manner:

> Other men war that they their rest may gayne;
> But wee will rest that wee may fight agayne.
> Those warrs the ignorant, these th'experienc'd love,
> There wee are alwayes under, here above.[1]

One is not aware, as one is in the dramatic elegies, as one is even in *His Picture*, which is almost a limiting case—one is not even momentarily aware of a person whom Donne is addressing and whose real or imaginary personality is to some extent dictating and qualifying what he says: one is aware only of Donne himself, wittily developing a paradox. He might just as well have addressed the elegy to a friend, have substituted the third person for the second, and have begun:

> Till I have peace with *her*, warr other men.

In the Eighteenth Elegy, *Loves Progress*, which begins:

[1] ll. 33–6.

> Who ever loves, if he do not propose
> The right true end of love, he's one that goes
> To sea for nothing but to make him sick

he describes the progress from the face, or better, he contends, from the feet, to the 'centrique part'. The impudence is Ovidian, but the ingenious comparisons Donne uses in order to describe the lover's progress in terms of a voyage could never possibly have occurred to Ovid or to any classical poet:

> The brow becalms us when 'tis smooth and plain,
> And when 'tis wrinckled, shipwracks us again.
> Smooth, 'tis a Paradice, where we would have
> Immortal stay, and wrinkled 'tis our grave.
> The Nose (like to the first Meridian) runs
> Not 'twixt an East and West, but 'twixt two suns;
> It leaves a Cheek, a rosie Hemisphere
> On either side, and then directs us where
> Upon the Islands fortunate we fall,
> (Not faynte *Canaries*, but *Ambrosiall*)
> Her swelling lips; To which when wee are come,
> We anchor there, and think our selves at home,
> For they seem all: there Syrens songs, and there
> Wise Delphick Oracles do fill the ear.[1]

The Nineteenth Elegy, *Going to Bed*, may perhaps have been suggested by the fifth in Ovid's First Book, where he describes how Corinna came to him one hot noon while he was resting on his couch, but it was not altogether without some kind of English precedent in Nashe's *Choice of Valentines*, a poem which never got into print, and for which Nashe and the noble patron for whom he wrote it were severely reproved by Hall and other satirists.

Let us now turn to those elegies which are still primarily witty rather than dramatic, but where the wit is not what I have called Ovidian, but logical, argumentative, scholastic, or, if you insist, metaphysical. We may begin with the two elegies which were particularly admired, the one by Drummond of Hawthornden and the other by Ben Jonson.

[1] ll. 43–56.

The Second Elegy, entitled *The Anagram*, defends by means of a series of ingenious analogies the preposterous proposition that an old and ugly woman will make a better wife than a young and handsome one. Drummond said of it: 'Compare Song, *Marry and Love*, &c. with *Tasso's Stanzas against Beauty*; one shall hardly know who hath the best.' But before offering a translation of Tasso's stanzas *Sopra La Bellezza*, I will say a word or two about the literary development of the paradox, of which Donne was by no means the inventor, although he seems to have been the first considerable English poet to exploit its possibilities.

Although the common meaning of Greek παράδοξος and Latin *paradoxus* was 'contrary to received opinion', the neuter substantives παράδοξον and *paradoxon* were used in rhetoric as technical terms to describe a conclusion or apodosis contrary to what the audience has been led to expect. But from early times paradoxes in the sense of opinions contrary to those generally received were often defended in academic debates and elsewhere as an exercise in argumentative skill, ingenuity and learning. As early, for example, as the fifth century of our era Synesius, one of the Fathers, wrote a *Calvitii Encomium* which was translated into English in 1579 by Abraham Fleming as *A Paradoxe, proving by reason and example, that Baldnesse is much better than bushie haire*; and about A.D. 880 the monk Hucbaldus dedicated to Charles the Bald a curious poem entitled *Ecloga de Laudibus Calvitii*, every word of which begins with the letter C. It was, however, in the Italy of the Cinquecento that the paradox first seems to have become a really popular literary form. In 1543 Ortensio Lando published his *Paradossi, cioè, Sententie fuori del comun parere*, which went through many editions and was translated into French by Charles Estienne in 1553. In 1593 this French version was translated into English by Anthony Munday as *The Defence of Contraries*. The topics praised or defended are: poverty, the hard-favoured face or foul complexion, blindness, the superiority of ignorance to knowledge, folly to wisdom, drunkenness to sobriety, barrenness to childbearing, banishment to liberty, sickness to health, weeping to laughter, scarcity to abundance, and that the loss of all goods and honours ought not to make us grieve. Berni and other Italians of the Cinquecento wrote many such paradoxes and encomia on trivial or ridiculous subjects, both in prose and in short poems in *terza rima* which they called *capitoli*.

The nature of these poems, of the men who wrote them, and of
the society which appreciated them is admirably suggested by De
Sanctis:

> Carnival songs [he writes] went the round of Italy, and
> buffoonery, obscene double-meanings, and gross jests became an
> important element in literature, in prose and in verse, the mark
> of the Italian spirit. The seed-bed, as it were, of these works was
> the academies. These Italian academies remind us of those merry
> companies of easy-going, idle people who inspired the *Decameron*,
> the model of its kind. Their members were literati and men of
> erudition, all of them completely idle intellectually, and ready
> to write in verse or prose on any subject, however frivolous, for
> their amusement. The more vulgar the material of these works,
> the more the treatment was admired for its liveliness and elegance.
> The names of these academies and academicians sound strangely
> to our ears to-day: the *Impastato* (sleepy-headed), the *Raggirato*
> (duped), the *Propaginato* (buried head downwards), the *Smarrito*
> (stray), and the like. And the members recited their talks, or as
> they called them, their 'prattlings', on salads, on cakes, on hypo-
> chondria: laborious trifles. Similar prattlings in verse were called
> *capitoli*. Casa sang of jealousy, Varchi of boiled eggs, Molza of
> figs, Mauro of lies, and Caro of a long nose: they sang of the
> vulgarest things and often the dirtiest, and often too with obscene
> double meanings and allusions in the manner of Lorenzo, who
> was supreme in that line. The carnival of the public square had
> retired to the academies, better and more neatly dressed, but more
> insipid. There was the academy of the Vignaiuoli at Rome,
> where Mauro, Casa, Molza, and Berni recited their works to
> priests and monsignors. And the most popular of all these writers
> was Berni, whose *capitoli* were discussed by every one, and were
> passed from hand to hand.[1]

When Sidney, in the *Apology for Poetry*, which he wrote about
1583, remarked that 'Wee know a playing wit can prayse the discre-
tion of an Asse, the comfortablenes of being in debt, and the iolly
commoditie of being sick of the plague',[2] he was almost certainly

---

[1] *History of Italian Literature*, transl. Joan Redfern, I, 440–1.
[2] *Eliz. Critical Essays*, ed. Gregory Smith, I, 181, l. 30.

referring to two *capitoli* by Berni in praise of the plague, to another in praise of debt, and to a longish *capitolo* ascribed sometimes to Berni and sometimes to a certain 'Messer B.' in praise of the ass.[1] The *capitolo* in praise of debt is very characteristic. After describing various serious and burlesque conceptions of the *summum bonum*, Berni declares that a bankrupt, ruined and desperate debtor leads a better life than the Grand Turk or the Emperor. He employs an absurd syllogistic argument, turning on the double meaning of *debito* as debt and as what is due or fitting: we are indebted to perform acts of courtesy, as, for example, to raise our caps and incline our heads to our elders: therefore to become indebted is a kind of well-doing. The worst that can happen to a debtor is to be carried away like a wax candle. The officer approaches him with a certain gracefulness and elegance, as though he would take him somewhere where he might go to sleep. And when he departs surrounded by such a crowd, what is the difference between him and the Pope? Suppose he is taken to prison—is he not locked up there like a precious jewel? And there he at last attains that condition which Aristotle imagined, where sense is suspended and only the mind alert. Berni also has *capitoli* in praise of peaches, gudgeons, eels, jellies, chamber-pots and needles, while others praise bed, the warmth of bed, beans, salads, excommunication, and thirst as being superior to drink just as the causes of good are superior to good itself. Nashe, defending his elaborate *Prayse of the Red Herring* in *Lenten Stuffe*, 1597, gives a long list of similar *encomia*: 'Homer,' he declares,

> of rats and frogs hath heroiqut it; other oaten pipers after him in praise of the Gnat, the Flea, the Hasill nut, the Grashopper, the Butterflie, the Parrot, the Popinjay, Phillip sparrow, and the Cuckowe ... Phylosophers come sneaking in with their paradoxes of pouertie, imprisonment, death, sickenesse, banishment, and baldnesse.[2]

Numerous collections of such paradoxes and *encomia*, many of them translations, were published in England during the later sixteenth

---

[1] *Opere Burlesche del Berni, del Casa, del Varchi,* etc., Usecht al Reno 1760, I, 9, 14, 85; II, 304.
[2] *Works,* ed. McKerrow, III, 176.

and during the seventeenth century, and their popularity is an interesting and important commentary on what that age understood
by 'wit' and how seriously it could devote itself to a kind of learned
and ingenious game. William Est, for example, a pious and solemn
person, in the Preface to his translation, in 1617, of Willibaldus
Pirckheimer's *Praise of the Gout*, defends himself for dealing with
such an apparent triviality by declaring that many learned men have
revealed in such *encomia* great acuteness of wit and not the least of
their learning. Moreover, the public disputations, which were still
an important part of University education, and in which various
theological or philosophical propositions were defended or im-
pugned, were often of a jocular or semi-jocular kind. One of
Milton's Latin poems, *Naturam non pati senium*, 'that Nature does
not grow old', seems to be the record of a disputation on one of the
most burning philosophical questions of the day, namely, whether
the world was decaying, running down like a clock, approaching
the end of its course; but his prolusion on the theme that Day is
preferable to Night proves that even he could occasionally, though
not very willingly, exercise his abilities upon less serious topics.
There is also a very interesting insertion in a passage in Udall's
translation of the *Apothegmata* of Erasmus, published in 1542. After
translating the following passage:

> Rhetoricians are wont for exercise, to handle matters inopin-
> able, as for example when thei make an oracion in the praise of
> *Busyris*, or of the *Fever quartane*, or when they praise ingratitude,

Udall adds, in square brackets:

> So did Homere write the battail between the Frogges and
> Mice. Erasmus wrote the praise of foolishnesse, an other the praise
> of baldenesse, an other of drunkenship: and this last argument,
> I handled for mine exercise, being a young student, albeit the
> same declamacion now lieth all worme eaten as right worthie it
> is.[1]

It was, then, in this tradition of academic or scholastic wit that
Tasso wrote those stanzas *Sopra La Bellezza*, of which and of

[1] 1877, 362.

Donne's *Anagram* Drummond of Hawthornden could not say which was the better, and which, though written in graceful and flowing *ottava rima*, are scarcely, I think, what most readers would expect from the author of the *Gerusalemme Liberata*.

That which the blind vulgar rate so highly, sole delight and sole care of women, fading and most fragile beauty, is a vile natural impediment. The wretched lover whom foolish charm puts at the mercy of an angelic face, how much easier the wretch would find it within the gates of hell to placate death!

As in a fair meadow among flowers and grass there often lurks a malignly hidden snake; as in a fair golden vessel bitter food is often hidden, or wicked and poisonous juice: as in a fair apple is often preserved a putrid worm by which the fruit is tainted and gnawed: even so some conceal beneath a veil of beauty wicked desires and thoughts and works.

Where beauty appears, courtesy departs, humility, pity, kindness flee; where beauty is resort, as to their proper place, pride and ingratitude; the evil shade of beauty causes the seed, the flower of every virtue, every art to wither: beauty is an infamous, a filthy monster, Heaven's scourge, with which it lashes the world.

Just as a bitter nut or sour apple can be better preserved than any ripe and sweet fruit and is desired and dear when that is already wasted and destroyed: even so in the sweetness of his clear nectar Love better preserves the ugliness that is tart in itself than the beauty that shies and rebels against all external sweetness.

Let my mistress be ugly, with a large nose that casts a shadow to her chin; let her mouth be so capacious a vessel that the largest object may find room therein; let her teeth be few and her eyes placed by chance, her teeth of ebony and her eyes of silver, and may what appears and what is hidden correspond to these worthy parts.

I shall have no fear that she may be loved by another, that another may follow her, or even look at her; I shall have no fear if she watches for someone else or if at times she seems to sigh in sadness: I shall not always be calling her proud, ungrateful, perverse and recalcitrant to my desires: her thoughts will be in conformity with mine: she will be entirely mine, and I entirely hers.[1]

Donne almost certainly had these stanzas of Tasso in mind, but, compared with his treatment of the subject, Tasso's is almost obvious. In fact, one might almost say that the only really astonishing thing about Tasso's poem is the initial paradox that ugliness in a woman is better than beauty, for his defence of this paradox is almost classical in its limpidity, one might almost say its naturalness. Donne, on the other hand, is breath-takingly ingenious from beginning to end: in comparison with the intense energy and mental agility he brings to the defence of his paradox Tasso seems almost languid and automatic. For example:

> If red and white and each good quality
> Be in thy wench, ne'r aske where it doth lye.
> In buying things perfum'd, we aske; if there
> Be muske and amber in it, but not where.
> Though all her parts be not in th'usuall place,
> She'hath yet an Anagram of a good face.
> If we might put the letters but one way,
> In the leane dearth of words, what could wee say?
> When by the Gamut some Musitions make
> A perfect song, others will undertake
> By the same Gamut chang'd, to equall it.
> Things simply good, can never be unfit.
> She's faire as any, if all be like her,
> And if none bee, then she is singular.
> All love is wonder; if wee justly doe
> Account her wonderfull, why not lovely too?
> Love built on beauty, soone as beauty, dies,
> Chuse this face, chang'd by no deformities.
> Women are all like Angels; the faire be
> Like those which fell to worse; but such as shee,
> Like to good Angels, nothing can impaire:
> 'Tis lesse griefe to be foule, then to'have been faire.[2]

[1] *Opere*, ed. Rosini, Pisa, 1822, IV, 151. Drummond himself has a verse translation of the poem, *Poetical Works*, ed. Kastner, I, 131–2.
[2] ll. 11–32.

While Tasso confines himself mainly to statements ('Where beauty appears, courtesy departs') or to arguments in which we can perceive at least some truth ('If my mistress is ugly, she will be less likely to make me jealous'), while, in fact, there remains a certain reasonableness and moderation in his paradox, Donne flings moderation to the winds and overwhelms us with a continuous fire of short analogical or syllogistic arguments which follow one another so rapidly that we have scarcely time to detect or to protest against their fallaciousness. He is, to borrow a phrase of Dryden's, like a juggler 'who is always staring us in the face, and overwhelming us with gibberish, only that he may gain the opportunity of making the cleaner conveyance of his trick'. Most of his analogies are compressed syllogisms, which, as he knows very well, for that is part of the fun, continually commit the fallacy of the undistributed middle.

> All love is wonder; if we justly doe
> Account her wonderfull, why not lovely too?

If this were expressed as a formal syllogism, it would run:

> All that is lovable is wonderful;
> Your mistress is wonderful:
> Therefore your mistress is lovable.

Here, though, there is an undistributed middle: the proposition that 'All that is lovable is wonderful' does not include the further proposition, which is necessary to the conclusion, 'All that is wonderful is lovable'. All that can be inferred from it is 'Your mistress *may* be lovable', a conclusion reasonable enough, but most lame and impotent in this context. Had Donne written

> All wonder's loved: if then wee justly doe
> Account her wonderfull, why not lovely too?

the proposition 'All wonder's loved' would in itself have seemed so patently absurd that our reason would have stopped there. Donne has to begin with a plausible statement or proposition and then to trick us (or make us pretend that we are tricked) into a fallacious conclusion. This kind of wit might more appropriately be called scholastic, or academic, than metaphysical. I have already shown its affinities with the paradoxes and *encomia*, the learned fooling, of the later Renaissance; but Donne, who probably returned at the age of nineteen or so from an Italy where the game had been made very popular by Berni and others, seems, as I have said, to have been the first considerable English poet to exploit its possibilities, and his originality here consists largely in the fact that he introduced into the already popular game something of the rigidly logical and systematic method of the academic or theological disputation. One might say, in fact, that he played the game according to far stricter and more difficult rules than it had ever been played before.

Let us turn next to the Eleventh Elegy, *The Bracelet. Vpon the losse of his Mistresses Chaine, for which he made satisfaction*, a poem which Ben Jonson, according to Drummond, had by heart, and which, although it was so utterly unlike his own poetry, was evidently one of those 'some things' for which he esteemed Donne 'the first poet in the world'. It is perhaps Donne's most astonishingly successful exercise in sheer wit. Punning throughout, as the Elizabethans were so fond of doing, upon the double meaning of 'angel', the spirit and the coin, he declares that his chief regret is that twelve righteous Angels, which Heaven commanded to be his providers and guides, must be damned for offences not their own, cast into the fire, and melted down to restore the lost chain. The following passage, turning as it does upon the kind of wisdom and knowledge possessed by fallen angels and upon the dependence of substance, or being, on form, may perhaps more appropriately be called metaphysical than anything we have yet encountered, although I still think that 'scholastic' or 'dialectical' is the better term, for just as in *The Anagram* Donne has employed something of the argumentative method, so here he employs some of the doctrines, of the Schools:

> Thou say'st (alas) the gold doth still remaine,
> Though it be chang'd, and put into a chaine;
> So in the first falne angels, resteth still
> Wisdome and knowledge; but 'tis turn'd to ill:
> As these[1] should doe good works; and should provide

[1] 'Just as these angels of mine'.

Necessities; but now must nurse thy pride.
And they are still bad angels;[1] Mine are none;
For, forme gives being, and their forme is gone.[2]

And Donne concludes with a most characteristically exuberant and
exaggerated curse upon the stealer-by-finding:

> But ô thou wretched finder whom I hate
> So, that I almost pitty thy estate:
> Gold being the heaviest metal amongst all,
> May my most heavy curse upon thee fall:
> Here fetter'd, manacled, and hang'd in chains,
> First mayst thou bee; then chaind to hellish panies;
> Or be with forraine gold brib'd to betray
> Thy Countrey, and faile both of that and thy pay.
> May the next thing thou stoop'st to reach, containe
> Poyson, whose nimble fume rot thy moist braine;
> Or libels, or some interdicted thing,
> Which negligently kept, thy ruine bring.
> Lust-bred diseases rot thee; and dwell with thee
> Itching desire, and no abilitie.
> May all the evils that gold ever wrought;
> All mischiefes that all devils ever thought;
> Want after plenty; poore and gouty age;
> The plagues of travellers; love; marriage
> Afflict thee, and at thy lives last moment,
> May thy swolne sinnes themselves to thee present.
> But, I forgive; repent thee honest man:
> Gold is Restorative, restore it than:
> But if from it thou beest loath to depart,
> Because 'tis cordiall, would twere at thy heart.

Need I pause to insist that the only biographical fact that may be
legitimately inferred from these two poems is that Donne had wit
enough to write them? *The Anagram*, no doubt, is a limiting case;
no one in his senses would regard it as serious evidence that Donne
preferred ugliness to beauty. Nevertheless, the existence of such

---

[1] The fallen angels, though bad, are at least still angels.
[2] ll. 69–76.

limiting cases should make us very careful about drawing any conclusions from the more outrageous of the *Songs and Sonets* about Donne's convictions, morals, habits and general attitude to life. One must always be prepared, as I have already insisted, to make very great allowance for the element of sheer wit.

Of the other scholastically witty elegies, the Third, *Change*, is a continuous and not very serious argument. He fears that his mistress will be untrue to him, since another may capture her by the same means as he has done, and women were made, not for one man, but for all men, just as the sea was made to receive all rivers. Love is cemented by likeness, but must he, in order that she may love him, become as changeable as she? No, he will be changeable but not, like her, promiscuous.

The Sixth Elegy, 'Oh, let me not serve so', seems to exist chiefly for the sake of the ingenious comparisons, one of them very long and elaborate, in the middle of it. She is like a whirlpool which sucks down careless flowers afloat on its surface; like a taper which attracts and burns a fly; like a stream which chides and swells if any bough tries to kiss it, but which, if its own kisses cause the treacherous bank to gape, rushes violently in, leaving its channel dry. Elaborately worked out similes like this, which we also find in some of Shakespeare's earlier plays, do not occur in Ovid's *Amores*: he will say, indeed, that an attractive woman looks for those qualities in a lover which a superior officer looks for in a soldier, but, in contrast to Donne's, such comparisons are what one who accepted the classical tradition would call 'natural'; they are, as it were, in *pari materia*: the comparison is between qualities proper to two human vocations, not between the real actions of a human being and the pretended actions of an inanimate object. Moreover, Ovid's wit consists rather in (often preposterous) epigrammatic statements and generalizations than in ingenious comparisons. The Eighth Elegy, *The Comparison*, is full of them, for it consists of a series of ingenious and often rather nauseous comparisons between Donne's mistress (or pretended mistress) and someone else's. My mistress's sweat, he declares, is like (among many other nice things) attar of roses; your mistress's sweat is like (among many other nasty things) the scum which Sancerra's starving citizens extracted from parboiled boots. My mistress's head is as round as the apple which Paris awarded to Venus, or the apple which Eve tasted; your mistress's head is like that of a rough-hewn jet statue. And so on, for more than fifty lines. The vivid and concentrated detail in several of these comparisons, together with the element of exaggeration and caricature, is quite in the manner of some of the descriptions in Jonson's comedies, or, one might almost say, in Falstaff's descriptions of his ragged regiment and of Justice Shallow:

> Like Sun-parch'd quarters on the citie gate,
> Such is thy tann'd skins lamentable state.
> And like a bunch of ragged carrets stand
> The short swolne fingers of thy gouty hand.[1]

And now, my whole Charge consists of Ancients, Corporals, Lieutenants, Gentlemen of Companies, Slaues as ragged as *Lazarus* in the painted Cloth, where the Gluttons Dogges licked his Sores.[2]

Shakespeare's comparison is as striking and as ingenious as Donne's, but, while Shakespeare's is a characteristic Falstaffism and is uttered by Falstaff at the right time and in the right place, some of Donne's elegies, and several of the poems of Donne's later imitators, especially Cleveland, exist merely for the sake of such ingenious comparisons. What in Shakespeare was merely incidental became with them essential.

We have now reviewed in sufficient detail a sufficient number of Donne's earlier Elegies to be able to reach certain useful conclusions. Most of the qualities we have noticed are also present in the *Songs and Sonets*, although there they are often combined with a much greater degree of seriousness. Nevertheless, many of the *Songs and Sonets* are also quite unserious, or only half-serious, a fact which we shall perceive more easily if we approach them after having familiarized ourselves with the Elegies. For it is easier to demonstrate that the Elegies are not to be interpreted autobiographically, are not to be regarded as expressions of Donne's personality, attitude to life, and so forth, than it is to demonstrate that the *Songs and Sonets*, or many of them, are not to be so regarded. It is easier to perceive in the Elegies the very great part played by sheer wit,

[1] ll. 31–4.
[2] *I Henry IV*, IV, ii, 22–6.

and, having perceived it there, we should always be prepared to find it again, in greater or lesser degree, in the rest of Donne's poetry. Moreover, to one who has carefully studied the Elegies the question, How appropriately may Donne be called a metaphysical poet? will be likely ever afterwards to present itself in a rather more questionable shape.

Of the many striking characteristics we have noticed in the course of this review, characteristics which, though sometimes combined in varying proportions, have never appeared all together in any single poem, which is most striking? Which is most important? Which—this, perhaps, is an easier question—is most pervasive? Most pervasive, I think it will be agreed, is the colloquial vigour of the language, together with the absence of classical allusions, traditional ornaments, and, generally speaking, of anything obviously 'poetical'—seventeenth-century qualities these, in respect of which Donne differs only in degree from Jonson and many other seventeenth-century poets. Then there is the dramatic element, apparent not only in the devising of imaginary situations, but in the rhythms and inflexions of the verse, in the characteristic and unmistakable tone of voice Donne has adopted for the occasion. Even in *The Anagram*, that preposterous defence of a preposterous proposition, which I classified as a dialectically witty rather than as a dramatic elegy—even there there is something dramatic, for Donne is not merely maintaining a paradox, but also, as it were, playing the part of the sort of man who would maintain such a paradox. How difficult it is to keep these elements apart! I mentioned *The Anagram* as an example of Donne's dialectical or scholastic method of arguing in verse, and yet even in some of the most dramatic elegies there is a strong argumentative element, although the argument there is not formal or scholastic: Donne *argues* with one imaginary mistress that she was merely 'natures lay Ideot' until he taught her how to love, and he argues with another that she must not think of accompanying him on a foreign journey disguised as a page. Again, although Donne is not always formally maintaining a formal paradox, there is a strong element of paradox, impudence, or outrageousness in some of the most essentially dramatic elegies. As for the ingenious comparison, that perception of occult resemblances between things apparently unlike, which seemed to Dr. Johnson the chief characteristic of the poets he called metaphysical, I think it is only in the Sixth Elegy, in the Eighth (*The Comparison*), and in the Eighteenth (*Loves Progress*) that it can be said to predominate and to appear as the most striking, the most noticeable, characteristic. In many of the other elegies it is scarcely present at all, and in such an elegy as *The Anagram* it is the paradoxical, syllogistic argument itself that strikes us rather than the ingenious analogies by which that argument is sometimes supported.

How difficult, I repeat, to achieve a really clear and balanced impression of Donne's Elegies! For we must first try to *perceive* what qualities are really there, and even to do that requires a good deal of patient analysis and concentration. Then we must try to *remember* what qualities are really there: by which I mean that we must not only try to hold them *together* in our memories, but that we must also, at the same time, try to hold them *apart*, try to prevent any one that has particularly struck us from swallowing up and obliterating the others. Then we must try to perceive how these various qualities are interrelated and try to decide what is their relative importance. Colloquial, dramatic, argumentative, impudent, paradoxical, dialectical, ingenious—the Donne of the Elegies is all these things, but can he, in respect of any or all of them, be appropriately called metaphysical? Only in so far as in *The Anagram*, and occasionally elsewhere, he has introduced into the popular pastime of defending paradoxes something of the rigorously logical and syllogistic method of the academic or theological disputation, and only in so far as such disputations, because of their philosophical or semi-philosophical subject-matter, might be loosely described as metaphysical. Since, though, it is the method and not (except, as it were, parodyingly) the matter of such disputations which Donne has imitated, the terms academic, scholastic, or dialectical would here be far more appropriate than the term metaphysical.

The various qualities which in this review of the earlier Elegies I have been trying to distinguish and interrelate might also be regarded as various aspects of Donne's wit. For Donne, in these elegies, whether he is being mainly dramatic, argumentative, impudent, paradoxical, dialectical, or ingenious, is always being witty. Spenser, it is true, was also praised by his contemporaries for his wit: Nashe wrote of 'divine Master *Spencer*, the miracle of wit';[1] but the word 'wit' was now beginning to acquire a different

[1] *Works*, ed. McKerrow, III, 323.

meaning. Spenser is never witty in the way in which Donne, in these elegies, is witty; neither, for that matter, is Wordsworth, or Keats, or Tennyson. Some of the qualities of this wit I have tried to analyse and describe, but there still remains something more fundamental, more general, and that is the author's attitude to his subject. His attitude is never wholly serious—indeed, in the Elegies, it is almost wholly unserious, is never more, one might almost say, than a kind of serious trifling. In the *Songs and Sonets*, as we shall see, this element of playfulness and trifling is by no means incompatible with varying degrees of seriousness; nevertheless, even in the most serious of the *Songs and Sonets* there nearly always remains something of play, of detachment, of conscious hyperbole. In the Elegies, though, the element of play, or of display, predominates: the reader's attention is directed, not so much upon the subject, as upon what Donne is able to make of it—upon what seemed to many of his contemporaries his miraculous ingenuity and cleverness. Now before one can safely generalize about Donne's poetry and the nature of Donne's wit, it is very necessary to attempt some classification of his poems according to their degrees of seriousness. For it seems to me that this important distinction between the serious and the unserious, the controlled and the uncontrolled, wit of Donne and his successors has been rather overlooked by Mr. T. S. Eliot and others in some of their generalizations about the wit of seventeenth-century poetry and in some of their remarks about that 'dissociation of sensibility' which, they tell us, set in during the latter half of the century and is apparent in the poetry of Milton and Dryden.

Let us remind ourselves of some of Mr. Eliot's very influential observations upon seventeenth-century poetry. Most of them occur in two essays which originally appeared as leading articles in the *Times Literary Supplement* in 1921: the first, entitled *The Metaphysical Poets*, was occasioned by the publication of Sir Herbert Grierson's anthology, *Metaphysical Lyrics and Poems of the Seventeenth Century*, and the second, *Andrew Marvell*, was occasioned by the tercentenary of that poet's birth. For good or ill, these two essays have probably exerted more influence upon those who have subsequently written on the history of English poetry, especially seventeenth-century poetry, than all the rest of Mr. Eliot's critical writings. They contain much that is illuminating and much that is true, and any student of seventeenth-century poetry—I might even say, any professed scholar in that field—who should be unwilling to admit that he had owed much to them must be either very stupid or very dishonest. Nevertheless, these essays also contain much that is either demonstrably untrue, or true only to a very limited extent and after having been subjected to very great qualification. They were, in fact, written under certain limitations which the author nowhere admits and of which only a few of his readers can be expected to be aware. In the first place, it is difficult not to suppose that Mr. Eliot's knowledge of so-called metaphysical poetry did not at that time extend very much further than Sir Herbert Grierson's anthology, and that his very high estimate of it and his readiness to praise it at the expense of other kinds of English poetry were partly determined by the fact that he knew it only at its best. In the second place, both in these essays and elsewhere, Mr. Eliot was writing not merely in a spirit of disinterested curiosity, but (though he never explicitly admits it) with something of an axe to grind. He was writing, not merely as a critic, but as a poet, or as what he himself calls a 'poetical practitioner', and a question always at the back of his mind was this: 'From what earlier English poets can a modern English poet most profitably learn?' His preoccupation with this question largely explains both his exaltation of the so-called metaphysical poets and that denigration of Milton which he continued intermittently for the next twenty years. Mr. Eliot believed (probably rightly) that a modern poet should above all not try to be 'poetical' in inverted commas, that he should try to rid himself of any tendency to distinguish between 'poetical' and 'unpoetical' subjects, and that he should deal in familiar and colloquial language with immediate experience. He should not, like Milton—and here I am trying to suggest how Milton appeared to Mr. Eliot—he should not choose an obviously 'poetical' subject and then proceed to treat it in an elaborately 'poetical' style.

Plato, in the *Republic*, declared that poetry could be very dangerous to those who did not possess, as a kind of antidote, a knowledge of its nature: one might say much the same of Mr. Eliot's observations on seventeenth-century poetry. Now, though, that we possess the necessary antidote we may safely consider some of the things he has to say.

Let us first try to make clear to ourselves what Mr. Eliot regards (or regarded) as the chief virtue of the so-called metaphysical poets. In his first essay, after noticing Dr. Johnson's failure to define their poetry by its faults, he attempts to define it by its virtues, and asks us to consider whether its chief virtue 'was not something permanently valuable, which subsequently disappeared, but ought not to have disappeared'. A comparison and collocation of various passages suggests that what seemed to Mr. Eliot the great virtue of these poets was that they were explorers rather than expounders, that their subject-matter, their thought and their feeling were almost inseparable, and that their poetry was essentially present and immediate. Their subject-matter, that is to say, was not something remote or external, something, as it were, pre-existing, but something immediately experienced in themselves or in the world around them; and they did not, as it were, begin to write with thoughts and feelings ready-made, did not expound already completed thoughts or communicate the results of past reflections, but created thought out of feeling and feeling out of thought in the very act of composition. We are not so much invited to admire a finished product as to share in a process, to observe, as we often do in the Elizabethan dramatists, of whom Mr. Eliot would have us regard these poets as the successors, what he calls 'a direct sensuous apprehension of thought, or a recreation of thought into feeling'.[1] Mr. Eliot's whole emphasis is upon experience, and throughout he seems to be praising these poets for exploring, illuminating and relating the greatest possible variety and complexity of individual experience—praising them, in fact, for doing what he thinks (or thought) modern poets ought to be doing. For to him as to many others the chief characteristic of the modern world, of modern life, is its complexity and unintelligibility, and the chief function and duty of a modern poet is to introduce, or to enable us to perceive, some order and meaning and relationship into all this complexity. 'When,' he declares,

> a poet's mind is perfectly equipped for its work, it is constantly amalgamating disparate experience; the ordinary man's experience is chaotic, irregular, fragmentary. The latter falls in love, or reads Spinoza, and these two experiences have nothing to do with each other, or with the noise of the typewriter or the smell of cooking;

[1] *Selected Essays*, 272.

in the mind of the poet these experiences are always forming new wholes.[1]

The example of Milton, Mr. Eliot seems to mean, although he never plainly says so, the example of Milton cannot help a modern poet to relate love and typewriting, Sweeney's nightingales and Aga-memnon's nightingales, culture and coffee-cups, but the example of Donne, Marvell and others may. For Mr. Eliot a modern poet should be above all an exploring and experiencing poet: if he should attempt to write an epic on the subject, say, of King Arthur, in an elaborately beautiful style he would be escaping from his responsibilities and neglecting his proper task. He would at best— in Mr. Eliot's then way of putting it—be a mere Milton. For in comparison with that 'mechanism of sensibility which could devour any kind of experience' which Mr. Eliot found in the so-called metaphysical poets, the sensibilities of Milton, of Dryden, and of most succeeding poets seemed to him simplified, limited, and even crude. In his essay on Marvell he declared that the wit of the so-called metaphysicals 'involves, probably, a recognition, implicit in the expression of every experience, of other kinds of experience which are possible', and that although Marvell had various errors of taste, 'they never consist in taking a subject too seriously or too lightly'.[2] The absence of this wit, of this perpetual awareness of other possible experiences besides the one actually being expressed, and a consequent unwillingness to express what the author has more immediately in mind either too lightly or too seriously, and without, so to speak, a certain reserve—the absence of this wit, this balance, this comprehensiveness is what Mr. Eliot most deplored in the work of Milton and later poets; and in order to account for its absence he invented what has become one of the most famous phrases— I might almost say one of the most famous clichés—of modern criticism: 'In the seventeenth century', he declared,

> a dissociation of sensibility set in, from which we have never recovered; and this dissociation, as is natural, was aggravated by the influence of the two most powerful poets of the century, Milton and Dryden. Each of these men performed certain poetic

[1] *Selected Essays*, 273.
[2] *Op. cit.* 289–90.

functions so magnificently well that the magnitude of the effect concealed the absence of others. The language went on and in some respects improved; the best verse of Collins, Gray, Johnson, and even Goldsmith satisfies some of our fastidious demands better than that of Donne or Marvell or King. But while the language became more refined, the feeling became more crude. The feeling, the sensibility, expressed in the *Country Churchyard* (to say nothing of Tennyson and Browning) is cruder than that in the *Coy Mistress*.[1]

This famous *pronunciamento* occurs in the essay on *The Metaphysical Poets*; in his essay on Marvell Mr. Eliot returns to this picture and fills in some of the detail: Dryden, he there declares, isolated the element of wit and exaggerated it into something like pure fun, while Milton dispensed with it altogether and contented himself (if I understand Mr. Eliot aright) with mere magniloquence. The phrase 'dissociation of sensibility', which Mr. Eliot coined to describe the process he deplored, and to which he accused Milton and Dryden of contributing, soon led to the coinage (not, I think, by Mr. Eliot himself) of the phrase 'unified sensibility' to describe that 'mechanism of sensibility' which the earlier seventeenth-century poets possessed, or were supposed to have possessed; and it is perhaps not going too far to say that these two phrases alone have enabled several later writers to set up in business and drive quite a prosperous trade as literary and historical critics.

In these views, these very influential views, on seventeenth-century poetry, which I have tried to expound and explain as clearly and fairly as I could, there is, as I said at the outset, much that is true and illuminating together with much that is either very limited-ly true or almost wholly untrue. The question, though, which I chiefly want to raise is this: to *how much* of the work of our so-called metaphysical poets, and, in particular, to how much of Donne's poetry, does Mr. Eliot's definition of seventeenth-century wit and his praise of undissociated, or pre-dissociated, seventeenth-century sensibility really apply? Does it, for example, apply to any or all of Donne's Elegies, those poems which we have been reviewing and analysing so carefully? 'Fidelity to thought and feeling', 'a direct sensuous apprehension of thought, or a recreation of thought into

[1] *Selected Essays*, 274.

feeling', 'a recognition, implicit in the expression of every experience, of other kinds of experience which are possible': such phrases might well find a place in a description of the ideal modern poet, the kind of poet Mr. Eliot believes (or once believed) that a modern poet should be—uncommitted, unanchored, unaccommodated, with, ultimately, only one subject, his own direct experience of a very puzzling world; an essentially exploring poet, dealing in hints and guesses rather than in statements; not expounding, illustrating, or building upon some inherited world-picture, philosophy, religion or point of view common to himself and to his readers, but suggesting, glimpsing, various kinds of unity and relationship in a world which both to himself and to his readers is infinitely complex, puzzling, and questionable. They are indeed the kind of phrases I myself should be inclined to apply to the later work of Rilke. But Donne's Elegies, not only *The Anagram*, *The Comparison* and the rest, but even the splendidly dramatic ones—for them, with their fundamental unseriousness, is not this rather high language rather out of place? Although it is perhaps not out of place for some of the *Songs and Sonets*, some of the *Divine Poems*, some of Marvell's poems—in a word, for some of the very best seventeenth-century poetry. Is it, though, quite fair, or even quite sensible, to generalize about our so-called metaphysical poetry on the basis of a few anthology pieces, and then to condemn other poets and other poetry for not normally displaying the same virtues? And are even the best pieces, the anthology pieces, quite what Mr. Eliot in these two essays implies? Is he not, to some considerable extent, describing an ideal of poetry which the best work of these poets has suggested to him, and does there not still remain some gap between his praise and even their finest achievements? It is true that he praises them for taking no subject either too lightly or too seriously, but, in his continual insistence on experience and exploration, is he not, perhaps, taking even their more serious poems too seriously, and neglecting, or under-emphasizing, even their very considerable element of play? For although, in comparison with Milton, Donne and Marvell are explorers rather than expounders, they were not explorers in the sense in which Rilke was an explorer: they were never so disinherited, so dependent on their own resources, so naked, so without all hope of receiving any answer from outside themselves as was the poet who exclaimed:

> Who, if I cried, from among the angelic orders
> would hear me?

Beneath all their disinterested curiosity and play of mind there is a fundamental assurance about ultimate things, and even in their most apparently serious explorations there is nearly always something of light-heartedness, something of play.

But I do not propose to use the example of Rilke in order to depreciate the achievements of Donne and Marvell, as Mr. Eliot used the examples of Donne and Marvell to depreciate the achievement of Milton: all I want to do is to examine the achievement of our so-called metaphysical poets, especially of Donne, rather more disinterestedly, and, in particular, to examine Mr. Eliot's theory and to decide how much of Donne's characteristic wit may be regarded as the expression of what has been called a unified sensibility.

This theory of a dissociation of sensibility which set in during the seventeenth century is still widely accepted as a proven fact, as a firm foundation upon which to build, but to what extent Mr. Eliot himself still believes in it I do not know; neither, if he does still believe in it, do I know which seventeenth-century poets he still regards as possessing, in contrast to Milton and Dryden, a sensibility that was as yet undissociated. For between 1921 and 1931 Mr. Eliot seems to have lost some of his earlier enthusiasm for Donne. In 1931, in an essay on *Donne in our Time* which he contributed to a volume entitled *A Garland for John Donne*, he declared, as proof that Donne's mind was essentially unmedieval, that, while the encyclopaedic knowledge of the Schoolmen was always directed towards unification, 'in Donne there is a manifest fissure between thought and sensibility'—words which, whatever else they may mean, seem to mean the opposite of that 'direct sensuous apprehension of thought, or recreation of thought into feeling' which in 1921 Mr. Eliot found in Chapman and which, he added, 'is exactly what we find in Donne'.[1] 'One reason,' continues Mr. Eliot, in his 1931 essay,

> one reason why Donne has appealed so powerfully to the recent time is that there is in his poetry hardly any attempt at organization; rather a puzzled and humorous shuffling of the pieces; and

[1] *Selected Essays*, 272.

we are inclined to read our own more conscious awareness of the apparent irrelevance and unrelatedness of things into the mind of Donne.[1]

I think I am probably right in supposing that this passage contains a kind of oblique confession, or recantation, and that when Mr. Eliot speaks of Donne's having 'appealed so powerfully to the recent time' he means, partly at least, 'appealed so powerfully to me ten years ago and to many of my readers'; also that, as the result of deepened insight, he has found the 'apparent irrelevance and unrelatedness of things' more merely apparent and less real, and is therefore less inclined to read a conscious awareness of such irrelevance and unrelatedness into the mind of Donne. As I say, I do not know whether Mr. Eliot still believes that a dissociation of sensibility set in during the seventeenth century; neither do I know which, if any, of our seventeenth-century poets he would still regard as exempt from that infection. At any rate, by 1931 he had discovered in Donne 'a manifest fissure between thought and sensibility', which would seem to mean, in the terminology of 1921, that Donne's sensibility was dissociated. Nevertheless, whatever Mr. Eliot's present position may be, his 1921 pronouncement, that a dissociation of sensibility set in during the seventeenth century, almost immediately found many echoes, and is still accepted by many critics as a proven truth. And most of these critics have not, like Mr. Eliot himself, given up Donne: Donne's poetry, no less than Marvell's, they still regard as an example of 'unified sensibility', and they are still ready to exalt Donne at the expense of Milton. It seems, therefore, worth while, before leaving the Elegies, to consider one very remarkable example of Donne's wit and Donne's sensibility, or, in Mr. Eliot's 1921 terminology, 'mechanism of sensibility', rather closely. The elegies we have been reviewing are all youthful work, and are all, in one way or another, what Donne in his later years would have called 'evaporations'. They are, as I have insisted, fundamentally unserious, and only a very dull reader should find in this fact matter for complaint. It is though—or at least I think it ought to be—rather surprising to find the mature Donne treating in the Ninth Elegy, *The Autumnall*, a serious subject with the same fundamental unseriousness.

[1] *op. cit.*, 8.

Walton, in his *Life* of Herbert, declares (or, rather, implies) that Donne addressed this poem to Mrs. Magdalene Herbert,[1] mother of the poet, and that it was written towards the beginning of their friendship, on an occasion when Donne, who was then 'near to the Fortieth year of his Age', came accidentally to Oxford, where Mrs. Herbert was then living and looking after her eldest son Edward (later Lord Herbert of Cherbury). This Edward, however, matriculated from University College (not, as Walton says, from Queen's) in May 1596, and was not accompanied by his mother until his return, after an absence, in February 1599. Walton's collocation of names, dates and ages is clearly impossible, and Mr. Garrod, in an important article on *Donne and Mrs. Herbert*,[2] is almost certainly right in suggesting that Walton, searching the Register of Metriculations, confused Edward Herbert, Lord Cherbury, of University, with his cousin Edward Herbert, who, together with Mrs. Herbert's third son, William, matriculated from Queen's on 1st July, 1608, that it was these two youths whom Mrs. Herbert, with her seemingly small confidence in the morals of undergraduates, was then superintending, and that it was at this time that Donne happened to visit Oxford, renewed the friendship which seems to have been begun a year earlier, and wrote *The Autumnall*. 'Both he and she', says Walton, 'were then past the meridian of mans life': Donne, as a matter of fact, was about thirty-six and Mrs. Herbert about forty-four. 'This amity', continues Walton,

> was not an *Amity* that polluted their Souls; but an *Amity* made up of a chain of suitable inclinations and vertues; an *Amity*, like that of St. *Chrysostoms* to his dear and vertuous *Olimpias*; whom, in his Letters, he calls his *Saint*: Or, an *Amity* indeed more like that of St. *Hierom* to his *Paula*; whose affection to her was such, that he turn'd Poet in his old Age.[3]

This poem, which Donne addressed to her whom Walton calls his Paula, and in which, Walton declares, after briefly alluding to it, 'the rest of her character may be read', ought, I think, to cause one at least some surprise (although, apparently, it did not surprise

[1] 'And he at his leaving *Oxford*, writ and left there in verse a Character of the Beauties of her body, and mind.'
[2] *R.E.S.*, July 1945.
[3] *World's Classics* ed., 265.

Walton) and to stimulate one to some interesting reflections about Donne and about what he and many of his cultivated contemporaries understood and appreciated as 'wit'. The opening lines, though characteristically ingenious, are tender and beautiful:

> No *Spring*, nor *Summer* Beauty hath such grace,
>> As I have seen in one *Autumnall* face.
> Yong *Beauties* force our love, and that's a *Rape*,
>> This doth but *counsaile*, yet you cannot scape.
> If t'were a *shame* to love, here t'were no *shame*,
>> *Affection* here takes *Reverences* name.
> Were her first yeares the *Golden Age*; That's true,
>> But now shee's *gold* oft tried, and ever new.
> That was her torrid and inflaming time,
>> This is her tolerable *Tropique clyme*.

Here (to borrow Wordsworth's famous phrase) Donne's eye is fixed steadily, or more or less steadily, upon his object; but in what immediately follows Mrs. Herbert seems, as it were, to fade out, and sheer wit takes control. Mrs. Herbert's wrinkles, he declares, are not to be called graves; although, if they were, they would be Love's graves; for there indeed Love is, not lying dead in them, but sitting in them, like an anchorite in his trench. Or, rather, Love is not digging a grave but building a tomb, for when she dies Love will die too. Or ratherest, Love, although he goes everywhere on visits, makes Mrs. Herbert's wrinkles his permanent address. Is not all this, to us at any rate, rather surprising?[1] Even Mrs. Herbert, Donne's Olympias, his Paula, as Walton calls her, between whom and himself there had been 'many sacred Indearments', becomes, after a few lines, a mere topic for wit, a mere broomstick, as fundamentally indifferent, one might be inclined to say, as, in the earlier elegies, the characteristics of Donne's pretended friend's pretended mistress, or the angels which had to be melted down to remake the lost chain. Is this, I wonder, an example of that 'unified sensibility'

---

[1] In an important article in *The Modern Language Review*, April 1961, pp. 213 ff., Mrs. E. E. Duncan-Jones has shown that both the idea of 'autumnal beauty' and the image of Love as 'sitting' even upon the wrinkles of such beauty occur in two epigrams (V, 258; VII, 217) in the Greek Anthology, and that Latin versions of these epigrams almost certainly provided the starting-point for Donne's elaborations in this poem.

about which we have heard so much? Let us proceed with our examination, allowing, in Arnold's phrase, a stream of thought to play freely about Donne's thought as it plays around Mrs. Herbert. After this firework display Donne's eye returns, for at least two lines, to his object, although in the next passage I will quote it is fascinating to observe how wit first mingles with the tenderness, then gradually predominates over it, and is soon once more bombinating in a void from which Mrs. Herbert has completely vanished.

> Here, where still *Evening* is; not *noone*, nor *night*;
>   Where no *voluptuousnesse*, yet all *delight*.
> In all her words, unto all hearers fit,
>   You may at *Revels*, you at *Counsaile*, sit.
> This is loves timber, youth his under-wood;
>   There he, as wine in *Iune*, enrages blood,
> Which then comes seasonabliest, when our tast
>   And appetite to other things, is past.
> *Xerxes* strange *Lydian* love, the *Platane* tree,
>   Was lov'd for age, none being so large as shee,
> Or else because, being young, nature did blesse
>   Her youth with ages glory, *Barrennesse*.[1]

Then come two syllogistic arguments in favour of loving what is old, arguments which might equally well have appeared in the Second Elegy, *The Anagram*, where, as we have seen, Donne sets out to prove that it is better to marry an old and ugly woman than a young and handsome one:

> If we love things long sought, *Age* is a thing
>   Which we are fifty yeares in compassing.
> If transitory things, which soone decay,
>   *Age* must be lovelyest at the latest day.

At this point, returning momentarily to his object, Donne seems to feel that he has, perhaps, rather over-emphasized, rather rubbed-in, Mrs. Herbert's age and her wrinkles (she was, as I have said, about forty-four), so he hastens to assure her that when he said he loved

[1] ll. 21–32.

autumnal faces he did not mean that he loved winter faces, and
that in calling her old he would not have her think that he regarded
her as what one of Congreve's characters might have called a positive ruin:

> But name not *Winter-faces*, whose skin's slacke;
>   Lanke, as an unthrifts purse; but a soules sacke;
> Whose *Eyes* seek light within, for all here's shade;
>   Whose *mouthes* are holes, rather worne out, then made;
> Whose every tooth to a severall place is gone,
>   To vexe their soules at *Resurrection*;
> Name not these living *Deaths-heads* unto mee,
>   For these, not *Ancient*, but *Antique* be.[1]

An apology which, although it might perhaps have reconciled
Mrs. Herbert to the fact of being what Donne calls 'ancient',
could scarcely have helped her to regard with equanimity the
prospect of becoming what he calls 'antique'. In the last six lines,
however, his eye returns to his object and tenderness mingles with
his wit:

> I hate extreames; yet I had rather stay
>   With *Tombs*, then *Cradles*, to weare out a day.
> Since such loves naturall lation[2] is, may still
>   My love descend, and journey downe the hill,
> Not panting after growing beauties, so,
>   I shall ebbe out with them, who home-ward goe.

'A thought to Donne was an experience', wrote Mr. Eliot in
1921; 'it modified his sensibility'.[3] Well, if Donne's sensibility
towards Mrs. Herbert was as great as Walton would have us suppose,
and as some even of the lines in this poem seem to indicate, his
thoughts. such ingenious thoughts as that her wrinkles are love's
graves and that Xerxes loved a plane-tree because of its age, seem
not so much to have modified that sensibility, as, for the time being,
to have suppressed it, or to have escaped from it into a kind of void.

[1] ll. 37–44.
[2] Motion from one place to another.
[3] *Selected Essays*, 273.

Certainly, in this poem at any rate, his sensibility seems only very occasionally to modify his thought, which, as I have said, might as well have been directed upon a broomstick. And in what sense can Donne be said to 'feel' these ingenious thoughts? What, surely, to a modern reader, seems most remarkable about them is precisely that, as thoughts about one's Olympias, one's Paula, between whom and oneself there had passed many sacred endearments, they appear so unfelt, so unfeeling. To call such thoughts experiences, a word which, as Mr. Eliot uses it, seems to denote something more fundamental, more complex, more integrated than either pure thought or pure feeling, is surely the very opposite of the truth. Are they not, in fact, about as near to pure thought, as remote from feeling and, one might almost say, from living, as geometrical propositions or formal logic? I am aware, of course, that this was not the kind of poem Mr. Eliot had in mind: he was thinking, no doubt, of certain things in the *Songs and Sonets*, in the *Anniversaries*, in the *Divine Poems*, where conceptions have the intensity and palpability of perceptions and where thought and feeling are almost inseparable; nevertheless, both Mr. Eliot in 1921 and several of Mr. Eliot's disciples to-day, when they declare that Donne's thoughts were experiences and when they generalize about the characteristic differences between the poetry of Donne and other so-called metaphysicals and that of their successors, seem to forget how much of Donne's poetry and how much of the poetry of Donne's imitators is essentially of the same kind as these verses to Mrs. Herbert. We may perhaps be willing to agree with Mr. Eliot that the feeling, the sensibility, expressed in Gray's *Elegy* is, in a sense, cruder than that expressed in Marvell's *Coy Mistress*, but we should beware of basing upon a few such comparisons large generalizations about the differences between the poetry of the earlier seventeenth century and that of later periods, and in drawing from a few such comparisons inferences about the kinds of sensibility possessed not only by English poets but by English readers at different times.

Is, in fact, 'unified sensibility' the most appropriate phrase to describe the impression made upon us by *The Autumnall* and by what we may imagine to have been the mind and mood from which it proceeded? If 'unified sensibility' means, as those who use the phrase seem to intend it to mean, a peculiarly balanced, integrated and harmonious relationship between intellect and feeling, does not Donne's *Autumnall*, which, as I have so continuously insisted, was addressed, not to a broomstick, but to his Olympias, his Paula, seem, at any rate to us, to proceed from a strangely disunified sensibility, from one in which sheer intellect, sheer ingeniousness, sheer wit greatly predominates over feeling? Donne—one might almost be inclined to say, were one to generalize from this and similar poems as Mr. Eliot and his disciples have generalized from poems of a different kind—Donne seems to be continually distracted from the object of his contemplation by a kind of mental *tic*, a 'concupiscence of wit' (to borrow his own phrase), a restless, itching ingenuity which cannot fully occupy itself or identify itself with anything, not even with his Paula. One might, perhaps, be tempted into psychological explanations: one might declare, for example, that Donne was so self-haunted, so fundamentally incapable of being interested in anyone or anything but himself, that he could not keep his attention even upon Mrs. Herbert for more than a line or two at a time. Or, alternatively, one might suggest that his feelings for her were so strong that he suppressed them and escaped from them by indulging in sheer intellectual wit, just as we know that Coleridge deliberately escaped from his painful emotional life into the distractions of metaphysical speculation. One might, I say, be tempted into such explanations and suggestions, although I myself should not be inclined to put very much faith in them. There probably was some element of what is currently called 'escapism' in Donne's wit, an escaping from boredom, from depression, an urge to exercise his restless and not adequately occupied intellect upon *something*, however trivial, but I rather suspect that, strange as it may appear to us, such wit was expected and appreciated even by the grave Mrs. Herbert. It is certainly remarkable that Walton, himself a steady and serious man and one who, moreover, seems to have been a little old-fashioned in his poetic taste, does not seem to have found anything odd or incongruous in *The Autumnall*, for he simply remarks, after quoting the beautiful opening lines and two others, that 'the rest of her Character' may be read there. If, then, Walton and his contemporaries were distinguished by their unified sensibilities, they could, nevertheless, appreciate a kind of poetry which, when we consider it carefully, seems to us to proceed rather from a disunified one, from one in which, for the time being at any rate, sheer intellect and sheer wit greatly predominate over feeling.[1]

In his essay on Marvell Mr. Eliot accused Dryden of isolating the element of wit and exaggerating it into something like pure fun, and he quoted, as examples, from *MacFlecknoe*,

> The midwife placed her hand on his thick skull,
> With the prophetic blessing: Be thou dull;

and from *Absalom and Achitophel*:

> A numerous host of dreaming saints succeed,
> Of the true old enthusiastic breed.

And he seemed to imply, at any rate in this essay, that such wit,[2] wit that had become almost pure fun, was the most striking characteristic of Dryden's poetry as a whole—which is an example of what I meant when I said that these two very influential essays contained several statements that were either very limitedly true or almost wholly untrue. For, were we to analyse and classify Dryden's poetry as a whole as thoroughly and impartially as we have just been attempting to analyse and classify Donne's Elegies, should we really be compelled to decide that its most fundamental, its most striking,

---

[1] If only we knew how Mrs. Herbert 'took' *The Autumnall*, knew what, in modern phraseology, was her 'reaction' to it! Nay more, if only we knew how Mrs. Beata Poole, daughter of the fourth and sister of the fifth Lord Chandos, 'took' the poem addressed to her by her husband's relative Walton Poole, which begins 'If shaddowes be a pictures excellence', and which will be found in the Appendix to Grierson's edition of *Donne*, I, 460. Its great popularity is attested by the numerous manuscripts in which it exists; it was attributed at various times to Donne, to Ben Jonson, and to Bishop Corbet, and was variously entitled *On Black Hayre and Eyes*, *On a Gentlewomans black hair and eyes*, *On a black Gentlewoman*, etc. Beginning with a paradoxical encomium of dark, or black, beauty quite in the manner of Donne, Walton Poole passes suddenly from what is seen to what is *not* seen, and it was no doubt this wittily obscene turn which made the poem so popular. Variations on this apparently original theme were soon produced, and there can, I think, be no doubt that it was from this interesting example of unified sensibility that the song known during the eighteenth century as *The Coal-Black Joke* was ultimately derived. If, I repeat, we knew precisely how these two poems were 'taken' by their addressees, we could generalize more confidently than we can at present about the nature of seventeenth-century sensibility.

[2] 'Such wit': and yet it seems to me that what really distinguishes the two quotations Mr. Eliot has chosen is the fact that (within the sphere of discourse) their imagery expresses the idea and sentiment of their subjects so perfectly and so completely—in a word, that they are perfect examples of wit in which thought and feeling coalesce into a 'unified sensibility'.

characteristic was something like pure fun? Where, except in the lines *Upon the Death of the Lord Hastings*, an early, imitative, and rather feeble performance, can we find in Dryden any such continuous and elaborate examples of sheer wit, of pure fun (if anything so strenuously intellectual may appropriately be called fun), as we have been finding continually in the Elegies of that supposed exemplar of unified sensibility (as he once seemed to Mr. Eliot and as he still seems to many), John Donne? And, let us remember, it was two of the most sheerly witty, two of the most entirely unserious and unimpassioned, of these elegies that were especially admired by Ben Jonson and Drummond of Hawthornden, men whose sensibilities, unlike those of Dryden and Milton, had not yet (one must suppose) been 'dissociated'.

Again, in his essay on Marvell Mr. Eliot seemed to intend all or most of his praise of that poet to apply equally to the other so-called metaphysicals, and among other things for which he praised Marvell was that of never taking a subject too seriously or too lightly.[1] Now although this refusal to take any subject either too seriously or too lightly would seem to have been an almost essential and indispensable characteristic of that whole conception of seventeenth-century wit which Mr. Eliot was then trying to expound, it would perhaps be rather unfair to ask him now whether he then intended this portion of his encomium on Marvell to apply equally to Donne. For I take it that he was observing Matthew Arnold's distinction between the real and the historical estimate of literature, and that he meant, not merely that these poets, or some of them, seemed to their contemporaries to take no subject either too seriously or too lightly, but that they made that impression upon Mr. Eliot and ought to make that impression upon all cultivated readers at all times, in contrast to less balanced and unified poets such as Dryden, Milton, Tennyson and the rest. Would he, though, even in 1921, have been ready to maintain that a cultivated modern reader ought to find nothing more odd or strange in *The Autumnall* than Walton apparently did, and that a still handsome modern woman of forty-four who should be similarly addressed ought not to feel that she had been taken too lightly? I fear she would only feel that she had not been taken too seriously. Remembering, too, what Mr. Eliot has written about the mainly magniloquent and rhetorical Milton, it

[1] *Selected Essays*, 290.

seems not unfair to ask, which reveals the more unified sensibility—
The Autumnall or the celebrated description of Eve? For in his
role of a critic who is also a 'poetical practitioner', and in his eagerness to demonstrate that the so-called metaphysicals were far better
models for a contemporary poet than Milton, Mr. Eliot has tended
to concentrate far too exclusively upon what seemed to him the
defects and limitations of Milton, and upon what seemed to him
the merits of the metaphysicals, and has shown far too little awareness of—shall we say?—the contrast between Donne's *Autumnall*
and Milton's description of Eve.[1]

Mr. Eliot's praise of Marvell for taking no subject either too
seriously or too lightly is, as I have said, essentially connected with
his whole conception of seventeenth-century wit, the wit of the
so-called metaphysicals, which, he declares,

> involves, probably, a recognition, implicit in the expression of
> every experience, of other kinds of experience which are possible.[2]

This statement, except that it requires qualification, and should be
regarded as a definition of, as it were, the mean, not of the extremes,
of seventeenth-century wit, seems to me one of Mr. Eliot's most
illuminating generalizations, or—I might almost say—revelations.
It had, I fancy, been fruitfully working in the mind of Professor
Basil Willey when he declared, in his chapter on Sir Thomas Browne
in *The Seventeenth Century Background*, that the 'major interests of
life had not yet been mechanically apportioned to specialists, so that
one must dedicate oneself wholly to fact or wholly to value', and
that

> something of the peculiar quality of the 'metaphysical' mind is
> due to this fact of its not being *finally committed* to any one

---

[1] I hope no reader will be so dull as to suppose that I am presuming to censure
Mr. Eliot, either for changing his mind about Donne, or for occasionally expressing
himself in a manner which seems to me to require more qualification than he had,
perhaps, time or space to give. Indeed, it may well be that he himself has been surprised and sometimes embarrassed at the way in which some of his always stimulating
pronouncements have been taken up and erected almost into dogmas. Even on the
subject of Milton, where I feel that, in the past at any rate, he really has been too
narrow and dogmatic, I am not without a certain sympathy; for, greatly as I admire
Milton's later poetry, I must confess that, as Dr. Johnson said of clean linen, I have no
passion for it.

[2] *Selected Essays*, 289.

world. Instead, it could hold them all in a loose synthesis together, yielding itself, as only a mind in free poise can, to the passion of detecting analogies and correspondences between them.[1]

And later in the same chapter Professor Willey remarks that:

> The peculiar irony of Browne, his wistfulness, the air of compassion with which he ponders all time and all existence, proceed from his detachment from each and all of the worlds he contemplates; so that he can indulge his whim in fitting together what patterns he pleases with their fragments.

> 'The world that I regard is my selfe; it is the Microcosm of my own frame that I cast my eye on; for the other (*i.e.* the Macrocosm), *I use it but like my Globe, and turn it round sometimes for my recreation.*'

> It is a romantic falsification to 'relish' Browne for his 'quaintness'. It is more valuable, in reading him, to try to recover something of his own inclusiveness, in virtue of which his juxtapositions are *not* quaint, but symbols of his complex vision.[2]

Here, too, there is important truth, although it seems to me that certain distinctions and qualifications are necessary. In the first place, can what *seems* quaint, even if it ought not to seem so, be truly called classical? Does what is truly classical ever seem quaint? And, if not, must we not admit that much in Browne and other seventeenth-century writers is, though admirable in many ways, not really classical? I do not say that we should read and admire only what is classical, but I think it is most important that we should not lose the ability to distinguish between what is classical and what is not, for, if we do, we shall tend to become provincial and eccentric in our admirations. In the second place, even after some necessary historical correction has been made, do not the questions of relevance, proportion, decorum still remain? Is there not a distinction between those analogies where one world really illuminates another

---

[1] *Op. cit.*, 42–3.
[2] *Op. cit.*, 46.

(That was her torrid and inflaming time,
This is her tolerable *Tropique clyme*)

and those where nothing is really illuminated or revealed except the author's extreme ingenuity

(*Xerxes* strange *Lydian* love, the *Platane* tree,
Was lov'd for age, none being so large as shee)?

I may perhaps conclude this subject by remarking that much of that multiplicity of vision, that multi-mundity, which Mr. Eliot and Professor Willey have admired in the Metaphysicals and in Browne, is also apparent in Shakespeare, so many aspects of whose achievement in drama these later writers may be said to have reproduced in other *media*. Shakespeare, too, like Hamlet, for whom man is now the paragon of animals and now a quintessence of dust, has more than a little of that 'detachment from each and all of the worlds he contemplates' which Professor Willey has noticed in Browne. Shakespeare, too, especially in *Richard II*, often yields to what Professor Willey calls 'the passion of detecting analogies and correspondences' between different worlds. Indeed, in *Richard II* there are several excellent examples of how this kind of wit can degenerate into quaintness, into mere wit, when it sins against the canons of relevance, proportion and decorum and pursues analogies mechanically and for their own sakes.

In Winters tedious Nights sit by the fire
With good old folkes, and let them tell thee Tales
Of wofull Ages, long agoe betid:
And ere thou bid good-night, to quit their griefe,
Tell thou the lamentable tale of me,
And send the hearers weeping to their Beds:
For why? the sencelesse Brands will sympathize
The heauie accent of thy mouing Tongue,
And in compassion, weepe the fire out:
And some will mourne in ashes, some coale-black,
For the deposing of a rightfull King.[1]

[1] V, i. 40–50.

Of this speech Dr. Johnson remarked that Shakespeare should have ended with the line

> And send the hearers weeping to their Beds,

'and have spared his childish prattle about the fire'. It was of such passages that Johnson was thinking, when he wrote in the *Preface*, not indeed, as so often, without some considerable degree of exaggeration and failure to distinguish between Shakespeare's practice in his earlier and in his later plays:

> He is not long soft and pathetick without some idle conceit, or contemptible equivocation. He no sooner begins to move, than he counteracts himself; and terrour and pity, as they are rising in the mind, are checked and blasted by sudden frigidity.

'He no sooner begins to move, than he counteracts himself': words which describe precisely some passages in Shakespeare and some poems of Donne, notably, *The Autumnall*, to which, and to the reflections it suggested, I have perhaps devoted more than sufficient attention.

III. The Satires

The Satires, like most of the Elegies, belong to those pieces (we can only guess how many or how much of the Satires Jonson would have ranked among Donne's 'best pieces') which Donne wrote before he was twenty-five, that is to say, by 1597. On the back of the Harleian MS. 5110 in the British Museum is inscribed:

> Jhon Dunne his Satires
> Anno Domini 1593.

1593, or more probably 1593 to 1594, is indeed the earliest date assignable to any of the Satires, although some of them were demonstrably written later. External allusions in the first two suggest that they were written between 1593 and 1594. The Third, on the search for true religion, has no datable references, but it seems reasonable to assume that it was written during the period when Donne was himself investigating the claims of the Roman and Anglican Churches, and that period, too, was probably 1593 to 1594. The reference to 'the losse of Amyens' in the Fourth proves that it was written after March 1597, and the address to Sir Thomas Egerton in the Fifth proves that it had been written after Donne had entered his service towards the end of 1597.

Donne, therefore, although he can scarcely be regarded as the originator, has some title to be regarded as the precursor of that sudden outburst of formal satire and satirical comedy which distinguishes the last years of the sixteenth century, and in which we seem to perceive a new generation, especially of University and Inns of Court men, reacting against most of the literary ideals and fashions which had hitherto prevailed, and declaring, in so many words, that it is time to get down from one's stilts, to remove one's rose-coloured spectacles, and to see things as they really are. At times, when one reads their many satirical portraits of foolish courtiers, one might be tempted to describe the movement as a revolt of University and Inns of Court men against what was fashionable at Court; although this, perhaps, would be to over-particularize and to sacrifice too much to an antithesis. It would probably be safer and more accurate to speak of a reaction against the earlier romanticism and idealism; a disenchanted resolve to be at all costs realistic, to see things and show things as they really were, and to describe them (as Jonson put it) in 'language such as men do use'. Donne, whose earliest satires were written at least as early as 1594, seems to have been the first in the field, although in this case as in others it was only through their circulation in manuscript that his poems became known and admired. In 1595 Lodge published his *Fig for Momus*, a miscellaneous collection which included four satires; in 1597 Hall published his *Tooth-less Satyrs*, being the first three books of the collection which he called *Virgedemiae*; and then, in 1598, the year in which Jonson's *Every Man in his Humour* was acted, there was a regular spate of satires and epigrams—Hall's *Biting Satyres*, Marston's *Scourge of Villanie*, as well as the *Certaine Satyrs* appended to his *Metamorphosis of Pigmalion's Image*, Guilpin's *Skialetheia*, to name only those best known. The spate continued during 1599, 1600 and 1601, during which year the stages were being much be-rattled by the War of the Theatres, but seems to have been checked for a time by the Injunction of 1st June, 1599, against

libellous books, ordering various titles to be burnt, and command-
ing 'That noe *Satyres* or *Epigrams* be printed hereafter', and by the
attempts of the Stationers' Company to co-operate with the authorities in enforcing it.

Most of these satirists believed, no doubt, that they were imitating Horace, Juvenal and Persius, but, with a few occasional exceptions, it seems to me that all they really succeeded in reproducing
was the imaginary harshness of those poets' verses. In the Roman
satirists we have generalizations about human nature, its weaknesses
and ruling passions, illustrated by occasional examples which
seldom descend to minute detail; in the Elizabethan satirists generalization is almost completely absent, and we have page after page of
detailed, realistic descriptions of particular follies, affectations and
'abuses', and of the perpetrators thereof. On those occasions when,
without any particular object before him, an Elizabethan satirist
indulges in general invective, he nearly always gabbles like a thing
most brutish, unable to endow his purposes with words.

They had been taught that the model satirist was Persius, and
that his chief characteristics were harshness of style and hardness of
conceit. This supposedly indispensable harshness some of them,
notably Donne and Marston, though not Hall and Guilpin, deliberately cultivated. It cannot be too often insisted that the harshness
of which Dryden and others accused Donne, and which is most
apparent in his Satires, was deliberately cultivated, although, for
some reason which I cannot explain, it is much more apparent in
his last two satires, the Fourth and Fifth, written between 1597 and
1599, than in the first three, written between 1594 and 1595. And
we must remember that when Dryden and the eighteenth-century
critics accused Donne of harshness they were thinking chiefly, if
not exclusively, of his Satires. Saintsbury, in his Introduction to
the Muses' Library edition of Donne's poems, has some excellent
remarks on this subject:

It is now, I believe, pretty well admitted by all competent
judges that the astonishing roughness of the Satirists of the late
sixteenth century was not due to any general ignoring of the
principles of melodious English verse, but to a deliberate intention arising from the same sort of imperfect erudition which had
in other ways so much effect on the verse of the Renaissance

generally. Satiric verse among the ancients allowed itself, and even went out of its way to take, licences which no poet in other styles would have dreamt of taking. The Horace of the impeccable odes writes such a hideous hexameter as—

Non ego, namque parabilem amo Venerem facilemque,

and one of the Roman satirists who was then very popular, Persius, though he could rise to splendid style on occasion, is habitually as harsh, as obscure, and as wooden as a Latin poet well can be. It is not probable, it is certain, that Donne and the rest imitated these licences of malice prepense.

But it must be remembered that at the time when they assumed this greater licence, the normal structure of English verse was anything but fixed. Horace had in his contemporaries, Persius and Juvenal had still more in their forerunners, examples of versification than which Mr. Pope himself could do nothing more 'correct'; and their licences could therefore be kept within measure, and still be licentious enough to suit any preconceived idea of the ungirt character of the Satiric muse. In Donne's time the very precisians took a good deal of licence: the very Virgils and even Ovids were not apt to concern themselves very greatly about a short vowel before *s* with a consonant, or a trisyllable at the end of a pentameter. If therefore you meant to show that you were *sans gêne*, you had to make demonstrations of the most unequivocal character.[1]

In the First Satire Donne describes how he was persuaded to leave his books and take a walk with a foolish companion, who, after smiling at 'every fine silken painted foole' they met, left him, first for a celebrated tobacco-smoker, then for a celebrated judge of clothes, and finally for his mistress, in whose house he quarrelled with other gallants and was turned out of doors with a broken head. The bare outline of this, as also of the Fourth Satire, may possibly have been suggested by the Ninth Satire of Horace's First Book, where he describes how he was buttonholed by an unwelcome companion who hoped for an introduction to Maecenas and from

[1] *op. cit.*, pp. xx–xxi.

whom Horace only got free when the man's adversary in a lawsuit appeared on the scene.

Here realistic detail such as Jonson loved predominates over mere wit, although there is a passage at lines 37 to 48 which could (or would) have been written only by Donne—a passage in which he insists on his companion's inconsistency and absurdity in hating naked virtue although he loves his naked whore, and although souls only enter into felicity when they are naked of bodies, and although man was naked in the state of innocence. This argument, based on a deliberate confusion between the metaphorical and literal meaning of 'naked', is essentially similar to Berni's argument, in his *capitolo* in praise of debt, based on the double-meaning of *debito* as 'debt' and as what is owed as a duty or obligation:

> *Debito è far altrui le cose oneste,*
> *Come dir, ch'a'più vecchi si conviene*
> *Trar le berrette, ed abbassar le teste.*
> *Adunque far il debito è far bene:*
> *E quanto è fatto il debito più spesso,*
> *Tanto questa ragion più lega, e tiene.*

The poem (and here it is clear that Horace was Donne's model) is also much more dramatic than most Elizabethan satires, which generally deal in mere description and denunciation: consider, for example, the amount of action and dialogue in the following passage:

> Now leaps he upright, Joggs me, & cryes, Do you see
> Yonder well favoured youth? Which? Oh, 'tis hee
> That dances so divinely; Oh, said I,
> Stand still, must you dance here for company?
> Hee droopt, wee went, till one (which did excell
> Th'Indians, in drinking his Tobacco well)
> Met us; they talk'd; I whispered, let 'us goe,
> 'T may be you smell him not, truely I doe;
> He heares not mee, but, on the other side
> A many-coloured Peacock having spide,
> Leaves him and mee; I for my lost sheep stay;
> He followes, overtakes, goes on the way,
> Saying, him whom I last left, all repute

For his device, in hansoming a sute,
To judge of lace, pinke, panes, print, cut, and plight,
Of all the Court, to have the best conceit;
Our dull Comedians want him, let him goe;
But Oh, God strengthen thee, why stoop'st thou so?
Why? he hath travayld; Long? No; but to me
(Which understand none), he doth seeme to be
Perfect French, and Italian; I replyed,
So is the Poxe.[1]

The Second Satire, on poets and lawyers, is much less individual
and characteristic and much closer to the general run of Elizabethan
satires. Poets who starve themselves by writing for idiot actors
(Greene died in 1592, Marlowe in 1593), who 'write to Lords,
rewards to get' (Shakespeare? Nashe?), who plagiarize—these,
Donne declares, like other monstrous sinners (letchers, usurers,
drunkards, swearers), don't trouble him, for they punish themselves;
but he can't stand Coscus (the author of the anonymous sonnet
sequence *Zepheria*), who is so proud of being a lawyer that he
courts in the terminology of the law. Then, by a very abrupt and
obscure transition (lines 61–2), Donne proceeds to satirize men who
take up the practice of the law for mere gain, and who, like that
William Gardiner on whom Dr. Leslie Hotson flashed his lantern,
combining law with usury, cheat prodigal heirs out of their
estates.

The exhaustive and contemptuous detail in the simile at lines
81 to 86 is reminiscent of many things in Jonson's comedies:

For as a thrifty wench scrapes kitching-stuffe,
And barrelling the droppings, and the snuffe,
Of wasting candles, which in thirty yeare
(Relique-like kept) perchance buyes wedding geare;
Peecemeale he gets lands, and spends as much time
Wringing each Acre, as men pulling prime;

while the large exuberance of what follows, with its back-handed
satire on the reformed Churches, reminds us that Dryden to some
extent remained, as he had begun, one of Donne's disciples:

[1] ll. 83–104.

In parchments then, large as his fields, hee drawes
Assurances, bigge, as gloss'd civill lawes,
So huge, that men (in our times forwardnesse)
Are Fathers of the Church for writing lesse.
These hee writes not; nor for these written payes,
Therefore spares no length; as in those first dayes
When Luther was profest, He did desire
Short *Pater nosters*, saying as a Fryer
Each day his beads, but having left those lawes,
Addes to Christs prayer, the Power and glory clause.

Is there not a strong affinity between this, including its exploitation
of what Hopkins called 'the native thew and sinew of the English
language', and, for example, this?—

Beast of a bird, supinely when he might
Lye snugg and sleep, to rise before the light:
What if his dull Forefathers used that cry,
Cou'd he not let a Bad Example dye?
The World was fallen into an easier way;
This Age knew better, than to Fast and Pray.
Good Sense in Sacred Worship would appear
So to begin, as they might end the year.
Such feats in former times had wrought the falls
Of crowing Chanticleers in Cloyster'd Walls.
Expell'd for this and for their Lands, they fled;   ⎫
And Sister Partlet, with her hooded head   ⎬
Was hooted hence, because she would not pray a-bed. ⎭
The way to win the restiff World to God
Was to lay by the Disciplining Rod,
Unnatural Fasts, and Foreign Forms of Pray'r:
Religion frights us with a meen severe.
'Tis Prudence to reform her into Ease,
And put Her in Undress, to make Her pleas;
A lively Faith will bear aloft the Mind
And leave the Luggage of Good Works behind.[1]

The similes in that passage from Donne's Second Satire, which I have

[1] *The Hind and the Panther*, Third Part, ll. 1013-33.

invited the reader to compare with the one just quoted from *The Hind and the Panther*,—the similes, though ingenious, are kept subordinate to the subject, which they illuminate. Sir Herbert Grierson has said of Dryden that he scarcely ever writes as one inspired by his subject in itself; nevertheless, when Dryden has chosen a subject he usually keeps to it, and it does not become a mere topic for wit, as even Mrs. Herbert, his Paula, his Olympias, does for Donne. That is one of the great differences between Donne and Dryden: we often feel that Donne is far more concerned with the working out of his ingenious similes than with the subject (whatever it be) which they profess to be illustrating and illuminating.

However, in his Third Satire, on the search for true religion, Donne *is* inspired by his subject in itself, and his wit and his similes never get out of hand. He is not merely witty, but passionately witty, or wittily passionate, and the poem gives an unforgettable picture of an eager mind at work—for even here Donne is in a sense dramatic, as he is in nearly all his best and most characteristic work. The poem proves, too, that his investigation of the rival claims of the Roman and Anglican Churches, although it may have been begun partly, or even, perhaps, largely, from motives that we should call worldly, was nevertheless prosecuted with what we should call 'sincerity', a burning sincerity, for the rough lines of this satire are penetrated by an intense eagerness for truth, for what to the young Donne, no less than to Spenser, was saving truth, truth on the discovery of which the soul's salvation depended, and by a deep contempt for indifference. And (what cannot but seem strange to us, and, even after all necessary explanations have been given, somehow separating) this saving truth is, in a sense, factual rather than doctrinal, and to be attained, not in some beatific vision, but as the result of a long and laborious process of historical, or semi-historical, research; for truth, says Donne, is a little elder than falsehood; that is to say, the true religion is that which is nearest to the Primitive Church. Truth, then, saving truth, is to be attained by a careful comparison of rival arguments about a matter of fact: the question to be decided being, which Church is, as a matter of fact, nearest to the Primitive Church? And faith, in this context, consists in the belief that a really thorough and disinterested research will discover this factual truth, that God will guide such a disinterested effort to the truth, which, I repeat, is a truth of fact. It is, I suppose, this strange mingling, as it seems to us, of facts and ideas, of truths of religion and truths of history, that makes the religious consciousness of Donne and his contemporaries so difficult for us to understand—makes it, perhaps, above all difficult to understand why a mind so acute and sceptical as Donne's should not have perceived what seem to us manifest incongruities. Later, indeed, in his letters, though not, of course, in his sermons and public controversies, Donne seems almost to admit a feeling of unity, a partnership in saving truth, with all those, of whatever Church, who believe in God and in Christ; but this more modern conception of religion, as we should perhaps be tempted to call it, only emerges occasionally from that more old-fashioned, that essentially historical, factual, controversial, literal conception which was characteristic both of Donne and of his age. It is therefore, in speaking of Donne's religion, very difficult to deal with it, as it were, psychologically: to isolate those elements which seem to us typical of various manifestations of the religious consciousness at all times from those elements which were conditioned by particular time and place.

We must seek for truth, he exclaims, but where is she to be found? Some seek her at Rome, because she was there a thousand years ago, others at Geneva, others at home, while some are content to suppose that all religions are the same:

> but unmoved thou
> Of force must one, and forc'd but one allow;
> And the right; aske thy father which is shee,
> Let him aske his; though truth and falshood bee
> Neare twins, yet truth a little elder is;
> Be busie to seeke her, beleeve mee this,
> Hee's not of none, nor worst, that seekes the best.
> To adore, or scorne an image, or protest,
> May all be bad; doubt wisely; in strange way
> To stand inquiring right, is not to stray;
> To sleepe, or runne wrong, is. On a huge hill,
> Cragged, and steep, Truth stands, and hee that will
> Reach her, about must, and about must goe.[1]

[1] ll. 69–81.

An unforgettable picture, as I have said, an almost dramatic expression, of an eager mind at work.

Of the Fourth Satire, as of the First, the bare outline may have been suggested by the Ninth Satire of Horace's First Book, where Horace describes how he was buttonholed by an unwelcome companion who could not be got rid of until his adversary in a lawsuit happened to appear. Its subject is the Court and Courtiers. It is the longest of Donne's satires, the roughest in versification, and, on the whole, the least interesting, the nearest to the common run. Donne describes how, having been foolish enough to go to Court, he was unable to escape the unwelcome attentions of an absurdly dressed person who pretended to be a great traveller, linguist, and repository of secrets. Having got rid of him by lending him a crown, Donne went home and reflected on the folly and futility of those whom he had seen at Court. There is no clear plan or dominant idea, detail is piled upon detail, and although individual lines are often striking, they do not co-operate to produce a whole. Here, nevertheless, is an example of the kind of plum one may expect to find: one spruce creature approaches a woman who scarcely knows him:

> And unto her protests, protests, protests,
> So much as at Rome would serve to have throwne
> Ten Cardinalls into the Inquisition;
> And whispered by Jesu, so often, that A
> Pursevant would have ravish'd him away
> For saying of our Ladies psalter.[1]

Of another type, who affects what he calls a 'rough carelessnesse', Donne says

> And though his face be as ill
> As theirs which in old hangings whip Christ, still
> He strives to looke worse[2]—

one simile among many scattered through Donne's poems, especially the more realistic ones, which is sufficient in itself to disprove the notion, often expressed by others and very strongly by Professor

[1] ll. 212–17.
[2] ll. 225–7.

Crofts, in that brilliant essay to which I have already referred, that
Donne seems to have been little affected by visual impressions.
Professor Crofts is concerned to show that the nature of Donne's
rebellion against literary conventions was largely determined by
what he calls 'the extraordinary deficiencies of his equipment as a
poet'.

> The beauty of the visible world meant nothing to him and
> yielded him no imagery for serious purpose. I am not forgetting
>
> > Her pure and eloquent blood
> > Spoke in her cheeks, and so distinctly wrought
> > That one might almost say, her body thought.
>
> This is always quoted. But it is quoted because it is the only passage
> in all his works which seems to record an intense visual experience;
> the one oasis in a visual desert.[1]

Here Professor Crofts, like some other of Donne's critics, seems to
me to be using the word beauty in a rather naïve and limited sense,
which would have been rejected by numerous artists from Rem-
brandt to Picasso, and to be inferring from the fact that Donne has
recorded, whether directly or in similes, comparatively few visual
impressions of things obviously and immediately recognizable as
beautiful—beautiful faces, costumes, landscapes, and so forth—to
be, I say, inferring from this fact that Donne might as well have
been born blind. Descriptions of things obviously beautiful Donne,
I think, deliberately rejected, along with the tales of Ovid's *Metamorphoses*, which, as Carew said, he silenced, and the goodly train
of gods and goddesses, which he exiled; but of things not obviously
beautiful, but nevertheless strange and arresting, even though sometimes repulsive, of 'things counter, original, spare, strange', many a
passage in Donne's poetry proves that he had had most intense
visual experiences. That Donne was not insensible to visual beauty
of a more obvious kind is proved by the Palatine and Somerset
Epithalamia, both written as late as 1613. Consider the description
of the birds, Bishop Valentine's parishioners, in the first stanza of
the Palatine *Epithalamion*:

[1] *Essays and Studies by Members of the English Association*, 1936, 136–7.

> The Lirique Larke, and the grave whispering Dove,
> The Sparrow that neglects his life for love,
> The household Bird, with the red stomacher.

Or consider the description of the bride in the Eclogue which precedes the Somerset *Epithalamion*:

> First her eyes kindle other Ladies eyes,
>   Then from their beames their jewels lusters rise,
> And from their jewels torches do take fire,
>   And all is warmth, and light, and good desire.

Grierson, in his Commentary, simply remarks that here Donne comes nearer than elsewhere to Spenser, and that 'in glow and colour nothing he has written surpasses the Somerset Epithalamium'. He might have added that if Donne did not more often write like this, it was not because he could not, but because he did not want to.

But let us return from this digression to the Fifth and last of Donne's satires, on suitors and law officers. Here I feel continually that the particular abuse Donne professes to be satirizing is merely a topic for the display of his wit, which, as I have remarked before, is a thing we almost never feel in reading Dryden's satires, however true it may be that he never writes as one inspired by his subject in itself. Almost the whole point of the following passage turns on the exploitation of the double meaning of the word angel:

> Judges are Gods; he who made and said them so,
> Meant not that men should be forc'd to them to goe,
> By meanes of Angels; When supplications
> We send to God, to Dominations,
> Powers, Cherubins, and all heavens Courts, if wee
> Should pay fees as here, Daily bread would be
> Scarce to Kings.[1]

And here and throughout such enjoyment as the mere play of wit

[1] ll. 57–63.

affords is marred by the deliberately achieved harshness of the verse:[1]

> If all things be in all,
> As I thinke, since all, which were, are, and shall
> Bee, be made of the same elements:
> Each thing, each thing implyes or represents.
> Then man is a world; in which, Officers
> Are the vast ravishing seas; and Suiters,
> Springs; now full, now shallow, now drye; which, to
> That which drownes them, run.[2]

To summarize the results of this survey of Donne's Satires, we may say that it is only in the Third, on the search for true religion, that he is consistently inspired by his subject in itself; and there, too, he writes with that moral earnestness which inspires most of Jonson's best work in the heroic couplet. In the other satires there are many touches of vivid realism, which remind us of Jonson, both in his comedies and in some of his epigrams and epistles, but there is much that is not clearly distinguishable from the general run of Elizabethan satire, including an absence of clear outline and plan, a tendency to pile detail upon detail and to present us with just one damned thing after another. What is more characteristic of Donne is that dramatic quality which I noticed in the First, and that tendency to indulge in mere wit for its own sake which is especially noticeable in the Fifth. In fact, with the exception of the Third, the Satires

[1] Pierre Legouis's suggestion, based on what is probably a misunderstanding of a remark of Gray's, that many of the lines in Donne's Satires are deliberately intended, like those in Spenser's August Eclogue, to be scanned as four-foot, not as five-foot, lines, seems to me totally unacceptable: *Donne the Craftsman*, Appendix I. Spenser was deliberately imitating what he understood to be the metre of Chaucer, for he (like Dryden after him) read Chaucer's decasyllabic couplets precisely as a modern reader would who had received no preliminary instruction about the pronunciation of final -e and -es: he read them, that is to say, not as five-beat, but as four-beat, lines. Donne, on the other hand, was not imitating Chaucer, but (with intolerable exaggeration) the 'harshness' of the Roman satirical hexameter. The fact that many of his lines can only with great difficulty be scanned as five-foot lines is precisely what he intended: he *intended* the reader to find as much difficulty in reading them as he himself found in reading such hexameters as the one quoted by Saintsbury. This was what Dryden meant when he declared that Donne had followed Horace too closely: 'Would not Donne's *Satires*, which abound with so much wit, appear more charming, if he had taken care of his words, and of his numbers? But he followed Horace so very close, that of necessity he must fall with him' (*Essays*, ed. Ker, II, 102).
[2] ll. 9–16.

are far less characteristic of Donne than the Elegies. In what I have called the dramatic elegies one important aspect of his poetic gift finds far completer expression than in the Satires, while in elegies such as *The Anagram* and *The Bracelet* his capacity for sheer wit is at least more appropriately employed than in the Satires, even if to-day most of us find, like Dr. Johnson, that we are rather surprised by it than delighted.

IV. *'Letters to Severall Personages'*

Leaving the two *Anniversaries* for separate consideration, as a kind of link between the secular and the religious poems, I will conclude this survey of Donne's couplet poems with an examination of some of those verse epistles (it is not necessary to consider them all) which he wrote at various times between 1597 and 1612, and which in the early editions of his poems were classified as *Letters to Severall Personages*. It so happens that most of those I propose to consider are written, not in couplets, but in quatrains or in triplets —a fact which does not, however, affect the appropriateness of considering them here. They fall naturally into two main kinds: those which, like several of the Elegies, are, as it were, discourses upon a broomstick, where the subject, whatever it be, is mainly an opportunity for the display of wit, and those which are written in a more serious and Jonsonian manner.

Taking first those which are mainly witty, we may begin with two very famous poems, one of which professes to describe the storm which drove the Islands Expedition back to Plymouth in the late summer of 1597, while the other professes to describe how the fleet was later becalmed. The first certainly, and probably the second as well, was addressed to Donne's friend and chamber-fellow at Lincoln's Inn, Christopher Brooke, who was later to give away Donne's bride while his clerical brother performed the ceremony. The poems are entitled, respectively, *The Storme* and *The Calme*, and they profess, as I have said, to describe those events. Nevertheless, if this be descriptive poetry, it is very unlike what either Milton or Thomson or Wordsworth or Tennyson understood thereby. Not, though, so very unlike Marvell's descriptive poetry in, for example, *Appleton House*, and very like that of many of Donne's immediate successors. Donne indeed, especially in these two poems, may perhaps be regarded as the originator of a kind of descriptive, or professedly descriptive, poetry which became very popular during the seventeenth century, and of which the formula would seem to be: to how many other things, ideas, experiences can this particular experience, or this particular object in front of me, be related? True, the experiences here described are not completely indifferent to Donne, not mere broomsticks, and he cannot be said to be writing entirely without his eye on the object. Nevertheless, he only looks at it, as it were, intermittently, and is concerned less with the object itself than with the ingenious things he can find to say about it, with the relationships and analogies he can establish between it and things, ideas or experiences that would have been very unlikely to occur to anyone else. It was for this kind of wit that Dr. Johnson, in his *Life of Cowley*, expressed a particular dislike, and seems to have regarded as *the* characteristic wit of the poets whom he called metaphysical; he contrasted it with the conception of wit as that 'which is at once natural and new, that which, though not obvious, is, upon its first production, acknowledged to be just', and declared that the thoughts of these poets 'are often new, but seldom natural; they are not obvious, but neither are they just; and the reader, far from wondering that he missed them, wonders more frequently by what perverseness of industry they were ever found'. It has not, I think, been generally observed that Johnson's objection to this kind of wit would seem to have been almost as much moral as aesthetic. He was offended, not merely by its unclassicality, its lack of proportion and *decorum*, but by its fundamental unseriousness, its detachment, its amorality. 'They never', he declared, 'inquired what, on any occasion, they should have said or done; but wrote rather as beholders than partakers of human nature; as Beings looking upon good and evil, impassive and at leisure.' In saying that they were 'men of learning, and to show their learning was their whole endeavour' he was being wildly inaccurate, but his remark that 'their wish was only to say what they hoped had been never said before' is, though an unsympathetic, a not unjust description of such poems as we are now considering. With the doctrine of wit for wit's sake Dr. Johnson had as little sympathy as G. K. Chesterton, who in some ways resembled him, had with the doctrine of art for art's sake. Life, he felt, was too serious a business to be spent in such trifling. Did his namesake, who in his own best poetry was nearly always intensely serious, reveal, in regarding Donne as the first poet in the world for such things as *The Bracelet* and a passage from *The Calme* which he had by heart—did he reveal thereby a more catholic sympathy, or simply that he also, to some extent, shared a taste that should be regarded as corrupt?

This is how Donne, in *The Storme*, describes his sea-sick companions:

> Some coffin'd in their cabbins lye, 'equally
> Griev'd that they are not dead, and yet must dye;
> And as sin-burd'ned soules from graves will creepe,
> At the last day, some forth their cabbins peepe:
> And tremblingly 'aske what newes, and doe heare so,
> Like jealous husbands, what they would not know.[1]

Here, although he is writing with what Dr. Johnson would no doubt have regarded as heartless and inhuman detachment, Donne is writing with his eye on the object: even though he may be more concerned with the ingenious analogies it suggests than with the object itself, the analogies do really illuminate the object, and very vividly. On the other hand, in what immediately follows there is perhaps less proportion between the objects and the similes they suggest, and a more obvious predominance of sheer wit: the sick ship's mast is shaken with an ague, and its hold clogged with a salt dropsy; the tacklings are snapping like 'too-high-stretched treble strings',

> And from our totterd sailes, ragges drop down so,
> As from one hang'd in chaines, a yeare agoe.—

an ingenious simile, this last one, but intensely vivid and intensely visual—one, indeed, of the many I had in mind when, commenting upon a similar though less vivid one in the Fourth Satire, I ventured to criticize Professor Crofts's complaint that he could only find one passage in Donne's works which seemed to record an intense visual experience. Donne often, it is true, shows his wit by describing things visible and tangible in terms of things abstract or intellectual, things familiar in terms of things remote or outlandish; but it is by no means always so. Sometimes he describes things seen in terms of

[1] ll. 45–50.

things imagined as seen, comparing, for example, his sea-sick companions peering from their cabins to sinful souls emerging from their graves on the Day of Judgment, and, in their asking for news, to jealous husbands hearing, in reply to their questions, what they would prefer not to know. And sometimes, as in the simile I have just commented upon, he describes something actually seen in the present with something actually seen in the past: this, indeed, is what he is doing in the most striking passage in either of these poems, that one in *The Calme* which, I cannot but think, Ben Jonson loved to repeat in its entirety, although Drummond only mentions the last two lines:

> As water did in stormes, now pitch runs out:
> As lead, when a fir'd Church becomes one spout.
> And all our beauty, and our trimme, decayes,
> Like courts removing, or like ended playes.
> The fighting place now seamens ragges supply;
> And all the tackling is a frippery.
> No use of lanthornes;[1] and in one place lay
> Feathers and dust, to day and yesterday.

Is it really necessary to insist that these lines were written by a man who, even though his gaze might more often be directed inwards than outwards, was nevertheless accustomed to look at the visible detail of the world around him as sharply and as fascinatedly as Ben Jonson himself?

I have said that Donne in these two poems may perhaps be regarded as the originator of a kind of descriptive, or professedly descriptive, poetry which became very popular during the seventeenth century. The chief characteristic, one might almost say, the essence, of this kind of poetry is the ingenious simile, and it is most interesting to observe the varying relations between the simile and the professed subject, the simile sometimes really illuminating the subject, and sometimes merely displaying the author's ingenuity. Marvell, in *Appleton House*, preserves a better balance between illumination and sheer astonishment than Donne in these two poems, or, for that matter, in *The Autumnall*: however witty he

---

[1] The motionless ships, he means, no longer require lanterns suspended from their sterns to prevent their losing touch with one another at night.

may be, he is nearly always far less detached than Donne, and we can nearly always feel his genuine affection for what he is describing:

> And now to the Abbyss I pass
> Of that unfathomable Grass,
> Where Men like Grashoppers appear,
> But Grashoppers are Gyants there:
> They, in there squeking laugh contemn
> Us as we walk more low than them:
> And from the Precipices tall
> Of the green spir's, to us do call.
>
> To see Men through this Meadow Dive,
> We wonder how they rise alive.
> As, under Water, none does know
> Whether he fall through it or go.
> But, as the Marriners that sound,
> And show upon their Lead the Ground,
> They bring up Flow'rs so to be seen,
> And prove they've at the Bottom been.

Milton, in *L'Allegro* and *Il Penseroso*, almost entirely dispenses both with the ingenious simile and with the element of paradox and hyperbole. For, after the introductory abjurations of 'loathed Melancholy' and of 'vain deluding joys', the purely paradoxical or hyperbolical element ceases, if it is present at all, to be felt as paradox or hyperbole. In this respect *L'Allegro* and *Il Penseroso* differ greatly, not only from some of the outrageously and quite unseriously paradoxical poems of Donne, but even from such a poem as Marvell's *The Garden*.

> No white nor red was ever seen
> So am'rous as this lovely green.

Throughout Marvell's praise of the garden we are delightfully aware of the element of hyperbole and paradox, whereas Milton's praise of the pleasures of mirth and of melancholy is, in comparison, as unhyperbolical as, let us say, Ben Jonson's Virgilian and Horatian praise of a country life in his epistle to Sir Robert Wroth. All that remains of wit, of academic or scholastic wit, is the element of contrast and debate, whether mirth is superior to melancholy or melancholy to mirth. Milton in these poems treats his subject more seriously, more whole-heartedly, than either Donne or Marvell, and his method is that of straightforward, though carefully selected and generalized, description. He is writing, not in the tradition of Donne, but in that of Fletcher, the Fletcher of *The Faithful Shepherdess* and of those lines on melancholy, beginning 'Hence, all you vaine Delights', which were first printed in his play *The Nice Valour*, or, *The Passionate Mad-man*, in the folio of 1647, but which long before that date had become very popular and appear in several manuscript collections from about 1620 onwards. In one of these, MS. Malone 21 in the Bodleian, it is followed by a reply entitled *Against Melancholly* and ascribed to Dr. Strode, that is, to William Strode (1602–45), Canon of Christ Church, Chaplain to Bishop Corbet, and Public Orator in the University of Oxford, a complete edition of whose poems was published for the first time in 1908 by Bertram Dobell, the discoverer of Traherne. Both Fletcher's poem and Strode's reply to it were published in the miscellanies *Wits Interpreter*, 1655, and *Wit Restor'd*, 1658. Since not even Fletcher's poem, let alone Strode's, is so well known as it should be; since, as a paradox or a thesis, Fletcher's defence of melancholy is so utterly unlike Tasso's ingenious defence of ugliness and Donne's still more ingenious variation on the same theme, proceeding, as it does, not by ingenious but completely unserious syllogistic arguments and analogies, but by carefully selected descriptions of things obviously attractive, or, as one might even be inclined to say, romantic—since, in a word, it illuminates by contrast the kind of paradoxical poetry which Donne seems to have initiated with *The Anagram* and the kind of descriptive poetry he seems to have initiated with *The Storme* and *The Calme*, and is in method essentially similar to Milton's *L'Allegro* and *Il Penseroso*, which it may well have suggested, I will quote both Fletcher's poem and Strode's reply. I have had occasion to criticize Mr. Eliot, but I cannot too strongly endorse his remark that the critic's two chief tools are analysis and comparison; for often the best way to see what a particular kind of literature really is, to recognize what its author is really doing and what effect he is trying to produce, is to compare it with another kind, superficially

similar but essentially different: in this case, Fletcher's and Milton's
method of debate and description with Donne's. And when once we
have recognized the fundamental contrast between, as it were, the
two extremes, between Donne, for example, and Milton, we begin
to perceive in the relationship of other writers to these two extremes
various illuminating similarities within what is still essentially difference—to perceive, for example, that in at least one respect, affection
for his subject, choice of things obviously pleasing or attractive,
Marvell in *Appleton House* is nearer to Milton than to Donne.
And when we have done that we have seen Marvell's poem more
clearly than we did before. Here, then, is Fletcher's poem:

> Hence, all you vaine Delights,
> As short as are the nights,
>   Wherein you spend your folly,
> Ther's nought in this life sweet,
> If man were wise to see't,
>   But onely Melancholy,
>   O sweetest melancholy.
> Welcome folded Armes, and fixed eyes,
> A sigh that piercing mortifies,
> A look that's fastned to the ground,
> A tongue chain'd up without a sound.
> Fountaine heads, and pathlesse Groves,
> Places which pale passion loves:
> Moon-light walkes,, when all the fowles
> Are warmly hous'd, save Bats and Owles;
>   A mid-night Bell, a parting groane,
>   These are the sounds we feed upon;
> Then stretch our bones in a still gloomy valley,
> Nothing's so daintie sweet as lovely melancholy.

Strode's reply is not a very notable poem, but I will quote it because
its co-existence with Fletcher's may well have suggested to Milton
the idea of *L'Allegro* and *Il Penseroso*. It is less romantic, less pictorial,
than Fletcher's, and in style—or so it seems to me—thoroughly
Jonsonian, for does not its concise and almost epigrammatic
catalogue of qualities recall that in Hermogenes's song at the end
of the second act of *Poetaster*, beginning

If I freely may discover
What would please me in my lover?

Against Melancholly

Returne my joyes & hither bring
A heart not taught to speak but sing,
A jolly spleen, an inward feast
A causelesse laugh without a jest;
A face which gladnesse doth anoint,
An arme for joy flung out of joynt;
A sprightfull gate yt leaves no print,
And makes a feather of a flint;
A heart yt's lighter then the aire,
An eye still daunceing in its spheare;
Strong mirth wch nothing can controule,
A body nimbler then a Soule;
ffree wandring thoughts not ty'de to muse,
W^ch thinke on all things, nothing choose,
W^ch are [=ere] wee see them come are gone:
These life itselfe doth live upon.
    Then take no care, but only to be jolly:
    To be more wretched then we must is folly.

If I have seemed to wander rather far from Donne's *Storme* and *Calme*, my apology must be that Donne's poetry can best be appreciated and understood in the context of seventeenth-century poetry as a whole, and that it is often both interesting and illuminating to read him with other seventeenth-century poets in mind, instead of waiting until we come to them chronologically or in some separate volume or chapter.

Another aspect of Donne's still fundamentally unserious wit, or serious trifling, rather different from anything we have yet encountered, is to be found in some of his verse letters to the Countess of Bedford and the Countess of Huntingdon. These are written in what may be called his scholastically or (though I am rather suspicious of that word) his metaphysically complimentary style. He assumes, or pretends to assume, that these noble friends and patronesses are divinities, and gravely deduces from this assumption their true relationship to others and to himself. Here we no longer find the ebullient and outrageous wit of Donne's earlier paradoxical verse, with its ingenious analogies fetched from here, there, and everywhere; although the whole procedure is still fundamentally unserious, Donne, having made the initial assumption, contrives to maintain an illusion of seriousness, as though he were demonstrating theological truths of the first importance. For the similes and analogies with which he supports his argument are now drawn almost exclusively from the realm of theology and school divinity. These epistles were, indeed, all written during his theological but pre-clerical period, during the years when he was assisting Morton in his controversy with the Recusants, and they may perhaps tempt us to ask that question which in my introductory chapter I said we might often feel tempted to ask, namely, how much did even the things to which he apparently devoted himself most seriously really mean to Donne? It is impossible to date these letters precisely, but Donne does not seem to have become intimately acquainted with the Countess of Bedford until about 1608, and although he had known the Countess of Huntingdon since about 1600, when her mother married, as her second husband, Sir Thomas Egerton, it seems not improbable that the very elaborate epistle to her which I propose to discuss may have been written after the publication, in 1611 and 1612, of his extravagant eulogies of young Mistress Elizabeth Drury had offended the Countess and other noble friends, and that it was to appease these offended divinities that Donne wrote some of his more hyperbolical epistles, to show, as Grierson puts it, the pitch he was capable of soaring to in praise of their maturer virtues.[1]

We may confine ourselves to two of these epistles, of which a mere prose analysis will make sufficiently clear how Donne is there exercising his wit. First, the one to the Countess of Bedford, beginning

Reason is our Soules left hand, Faith her right.

The Countess, declares Donne, is a divinity, and divinity is apprehended partly by faith and partly by reason. Her friends, that is to say, her saints, whom her election has glorified and her presence

[1] II, 132.

illuminates, have apprehended her by reason, but Donne has had to be content with a distant faith. Nevertheless, in order to make that faith as intelligible as possible, he has studied her in her saints, in her deeds, in her writings; but soon the reasons why all love her grow infinite and transcend reason, so he falls back once more upon an implicit faith.

If Ben Jonson declared of Donne's *Anniversaries*, of which, after all, fifteen-year-old Mistress Elizabeth Drury was merely the starting point and occasion, just as King was the occasion of Milton's *Lycidas*—if Ben Jonson declared of Donne's *Anniversaries* that they were 'profane and full of blasphemies', and that 'if it had been written of the Virgin Mary it had been something', what, we may wonder, would he have said of this epistle? He could admire unstintedly the argumentative wit of *The Bracelet* and the descriptive wit of *The Calme*, and, although he blamed Donne for the harshness and obscurity of his verse, he never, so far as we know, objected to the morality of those early poems which he regarded as Donne's best; nevertheless, knowing what he said of the *Anniversaries*, we may assume that this solemn trifling with matters which he held sacred would have been too much even for the not very strait-laced Ben, who was not capable of Donne's complete detachment.

The epistle to the Countess of Huntingdon beginning

Man to Gods image; *Eve*, to mans was made,

which Grierson thinks was probably written just before Donne entered holy orders, is much more elaborate and almost as daring, or, as Ben Jonson would have held, as profane and blasphemous, in its conceits as that epistle to the Countess of Bedford which I have just mentioned. It is also a most remarkable piece of consecutive syllogistic reasoning.

Since, Donne tells the Countess, God made woman not in his own image but in man's, and, so far as we know, did not breathe a soul into her, innocence in a woman, like a new comet, is matter for wonder, but active goodness in a woman is miraculous, like a new star in the unchanging firmament. And just as such a star led the Magi to behold God made man, your reputation may lead all souls to know what virtue is. It is true that, just as the decline of the sun, which New Philosophy has degraded from the summit to the centre of the universe, might seem to imply the old age and approaching end of the world, even so the decline of virtue from men to women might seem to imply that virtue too was near her end: this, though, would be a false conclusion, for virtue has not stooped but risen: exiled by men, she has fled to Heaven, that is, to yourself. Dispersed in men, she is now concentrated in you: us she merely informed, you she transubstantiates. Although you are still a wife and a mother, that is merely in order that you and the virtue you incorporate may be visible to mortal sight, just as water rarefied into air is only visible when it forms a cloud. Moreover, you are like those constellations, those groups of stars, which are content with humble names such as Crab and Bull, while mere single planets assume the names of gods. Only one being, your husband, comprehends you as you really are; others must be content with progressively imperfect revelations of you. To me you appear as a virtuous prince does to a subject, and I pay you the tribute of these lines. If you think they flatter you, then indeed they do, for by so thinking you reveal less judgment than I supposed you to possess. Flattery, though, can often direct the will to goodness as efficaciously as advice, and it was certainly not my intention to flatter you. If I flatter anyone, it is my own judgment, which long ago prophesied that your virtue would come to excel both your beauty and your birth; and now that this prophecy has been fulfilled it is your duty to agree with what I say, since otherwise you would be depriving God of the praise and gratitude due to him for what he has bestowed. In fact, I, who was formerly your prophet, am now your chaplain, praising God in you.[1]

This solemn trifle is, I think, the most elaborately and rigidly argumentative of all Donne's poems, and as close as anything he ever wrote to what Dryden had in mind when, involuntary pro-

---

[1] Although Dryden censured Donne for affecting the metaphysics, he nevertheless (whether consciously or unconsciously) often imitated him, both in prose and verse, in this strain of hyperbolical eulogy: most notably, perhaps, in his Dedication of *The State of Innocence* to Mary of Modena, of which Dr. Johnson wrote: 'This composition is addressed to the princess of Modena, then duchess of York, in a strain of flattery which disgraces genius, and which it was wonderful that any man that knew the meaning of his own words, could use without self-detestation. It is an attempt to mingle earth and heaven, by praising human excellence in the language of religion.'

genitor of a long line, he first[1] associated Donne's name and poetry
with the word 'metaphysics'. Somewhere in the background,
perhaps (though I am by no means sure of this), is Petrarch with his
so often ecstatically and religiously celebrated Madonna Laura, and
behind Petrarch those poets of Courtly Love, who so often appro-
priated the language and liturgy of religion; but this tradition, if it
is really present, has been completely merged, or submerged, in
that tradition of paradoxical, scholastic and academic wit which
had long flourished intermittently among scholars, which Berni
and his contemporaries made fashionable, and which Donne, in
elegies such as *The Anagram* and *The Bracelet*, developed with an
intellectual agility and strenuousness that was all his own. It was
very casually, in that fulsomely flattering *Discourse concerning the
Original and Progress of Satire*, dedicated to the Earl of Dorset, and
in which the names of Homer, Shakespeare and your Lordship are
so closely associated, that Dryden let fall the famous phrase about
Donne's affecting the metaphysics:

> You equal Donne in the variety, multiplicity, and choice of
> thoughts; you excel him in the manner and the words. I read you
> both with the same admiration, but not with the same delight.
> He affects the metaphysics, not only in his satires, but in his
> amorous verses, where nature only should reign; and perplexes
> the minds of the fair sex with nice speculations of philosophy,
> when he should engage their hearts, and entertain them with the
> softnesses of love.[2]

The fact that Dryden immediately proceeds to declare that in this
respect Cowley, in *The Mistress*, has copied Donne to a fault,
makes it probable that he was thinking of the *Songs and Sonets*,
since it is those which Cowley has imitated in *The Mistress*, but
it is also possible that he may have had these and similar verse-
letters in mind, and that he regarded even those exalted and learned
ladies, the Countess of Bedford and the Countess of Huntingdon,
primarily as members of what he called 'the fair sex', who would

---

[1] I am not forgetting Drummond's letter to Dr. Arthur Johnston, quoted in my
footnote on p. 15; but, besides the fact that this letter was first published in 1711,
Drummond there refers neither to Donne nor to any other English poet *by name*, and
one cannot even be certain that he had Donne in mind.

[2] *Essays*, ed. W. P. Ker, II, 19.

have preferred to have been entertained with the softnesses of love rather than to have had their gentle minds perplexed with meta-physical, or metaphysico-theological, compliments on their divinity. However that may be, this casual phrase, like many another casual phrase of Dryden's, was taken up by Dr. Johnson, magnified, and developed into something like a literary-historical pronunciamento. 'About the beginning of the seventeenth century' he wrote, 'appeared a race of writers that may be termed the metaphysical poets; of whom, in a criticism on the works of Cowley, it is not improper to give some account'; and he proceeded, acutely, though not, as it seems to us, very sympathetically or discriminatingly, to describe what seemed to him their characteristics.

It is, by the way, amusing to observe how casual remarks of eminent writers have been developed, often through misunder-standing, into articles of literary belief. *Ut pictura poesis*, said Horace, innocently enough, in the *Ars Poetica*,

> *Ut pictura poesis: erit quae, si propius stes,*
> *Te capiat magis, et quaedam si longius abstes*

—lines neatly and accurately rendered by Conington as

> Some poems, like some paintings, take the eye
> Best at a distance, some when looked at nigh.

But the phrase *ut pictura poesis*, which, as Horace wrote it, meant no more than 'as with a painting, so with a poem', was taken out of its context, misunderstood, and, until the time of Lessing, it remained a current literary dogma that a poem should be like a picture. Where, too, did the tradition of Shakespeare's want of learning, of his almost total ignorance, originate—that tradition which flourished during the greater part of the eighteenth century and which led Rowe to declare that Shakespeare wrote under a kind of mere light of nature? 'Those who accuse him to have wanted learning,' declared Dryden, in that famous encomium in the *Essay of Dramatic Poesy*, 'those who accuse him to have wanted learning, give him the greater commendation; he was naturally learn'd; he needed not the spectacles of books to read Nature; he looked inward, and found her there.'[1] Who accused Shakespeare

[1] *Essays*, ed. Ker, I, 80.

to have wanted learning? At the very end of the Preface to *All for Love* Dryden tells us—lets, one might say, the cat out of the bag: 'But it is almost a miracle that much of his language remains so pure; and that he who began Dramatic Poetry amongst us, untaught by any, and as Ben Jonson tells us, without learning, should by the force of his own genius perform so much, that in a manner he has left no praise for any who come after him'.[1] Where does Ben Jonson tell us that Shakespeare was without learning?— Why, in a single line, the only line which most people seem able to remember, in the noble commemorative poem he contributed to the First Folio:

And though thou hadst small *Latine*, and lesse *Greeke*.

On that line, and on Dryden's misinterpretation of it, rests the whole tradition, the whole myth, of Shakespeare's illiteracy.

What mighty contests rise from trivial things!

But to return to that verse-letter to the Countess of Huntingdon which we were considering, whether or no Dryden had it in mind, it is, as I have said, as near as anything Donne ever wrote to what Dryden meant when he said that Donne affected the metaphysics and perplexed the minds of the fair sex with nice speculations of philosophy. The poem is, indeed, crammed full, almost totally consists, of philosophical, or, perhaps more accurately, Scholastic, concepts and arguments, but it remains an entirely unserious poem and is in no sense a philosophical one; for a philosophical poem is one in which the author, whether or no he employs traditional or technical philosophic concepts, is trying to express, according to the laws of poetic beauty and poetic truth, a vision, or part of a vision, of life, of existence, as a whole. In this poem, though, Donne is not trying to express any such vision, and this poem, like so many others, is only accidentally, only superficially, philosophical or metaphysical. Donne is merely playing with scholastic concepts, as in some of the Elegies we have seen him playing with paradoxes. Later, indeed, in the *Songs and Sonets* and elsewhere, we shall sometimes find him making a more serious use of scholastic or

[1] *op. cit.*, I, 201.

philosophical concepts, using them not merely for fun, as it were, but in order to illuminate portions of his experience; nevertheless, I doubt whether even on the strength of such poems he may appropriately be called a metaphysical poet. What is really remarkable about that verse-letter to the Countess of Huntingdon is the consecutiveness, the elaborateness, the concentration, the tight logic, the extreme ingenuity with which an entirely unserious argument is conducted. Most of Donne's poems, including even some of the best of the *Songs and Sonets*, are poetical arguments, sometimes serious, sometimes frivolous, and whether or no in such poems he makes use of theological, scholastic or so-called metaphysical concepts is almost accidental. He may, or he may not. In fact, he might far more appropriately be called an argumentative or dialectical than a metaphysical poet, and those whose poems in this respect resemble his might far more appropriately be called the argumentative, or the dialectical, than the metaphysical school. For it is not merely his logical or argumentative capacity that distinguishes and differentiates a philosopher or a philosophic poet: it is, as I have said, his capacity to see life as a whole, to apprehend the meaning of life as a whole. In this sense, Rilke's *Duino Elegies*, though far less consecutively logical than Donne's poems, and although they scarcely ever employ traditional or current philosophic concepts, are far more essentially philosophic or metaphysical than anything of Donne's. For Rilke here, unlike Donne, is inspired by a vision of life as a whole and by a passionate urge to express it. The arguments employed by Donne, however logical, concentrated and consecutive, are seldom more than half-serious; that element of wit, of detachment, on which I have so often insisted, is nearly always present.

When Mr. Eliot declared that the characteristic wit of Marvell and other seventeenth-century poets took no subject either too lightly or too seriously, and that it probably involved 'a recognition, implicit in the expression of every experience, of other kinds of experience which are possible', and when he professed to regard this wit as the characteristic expression of a unified sensibility which in the work of later poets seemed to him to have become disunified or dissociated, he was, I take it, objecting to a kind of one-sidedness or extremism, a monotony of feeling, which he perceived and disliked. Gray's *Elegy*, I take it, seemed to him, in comparison with Marvell's *Coy Mistress*, to be a rhetorical and one-note poem. Shelley, no doubt, seemed shrill, hectic and excessive, and he might well have remarked that he could not, for example, possibly imagine Donne or Marvell or any of their school exclaiming in all seriousness

> I fall upon the thorns of life, I bleed.

They never, he might have said, took themselves so seriously, so one-sidedly, as that. Similarly, Wordsworth in many of the *Lyrical Ballads* might be said to have taken various small incidents and encounters, and in *The Excursion* and later poems many commonplace moral and theological ideas, far more seriously and solemnly than they deserved. And Tennyson's grief in *In Memoriam* might be regarded as too monotonous, too continuous, too unrelieved. It was, I think, above all with the detachment of the metaphysical, or, as I should prefer to call them, the dialectical, poets, that Mr. Eliot sympathized; and, although he has underemphasized, or even, perhaps, failed to notice, the very considerable element of mere trifling, of mere elaborate fooling, especially in Donne, I must confess that I share to a considerable extent his admiration for these poets at their best. Nevertheless, I cannot see that mere wit is, in itself, more admirable than mere pathos, mere revolt, mere solemnity, or any of the various excesses Mr. Eliot objects to in later poets, and I cannot see why, in themselves, these defects should be regarded as any more evidence of a dissociated sensibility than is mere wit. After all, admirable as Donne may be at his best, the *Ode to the West Wind* is a much better, a much more poetical, poem than either *The Autumnall* or the Epistle to the Countess of Huntingdon.

Let us now turn to some of the verse-letters which are written in a more serious, and, one might perhaps say, a more Jonsonian manner. Take the one addressed to Sir Henry Wotton, 'Here's no more newes, then vertue', written, as we learn from two manuscripts, in 1598, on the vanity of life at court. Like some of Jonson's epistles, it is in triplets, and it has some tendency towards Jonsonian statement and generalization:

> Beleeve mee Sir, in my youths giddiest dayes,
> When to be like the Court, was a playes praise,
> Playes were not so like Courts, as Courts'are like playes.

Or take the letter *To Mr. Rowland Woodward*, who, it would appear, before he went to Venice with Wotton in 1604, had asked Donne, then living in retirement at Pyrford or Camberwell, for copies of love-poems and satires, a request with which Donne seems to have complied rather reluctantly. This poem, too, is in triplets, and its theme is the value of retiredness and self-examination. The following lines seem to me quite in Jonson's manner, the gravely Horatian Jonson seeking to measure life:

> Wee are but farmers of our selves, yet may,
> If we can stocke our selves, and thrive, uplay
> Much, much deare treasure for the great rent day.
>
> Manure thy selfe then, to thy selfe be'approv'd,
> And with vaine outward things be no more mov'd,
> But to know, that I love thee'and would be lov'd.

In the letter *To Sr Henry Goodyere* beginning

> Who makes the Past a patterne for next yeare,

and written some time during the Mitcham years, Donne recommends Goodyer, who, it would seem, had contracted expensive habits and was rather going to seed, to travel. Here Donne's wit is strictly subordinated to the task of imparting serious and practical advice to a person in whom he is genuinely interested. The poem contains that fulness, that 'high and noble matter', which Jonson nearly always aimed at and often achieved. There is more illustration, more simile and metaphor, more play of wit than is common in Jonson's moral epistles and addresses, but, as in Bacon's *Essays*, it is always strictly subordinate to the matter in hand. Take the first stanza:

> Who makes the Past a patterne for next yeare,
> Turnes no new leafe, but still the same thing reads,
> Seene things, he sees againe, heard things doth heare,
> And makes his life, but like a paire of beads.

This seems to me very much more like the manner of Bacon at his best than like the Donne whose subject, whatever it be, either begins as or soon becomes a mere occasion for the performance of intellectual gymnastics. In 1943 Mr. L. C. Knights published in *Scrutiny* an interesting essay on *Bacon and the Seventeenth-Century Dissociation of Sensibility*, a title which illustrates very well the almost matter-of-course way ('with remarkably little fuss') in which the phrase Mr. Eliot coined in 1921 has been accepted as the statement of an indisputable fact and his theory as a firm foundation for further disquisitions and hypotheses. In that essay Mr. Knights seems to me rather unfair to Bacon in the examples which he chooses and which lead him to conclude that 'the function of the images is not to intensify the meaning, to make it deeper or wider, but simply to make more effective a meaning that was already fully formed before the application of the illustrative device'.[1] I cannot feel that in such an example as, let us say, 'Vertue is like precious odours, sweetest when most incensed and crushed', there is none of that 'vivid feeling for both sides of the analogy' which Mr. Knights finds in the metaphors and similes of more representative Elizabethans and denies to Bacon's. Doubtless some of Bacon's illustrations are, as Mr. Knights would say, purely forensic, but, on the other hand, 'vivid feeling for both sides of the analogy' is equally wanting in many of Donne's ingenious comparisons—in, for example:

> Call not these wrinkles, *graves*; If *graves* they were,
>   They were *Loves graves*; for else he is no where.
> Yet lies not Love *dead* here, but here doth sit
>   Vow'd to this trench, like an *Anachorit*.

If Bacon is often entirely preoccupied with a clearly defined idea, Donne is often entirely preoccupied with the analogy which some idea or phenomenon has suggested to him, and I cannot see why the one case rather than the other should be regarded as evidence of 'dissociated sensibility'. But let us return to Donne's letter to Goodyer:

> Provide you manlyer dyet; you have seene
>   All libraries, which are Schools, Camps and Courts;
> But aske your Garners if you have not beene
>   In harvests, too indulgent to your sports.

[1] *Explorations*, p. 99.

Would you redeeme it? then your selfe transplant
  A while from hence. Perchance outlandish ground
Bears no more wit, then ours, but yet more scant
  Are those diversions there, which here abound.

To be a stranger hath that benefit,
  Wee can beginnings, but not habits chok'e.
Goe; whither? Hence; you get, if you forget;
  New faults, till they prescribe in us, are smoake.[1]

Here, it seems to me, Donne has achieved that just balance between form and matter which Jonson was always aiming at. And it is the fact that he *could* achieve it that makes me rather hesitate to advance purely psychological explanations of such poems as *The Autumnall* or the verse-letter to the Countess of Huntingdon. Can we assume that Donne, whatever he might imagine or profess, was, fundamentally, so little interested in Mrs. Herbert and the Countess that he could not, as it were, keep his attention upon them? Or that his feelings were so strong that he tried to escape from them by means of his wit? Or must we rather assume that wit of this kind was what they most appreciated, and that Donne was deliberately playing a kind of fashionable game, although, it is true, a game of which, in England at any rate, he himself was the inventor?

The letter *To Sr Edward Herbert, at Iulyers*, written in 1610, begins with an image (partly suggested by Plato) that man is an amalgam of all beasts. Wisdom can make him an ark, where they all agree; folly, a theatre, where they fight each other and make sport for spectators. The poem as a whole is rather gritty and abstract, but there is one couplet that might well have been written by Jonson:

How happy'is hee, which hath due place assign'd
  To'his beasts, and disaforested his minde!

In the letter *To the Countesse of Bedford*, beginning 'Honour is so sublime perfection', witty hyperbolical compliment is mingled with Jonsonian seriousness, statement, and generalization. Donne begins

[1] ll. 17–28.

very much in the manner of his so closely argued and so fundamentally unserious letter to the Countess of Huntingdon. Since, he
declares, all honour proceeds from inferiors, since God was without
honour before the Creation, since kings do not bestow honour but
merely direct it from us to those whom they would have honoured,
it does not matter how humble may be the station of those who
praise you. The pure essence of herbs is better distilled by the heat
of dung than by fire or the sun, God often finds more piety in
labourers' ballads than in *Te Deums*, and cannon fired from towers
make less noise than the subterranean fires in Sicily. All this is
characteristic Donnish ingenuity, but in what follows there is something almost equally characteristic of Jonson:

> You, for whose body God made better clay,
> Or tooke Soules stuffe such as shall late decay,
> Or such as needs small change at the last day.
>
> This, as an Amber drop enwraps a Bee,
> Covering discovers your quicke Soule; that we
> May in your through-shine front your hearts thoughts see.
>
> You teach (though wee learne not) a thing unknowne
> To our late times, the use of specular stone,[1]
> Through which all things within without were shown.
>
> Of such were Temples; so and of such you are;
> *Beeing* and *seeming* is your equal care,
> And *vertues* whole *summe* is but *know* and *dare*.[2]

The comparisons, perhaps, are rather more ingenious than one
would expect to find in Jonson, but the Jonsonian gravity and fulness, the 'high and noble matter', are there.

One of the pleasantest of Donne's verse-letters and the last I
shall refer to is *A Letter to the Lady Carey, and Mrs Essex Riche*,

[1] '*The heathens* served their Gods in Temples, *sub dio*, without roofs or coverings,
in a free opennesse; and, where they could, in temples made of *Specular stone*, that was
transparent as glasse, or crystall, so as they which walked without in the streets, might
see all that was done within.' (*Donne's Sermons*, ed. Pearsall Smith, 113–14.)

[2] ll. 22–33.

From Amyens, written during Donne's visit to the Continent with Sir Robert Drury in 1611 to 1612. Beginning in the same wittily hyperbolical manner as that letter *To the Countesse of Bedford* which we have just been considering, it, too, leads up to some fine examples of what I have called 'Jonsonian' statement and generalization. Here in France, says Donne, where everyone invokes saints, it would be too schismatic to avoid the custom altogether, but, on the other hand, to invoke any saint but you would be heretical; and, moreover, since Faith here is too much subordinated to Good Works, it will be some degree of apostleship in me to speak of what I only see by faith, to speak, that is to say, of you. After this not very serious introduction—in which, by the way, the wit, although it employs no theological or philosophical or metaphysical concepts more recondite than those of the invocation of saints and the relationship between faith and good works, is of precisely the same kind as that in the much more elaborately argued and illustrated letter to the Countess of Huntingdon—after this not very serious introduction Donne proceeds to his main subject, which is the distinction between the occasional performance of virtuous actions and the state of being truly virtuous, between, as it were, accidental and essential virtue: the kind of moral distinction whose development and illustration would, one can imagine, have been thoroughly congenial to Ben Jonson, or, for that matter, to Horace. The beginning, I said, was not very serious, although the catholic exaltation of works over faith, there light-heartedly referred to, is implicitly and seriously criticized in what follows:

> Others whom wee call vertuous, are not so
> In their whole substance, but, their vertues grow
> But in their humours, and at seasons show.
>
> For when through tasteless flat humilitie
> In dow bak'd men some harmelessenes we see,
> 'Tis but his *flegme* that's *Vertuous*, and not Hee.

And then, after devoting three more stanzas to the other humours, or complexions, or temperaments, after declaring that the man who, upon occasion, can be rashly brave, is no more than sanguinely virtuous, or virtuous in his blood; that those who retire from the

world to a cloister have no more than melancholy virtue; and that
choleric and uncharitable critics of all religions and all faults are
merely virtuous in their gall, Donne continues:

> We'are thus but parcel guilt; to Gold we'are growne
> When Vertue is our Soules complexion;
> Who knowes his Vertues name or place, hath none.
>
> Vertue'is but aguish, when 'tis severall,
> By occasion wak'd, and circumstantiall.
> True vertue is *Soule*, Alwaies in all deeds *All*.[1]

Here, indeed, there is that 'vivid feeling for both sides of the analogy'
which Mr. Knights regards as especially characteristic of what I
suppose he would call pre-dissociated sensibility, and which, unjustly
as it seems to me, he denies to most of Bacon's similes and metaphors.
Here Donne is not, as so often, playing with a more or less indifferent subject and extracting from it as many ingenious analogies
as he can; he is treating a serious subject seriously, although at the
same time wittily, and making one world really illuminate another.

In this review of Donne's *Elegies, Satires* and *Letters to Severall
Personages*, what are the chief qualities we have noticed? Language
such as men do use; deliberate rejection of traditional ornaments,
images, diction, and of the conventionally beautiful; drama (one
may wish, perhaps, that there had been more of it); occasionally—
two qualities, these, which Donne shares with Ben Jonson—a vivid
realism in imagery and in often satirical description, and a grave
and weighty, though often witty, treatment of moral ideas; but,
above all, wit: often deliberately outrageous and impudent and
coat-trailing, often breath-takingly ingenious in the discovery of
comparisons and analogies, but nearly always, in one way or another,
argumentative, sequaciously, rigidly, scholastically argumentative,
whether in the defence of preposterous paradoxes or in the mock-
serious devising of hyperbolical compliments. Little that can be
regarded as the direct expression of personal experience, or, indeed,
of more than a part, a small part, of the poet's self; little that is more
than half-serious; little that is what a modern reader is accustomed
(perhaps too accustomed) to call 'sincere'. A pervading detachment,

[1] ll. 16-21, 31-36.

an impression of one playing, albeit with remarkable skill and strenuousness, a kind of elaborate game. Certainly not, except accidentally,
and in so far as he often employs philosophic or theological concepts, a primarily philosophic or metaphysical poet, but, as I have
insisted, sometimes a dramatic, though more often an argumentative, a wittily argumentative or dialectical, one.

4

THE *SONGS AND SONETS*

I. Jest and Earnest

It is easier to generalize about the form and style of the *Songs and Sonets* than about their characteristics as a collection of love-poems, for while certain qualities of style are shared in varying degrees by them all, these qualities are combined in different poems with very different degrees of seriousness. While, that is to say, all the poems are characteristic expressions of Donne's wit, they cannot all be regarded as characteristic expressions of his actual feelings, values, convictions and ideals. What we may call Donne himself is not equally present in them all. Readers, though, who are insufficiently equipped with a knowledge of Donne and of his time may nevertheless be tempted to regard them all precisely as they would regard contemporary poems: to regard them all with equal seriousness as expressions of moods and feelings and convictions which, however different, were at different times equally real. This can only lead to a serious misunderstanding both of Donne and of his poetry, and, more especially, of Donne as a love-poet, as a serious love-poet; for many of the *Songs and Sonets* are not really love-poems at all, but simply ingenious or outrageous paradoxes, disquisitions, or what Donne himself called 'evaporations' on the subject of love. It is, therefore, very necessary to attempt to classify them and distinguish between them according to their degrees of seriousness.

Were I asked to enumerate in order of importance those more formal characteristics of the *Songs and Sonets* with which these different degrees of seriousness are combined, I should insist first of all upon their wit, that kind of wit of which we have already examined and tried to analyse so many examples in the Elegies, Satires, and *Letters to Severall Personages*—that wit which I have suggested might more appropriately be termed scholastic or dialectical than metaphysical, and which may be roughly defined as the development in logical (sometimes in syllogistic) form of general propositions or statements, often paradoxical, preposterous or hyperbolical, and the reinforcements and illustration of them by means of ingenious analogies. I should insist, in the second place, on their dramatic quality, their dramatization of actual or imaginary experiences, situations, attitudes; thirdly (a matter closely connected with their characteristic wit) on their logical construction, the untransposability of their lines and stanzas; and, lastly, on their colloquial diction, their approximation to 'language such as men do use', together with their deliberate rejection of conventional ornaments, of classical, mythological, and, in general, of all merely literary allusions.

In this list of formal characteristics, several of which Donne's contemporaries had in mind when they described much new, un-Spenserian, un-Elizabethan poetry—Jonson's no less than Donne's —as 'strong-lined', I have not included the commonly alleged multiplicity of 'learned' allusions; neither, had I done so, should I have been inclined to attach much importance to it. Dr. Johnson's declaration that 'the metaphysical poets were men of learning, and to show their learning was their whole endeavour' was a gross exaggeration: it would be far nearer the truth, though also an exaggeration, to say that they were men of wit, and that to show their wit was their whole endeavour. The number and importance of the learned allusions in the *Songs and Sonets*, of allusions to theological, philosophical, scientific or pseudo-scientific doctrines, and, in general, to matters which require a factual or documentary, as distinct from an interpretative, note, has often been greatly exaggerated. Occasional allusions to the scholastic doctrines of angels and of substance and to such conceptions as that of animal spirits would have been as immediately comprehensible to most of Donne's readers as would to-day allusions to what we call popular science. Neither are these allusions more striking or more ingenious than many other of Donne's comparisons and analogies. It was not the time and labour he had bestowed in acquiring them, but the wit and ingenuity he displayed in using them, that was new and remarkable in English poetry. It is the wit that is fundamental; the learning is only incidental, and, as here displayed, not really extraordinary. Indeed, in comparison with that displayed by Milton in *Paradise Lost* it is insignificant.

In a later section of this chapter I shall examine more closely the formal structure of the *Songs and Sonets*: first, though, I propose to attempt, in some considerable detail, to distinguish between them according to their degrees of seriousness, to decide what is jest and what is earnest, and to put the too-commonly exaggerated autobiographical element in its proper place; then, having decided which may be regarded as more or less serious love-poems, I shall attempt to decide what sort of love-poems they really are, to indicate what, as love-poems, seems to me their essential *this-ness*.

Although in all poetry style and matter, form and substance, the manner of saying and the thing said are ultimately inseparable, the balance between these two elements, their relative importance, can vary very greatly, and so too can the degree of importance which readers attach to these two ultimately inseparable elements at different times. It was the manner and style of his poems, their 'strong-lined' characteristics, that Donne's contemporaries chiefly admired; there is little evidence that they paid much attention to differences in substance and in seriousness. Modern readers, on the other hand, tend to have a much less disinterestedly artistic approach, to concentrate much more attention upon substance, and to regard the poems as personal expressions and confessions, as autobiographical or semi-autobiographical records. Donne's contemporaries perhaps, or some of them, tended to take the more serious poems too lightly; modern readers perhaps tend to take the lighter poems too seriously. If Donne's contemporaries had an excessive, a too exclusive, admiration for his sheer wit, modern readers often fail to recognize it for what it is and to make allowance for it.

Our study of the Elegies should already have taught us that Donne had an unusual liking and capacity for what children call 'dressing up', and that the fact that he can describe a situation or express an attitude with convincing realism and dramatic truth is no proof that he has actually been in that situation or seriously and habitually accepted that attitude. Just as the Elegies have sometimes been regarded as the record of actual intrigues, the *Songs and Sonets* have too often been regarded as the record of a kind of rake's progress from vice to virtue, from cynical libertinism to real and lasting and loyal affection—from, let us say, that married woman who appears in some of the Elegies and whom (although, as I have insisted, she was pretty certainly suggested by the triangular situation in Ovid's *Amores*) Gosse assumed to have been a real person—from that woman, to Ann More. Now, although one cannot dismiss the later Donne's oft-repeated regrets and repentances for the sins of his youth as mere rhetoric and self-dramatization, it is, I think, very unlikely that he ever actually conformed to the image which several of the more outrageous of the *Songs and Sonets* present. I think, therefore, that Professor Crofts, in that brilliant essay to which I have already had occasion to refer, has got the emphasis and the proportions wrong when he writes:

> And so in a number of studiously scandalous 'elegies' and 'songs' he unfolds his sage and serious doctrine of promiscuity; presents that view of human nature which Othello greeted simply with the words 'Goats and monkeys' as the only true view; describes his adventures on these unlit levels; boasts of his conquests, mocks at injured husbands, and, in short, is at pains to present himself as one of the most egregious and offensive young coxcombs that even the Elizabethan age produced.[1]

Here, I am sure, Professor Crofts, like so many modern readers, is taking the Elegies and the *Songs and Sonets* too seriously, and, in consequence, being taken in by them. This was not how Donne's contemporary admirers would have understood him; I doubt very much whether they would—in fact, I am almost certain they would not—have assumed that he was unfolding *his* doctrine, describing *his* adventures, boasting of *his* conquests, taking pains to present a clear and undistorted image of himself as he actually was, of the young man whom Sir Richard Baker remembered as 'not dissolute, but very neat, a great visiter of Ladies, a great frequenter of Playes, a great writer of conceited Verses'. What, I am sure, in those more outrageous *Songs and Sonets*, they assumed Donne to be doing, what, I am sure, he mainly was doing, was this: displaying his wit, maintaining, with the sequacious but only half-serious logic of a defendant in some academic disputation, the most outrageous paradoxes; cocking snooks at the Petrarchan adoration and Platonic idealism of Spenser and the Sonneteers, flouting conventions which he and many of his contemporaries felt to have lasted too long;

[1] *Essays and Studies*, 1936, 131.

inspired by something of that spirit which led a certain Athenian to vote for the ostracism of Aristides because he was tired of hearing him called 'the just', which led Marlowe, in his tavern, to declare that Moses was a juggler and that he that did not love tobacco and boys was a fool, and which has so often made young men feel (as Virginia Woolf said of James Joyce) that in order to breathe they must break the windows.

Let us consider some of the more outrageous of the *Songs and Sonets*, and let us begin with *The Indifferent*. We have already noticed the general and particular influence of Ovid's *Amores* upon the Elegies. In the Fourth Elegy of the Second Book Ovid declares that he can't avoid the weakness of loving, and that his love is not kindled by any one particular type. Whatever qualities a woman may have are so many different reasons for loving her: modesty ensnares him, impudence promises good sport, while rigid virtue suggests profoundly dissimulated desire. If she is learned, she pleases by her rare endowments, if ignorant, by her simplicity. A pale complexion can captivate him, so can an amber one, while there is something lovable even in deepest brown. If black locks fall from a snowy neck, he remembers that Leda was admired for her dark hair; if they are blond, that it was by her saffron locks that Aurora pleased. I think Donne may well have had this elegy in mind when he wrote *The Indifferent*; but, while he reproduces the witty depravity, the entirely unidealized and unspiritualized sensuality, of Ovid, mingled, as that is, with some degree of Saturnalianism, of deliberate outrageousness and coat-trailing, he introduces, in his attack on constancy and defence of inconstancy, an element of scholastic argument and paradox which is quite foreign to Ovid, and which Donne seems to have been the first English poet to exploit. And I doubt whether he really took this argument much more seriously than the arguments which he used in one of the Elegies to persuade a friend that it was better to marry an old and ugly woman than a young and handsome one, arguments which, as I have said, may well have been suggested to him by those stanzas of Tasso between which and Donne's elegy Drummond of Hawthornden found it so hard to choose.

I can love both faire and browne,
Her whom abundance melts, and her whom want betraies,

Her who loves lonenesse best, and her who maskes and
    plaies,
Her whom the country form'd, and whom the town,
Her who beleeves, and her who tries,
Her who still weepes with spungie eyes,
And her who is dry corke, and never cries;
I can love her, and her, and you and you,
I can love any, so she be not true.

Will no other vice content you?
Wil it not serve your turn to do, as did your mothers?
Or have you all old vices spent, and now would finde out
    others?
Or doth a feare, that men are true, torment you?
Oh we are not, be not you so,
Let mee, and doe you, twenty know.
Rob mee, but binde me not, and let me goe.
Must I, who came to travaile thorow you,
Grow your fixt subject, because you are true?

Venus heard me sigh this song,
And by Loves sweetest Part, Variety, she swore,
She heard not this till now; and that it should be so no more.
She went, examin'd, and return'd ere long,
And said, alas, Some two or three
Poore Heretiques in love there bee,
Which thinke to stablish dangerous constancie.
But I have told them, since you will be true,
You shall be true to them, who'are false to you.

We shall never be able to judge such poems properly, or appreciate
them for what they are worth, unless we are able to understand,
and in some measure to appreciate, what Donne and his contemporaries understood by 'wit'. I have already said a good deal on this
topic, but here, in order to remind ourselves that there once existed
an attitude to literature and an assessment of literary ability very
different from our own, let us listen to Nashe's defence of his
Lenten Stuffe, published in 1599, a pamphlet in which he celebrates
his native Yarmouth and praises its red herrings:

This is a light friskin of my witte, like the prayse of iniustice, the feuer quartaine, *Busiris*, or *Phalaris*, wherein I follow the trace of the famousest schollers of all ages, whom a wantonizing humour once in their life time hath possesst to play with strawes, and turne mole-hils into mountaines.

Euery man can say Bee to a Battledore, and write in prayse of Vertue and the seuen Liberall Sciences, thresh corne out of the full sheaues and fetch water out of the Thames; but out of drie stubble to make an after haruest, and a plentifull croppe without sowing, and wring iuice out of a flint, thats *Pierce a Gods name*, and the right tricke of a workman.[1]

We shall never, I repeat, be able to reach a just estimate of such poems as *The Indifferent* until we are able to recapture something of this attitude to literature and this conception of wit: never, that is to say, so long as we insist on demanding that poetry should be, first and foremost, what many modern readers and critics of it call 'sincere'; or so long as we insist on regarding it as an expression of the writer's personality, as a kind of autobiographical record. Donne's admirers did not value such a poem as *The Indifferent* as an expression of Donne's personality or principles or practice, but as an expression of Donne's wit, that wit which delighted Ben Jonson in *The Calme* and in the elegy on the loss of his Mistress's Chain, and Drummond in the paradoxical elegy in praise of ugliness. Neither did Donne himself or his contemporaries take these poems so seriously as we do. Donne, like many other good poets of his time, never regarded his poetry as the serious business of his life—never, in fact, regarded it as more than an occasional though agreeable diversion. He wrote, not for publication, but for the amusement of himself and his friends, and he does not even seem to have troubled to keep copies of his poems. Such casualness differs so completely from the appetite of even the most minor modern poet for print that it must seem to many readers almost unintelligible. We are puzzled by this careless expenditure of genius, this apparently irresponsible exercise of prodigious gifts; or rather, perhaps I should say, we are puzzled and incredulous when it is pointed out to us; for we tend to assume that Donne was as serious and singleminded about his poetry as any young modern poet in search of

[1] *Works*, ed. McKerrow, III, 151-2.

a publisher, and, consequently, we tend to take a good deal of
Donne's poetry far more seriously, far less light-heartedly, than I
am sure he did himself.

Immediately following *The Indifferent* is *Loves Vsury*, a
poem on very much the same theme and in very much the same
spirit.

> For every houre that thou wilt spare mee now,
>   I will allow,
> Usurious God of Love, twenty to thee,
> When with my browne, my gray haires equall bee;
> Till then, Love, let my body raigne, and let
> Mee travell, sojourne, snatch, plot, have, forget,
> Resume my last years relict: thinke that yet
>   We'had never met.

> Let mee thinke any rivalls letter mine,
>   And at next nine
> Keepe midnights promise; mistake by the way
> The maid, and tell the Lady of that delay;
> Onely let mee love none, no, not the sport;
> From country grasse, to comfitures of Court,
> Or cities quelque choses, let report
>   My minde transport.

> This bargaine's good; if when I'am old, I bee
>   Inflam'd by thee,
> If thine owne honour, or my shame, or paine,
> Thou covet, most at that age thou shalt gaine.
> Doe thy will then, then subject and degree,
> And fruit of love, Love I submit to thee,
> Spare mee till then, I'll beare it, though she bee
>   One that loves mee.

Surely we are being rather dull-witted and literal-minded if we
insist on reading as a serious description of Donne's actual behaviour
such lines as:

Let mee thinke any rivalls letter mine,
    And at next nine
Keepe mid nights promise: mistake by the way
The maid, and tell the Lady of that delay.

Are they not rather, like the 'grim eight-foot-high iron-bound serving-man' and the 'immortal mother' in one of the elegies, a piece of witty and outrageous drama? Indeed, as I have remarked before, the detailed, mock-serious exaggeration here and elsewhere in Donne's poetry has much affinity with that so often used with satiric intention by Ben Jonson in his comedies: as when, for example, he makes Sir Epicure Mammon exclaim:

> No. I'll ha' no bawds,
> But fathers, and mothers. They will doe it best.
> Best of all others. And, my flatterers
> Shall be the pure, and grauest of Diuines,
> That I can get for money . . .
>   I my selfe will haue
> The beards of barbels, seru'd, in stead of sallades;
> Oild mushromes; and the swelling vnctuous paps
> Of a fat pregnant sow, newly cut off,
> Drest with an exquisite, and poynant sauce;
> For which, Ile say vnto my cooke, there's gold,
> Goe forth, and be a knight.[1]

Perhaps still nearer to Donne in spirit, though far lighter and frothier in style, is the impudent exaggeration, or exaggerated impudence, of many of Fletcher's wild gallants—of Mirabel, for example, in *The Wild-Goose Chase*, when he says to Oriana, who has gratefully thanked him for having refused two proposed marriages out of loyalty, as she supposes, to herself:

> And let me tell thee, there was no such matter:
> Nothing intended that way of that nature;
> I have more to do with my honesty than to fool it,
> Or venture it in such leak barks as women;
> I put 'em off, because I lov'd 'em not,

[1] *The Alchemist*, II, ii, 57–87.

Because they are too queazie for my temper,
And not for thy sake, nor the Contract sake,
Nor vows, nor oathes; I have made a thousand of 'em,
They are things indifferent, whether kept or broken;
Mere veniall slips, that grow not near the Conscience . . .
For, as I think, there was never man yet hop'd for
Either constancie, or secrecie, from a woman,
Unless it were an Ass ordain'd for sufferance;
Nor to contract with such can be a Tiall;
So let them know again; for 'tis a Justice,
And a main point of civill policie,
Whate'er we say or swear, they being Reprobates,
Out of the state of faith, we are clear of all sides,
And 'tis a curious blindness to beleeve us.[1]

Most readers, I think, will agree with me that it is only possible to
enjoy this so long as one is not persuaded to take it seriously, so
long as one is able to regard it as the witty and outrageous exaggeration appropriate to a kind of moral holiday. Taken literally and
seriously it is, of course, sheer blackguardism. No doubt there was
an element of blackguardism in Fletcher, as there certainly was in
his audience, but, on the whole, I think that the main point of
passages such as I have quoted is that they should be felt to be
outrageous—that, indeed, a very large measure of immediately
perceptible outrageousness and exaggeration is of the very essence
of their wit.[2]

---

[1] II, i; 1652, E1ᵛ–E2.

[2] Here I would insist again, as I have already insisted in a foot-note on p. 55, that
such passages would have been quite pointless had not the writers of them been
thoroughly aware that they were being naughty, that many of their contemporaries
would think them very naughty indeed, and that those for whom they wrote would
experience in varying degrees various elements of a very complex pleasure: would
find a certain delicious thrill in the feeling that they ought to be shocked and yet were
not really so shocked as they felt they ought to be; would find a wicked pleasure in
the thought, 'How shocking this would seem to poor So-and-so or old So-and-so,'
etc., etc. Indeed, the pleasure both of the writers and readers (or hearers) of this kind
of writing is not unrelated to the kind of pleasure which small boys who ring door-
bells and fling gravel at windows find in the sudden appearance of an angry face.
The angry face, the Elder Cato, the policeman, the Ten Commandments must still
be there, must still be exacting some fear and respect, in order that such writing
should be able to achieve its object. There would be no point in expressing contempt
for law in a society that was completely lawless, or for morality in a society that was
completely amoral. There is no point, no pleasure, in being naughty unless you *know*
that you are being naughty.

This, then, is one of the elements in Donne's wit—exaggeration: in spirit (the flouting of traditional ideals and morals in sexual relationships) rather like Fletcher's; in style (the mock-serious elaboration of realistic detail) rather like Jonson's. Sometimes, in poems where this element of exaggeration predominates, it is combined with that scholastic, that almost syllogistic, argument, and that demonstration and illustration by means of ingenious analogies which we have already encountered in some of the paradoxical elegies and in some of the hyperbolical verse-letters to the Countess of Bedford and the Countess of Huntingdon, which is what people chiefly have in mind when they speak of 'metaphysical' poetry. This, though, is by no means always the case. The famous 'Goe, and catche a falling starre' has that sequaciousness, that untransposability, which is characteristic of nearly all Donne's poems, and which is one of the most important differences between seventeenth- and sixteenth-century lyric, but, apart from that, what chiefly distinguishes it is its rollicking exaggeration and high-spiritedness, its absolutely colloquial diction (defiantly colloquial, one feels, here and elsewhere), and the subordination, as in the best dramatic verse, of verse-pattern and metrical accent to the giving of maximum emphasis and intensity to a natural speech-rhythm, as of a man talking excitedly.

> Goe, and catche a falling starre,
>   Get with child a mandrake roote,
> Tell me, where all past yeares are,
>   Or who cleft the Divels foot,
> Teach me to heare Mermaides singing
> Or to keep off envies stinging,
>   And finde
>   What winde
> Serves to advance an honest minde.
>
> If thou beest borne to strange sights,
>   Things invisible to see,
> Ride ten thousand daies and nights,
>   Till age snow white haires on thee,
> Thou, when thou retorn'st, wilt tell mee
> All strange wonders that befell thee,

And sweare
No where
Lives a woman true, and faire.

If thou findst one, let mee know,
    Such a Pilgrimage were sweet;
Yet doe not, I would not goe,
    Though at next doore wee might meet,
Though shee were true, when you met her,
And last, till you write your letter,
    Yet shee
    Will bee
False, ere I come, to two, or three.

Loves Alchymie is more argumentative, though not distinctively scholastic or metaphysical. Neither need it be regarded, as it often has been, as the record of a mood of deep disenchantment and disgust. It is written with great gusto, I would almost say, with great animal spirits, and with admirable use of speech-rhythm. It should not, I think, be regarded as evidence that Donne at one time seriously believed that women had no minds, but rather as a deliberately exaggerated, provocative and paradoxical expression of what always remained his conviction, namely, that in love the physical and the spiritual were ultimately inseparable. Years later—in 1612, to be precise—he wrote to Sir Henry Wotton: 'You (I think) and I are much of one sect in the Philosophy of love; which though it be directed upon the minde, doth inhere in the body, and find prety entertainment there.'[1] In that sentence, as in several of his more philosophic poems, Donne is being serious as well as witty and is trying to express the whole complicated truth; whereas in *Loves Alchymie* and in many similar poems he is being mainly witty and paradoxical and insisting, partly in reaction against that Platonic and Petrarchan idealization which had degenerated into a mere fashion, on only one aspect of the truth, an aspect which he deliberately exaggerates and distorts and presents as though it were the whole truth. He confronts, as it were, agreeable but exaggerated half-truths, expressed in elaborate and sugared language, with disagreeable, though equally exaggerated, half-truths, expressed as directly

[1] *Letters to Severall Persons of Honour*, 1651, 211; Gosse, I, 291.

and unsugaredly as possible. In most of these poems, I feel, he is getting at someone, getting at the sugared sonneteer, whose too-repeated and too-conventional professions of eternal constancy elicit from an exasperated Donne professions of eternal inconstancy, and whose over-insistence on the spirituality of love provokes an almost brutal insistence on its carnality. The impulse behind such a poem as *Loves Alchymie* seems to me to be rather negative than positive, reactionary rather than doctrinal, destructive rather than constructive; Donne is moved, I think, not so much by a desire to express what he believes to be the whole truth, or even the half-truth, about love, as by a desire to shock, pillory and expose, for the delectation of himself and his friends, those loving wretches who swear in sugared sonnets that not the bodies marry but the minds.

Some that have deeper digg'd loves Myne then I,
Say, where his centrique happinesse doth lie:
  I have lov'd, and got, and told,
But should I love, get, tell, till I were old,
I should not finde that hidden mysterie;
    Oh, 'tis imposture all:
And as no chymique yet th'Elixar got,
    But glorifies his pregnant pot,
    If by the way to him befall
Some odoriferous thing, or medicinall,
  So, lovers dreame a rich and long delight,
  But get a winter-seeming summers night.

Our ease, our thrift, our honor, and our day,
Shall we, for this vaine Bubles shadow pay?
    Ends love in this, that my man,
Can be as happy'as I can; If he can
Endure the short scorne of a Bridegroomes play?
    That loving wretch that sweares,
'Tis not the bodies marry, but the mindes,
    Which he in her Angelique findes,
    Would sweare as justly, that he heares,
In that dayes rude hoarse minstralsey, the spheares.
  Hope not for minde in women; at their best
  Sweetnesse and wit, they'are but *Mummy*, possest.

The exaggeration—that element in Donne's wit with which I am now particularly concerned—is here not so very different from that of some of Fletcher's wild gallants, although its expression is far more brilliant, concentrated and intellectual. In *The Curse*, which is only a love-poem in so far as its maledictions are pronounced upon whoever guesses, thinks, or dreams he knows who is Donne's mistress, the exaggeration, in its mock-serious but exhaustive and precise elaboration of detail, is not unlike that which Ben Jonson often employs in his comedies:

> Who ever guesses, thinks, or dreames he knowes
> Who is my mistris, wither by this curse;
>   His only, and only his purse
>   May some dull heart to love dispose,
> And shee yeeld then to all that are his foes;
>   May he be scorn'd by one, whom all else scorne,
>   Forsweare to others, what to her he'hath sworne,
>   With feare of missing, shame of getting, torne:
>
> Madnesse his sorrow, gout his cramp, may hee
> Make, by but thinking, who hath made him such:
>   And may he feele no touch
>   Of conscience, but of fame,[1] and bee
> Anguish'd, not that'twas sinne, but that'twas shee:
>   In early and long scarcenesse may he rot,
>   For land which had been his, if he had not
>   Himselfe incestuously an heire begot:
>
> May he dreame Treason, and beleeve, that hee
> Meant to performe it, and confesse, and die,
>   And no record tell why:
>   His sonnes, which none of his may bee,
> Inherite nothing but his infamie:
>   Or may he so long Parasites have fed,
>   That he would faine be theirs, whom he hath bred,
>   And at the last be circumcis'd for bread:

[1] If the reading 'fame' is authentic, it can only mean 'public opinion', 'public reputation': 'may he be troubled, not by his conscience, but by what people think of him'. It seems probable that 'shame', the reading of several manuscripts, is a sophistication.

The venom of all stepdames, gamsters gall,
What Tyrans, and their subjects interwish,
　　　　What Plants, Mynes, Beasts, Foule, Fish,
　　　　Can contribute, all ill which all
Prophets, or Poets spake; And all which shall
　　Be annex'd in schedules unto this by mee,
　　Fall on that man; For if it be a shee
　　Nature before hand hath out-cursed mee.

Similar in style is that essentially dramatic poem *The Apparition*. It has often, because of its very dramatic truth, the power and convincingness with which Donne creates the situation and assumes the part, been regarded as autobiographical, as the record of an actual experience, perhaps as having been provoked by and addressed to that married woman who appears in some of the elegies, whom Gosse assumed to have been a real person, but whose original, as I have already suggested, is probably to be sought for partly in Ovid's *Amores* and partly in Donne's dramatic imagination. It is no more necessary to presuppose an actual experience as the basis of this and other of Donne's poems than it is necessary to presuppose such an experience as the basis of Shakespeare's most dramatic scenes. We have already seen how Donne could develop imaginatively and dramatically suggestions and situations which he probably found in Ovid; here, I think, he is developing with superb imaginative and dramatic power the situation suggested to him by such poems as those in which Horace and Propertius threaten an ungrateful Ligurinus or Cynthia with what will be their fate when their charms have fled.[1]

When by thy scorne, O murdresse, I am dead,
　　And that thou thinkst thee free
From all solicitation from mee,
Then shall my ghost come to thy bed,
And thee, fain'd vestall, in worse armes shall see;
Then thy sicke taper will begin to winke,
And he, whose thou art then, being tyr'd before,
Will, if thou stirre, or pinch to wake him, thinke
　　Thou call'st for more,

---

[1] The poetic possibilities of imprecation, serious and burlesque, may have been suggested to Donne by Ovid's *Ibis* and by some of Horace's Epodes.

And in false sleepe will from thee shrinke,
And then poore Aspen wretch, neglected thou
Bath'd in a cold quicksilver sweat wilt lye
    A veryer ghost then I;
What I will say, I will not tell thee now,
Lest that preserve thee'; and since my love is spent,[1]
I'had rather thou shouldst painfully repent,
Then by my threatnings rest still innocent.

I have included this poem among the examples of what I have
called the element of exaggeration in Donne's wit, although it
might equally well, or even, perhaps, more appropriately, be
regarded as an example of the dramatic element. Exaggeration and
dramatization—the two elements are often almost inseparable; for
often, when Donne seems to be mainly concerned with exercising
his wit in the defence of a paradox, he will work out the implications of the attitude he has adopted in a manner essentially dramatic,
and will display it in fleetingly presented but vividly and realistically
imagined *situations*

        (mistake by the way
The maid, and tell the Lady of that delay).

In *The Apparition* and in some of the Elegies the dramatic element
predominates, but it is present in much of Donne's poetry, as also
in much of George Herbert's, and in several poems by other seventeenth-century poets who are commonly regarded as belonging to
the School of Donne—notably, in Marvell's *To his Coy Mistress*.
Indeed, much of Herbert's best poetry, like much of Donne's,
might be far more accurately and illuminatingly described by some
such phrase as 'the dialectical expression of personal drama' than by
that vague and imprecise term 'metaphysical'. Just as in *The
Apparition* Donne has dramatized an imaginary, or mainly imaginary, experience, George Herbert in *The Collar* has dramatized an
actual one: in spirit the poems are poles apart, but in style there
is a remarkable similarity between them. Both have to be spoken
with, as it were, a single breath; in both there is one complex
dramatic rhythm running continuously from the first line to the
last.

[1] Why, it might be asked, if his love for her is spent, is her scorn going to kill him?

The Collar

I struck the board, and cry'd, no more.
        I will abroad.
    What? Shall I ever sigh and pine?
My lines and life are free; free as the rode,
        Loose as the winde, as large as store.
            Shall I be still in suit?
    Have I no harvest but a thorn
    To let my bloud, and not restore
    What I have lost with cordiall fruit?
            Sure there was wine
Before my sighs did drie it: there was corn
        Before my tears did drown it.
    Is the yeare onely lost to me?
        Have I no bayes to crown it?
No flowers, no garlands gay? all blasted?
            All wasted?
    Not so, my heart: but there is fruit
        And thou hast hands.
Recover all thy sigh-blown age
On double pleasures: leave thy cold dispute
Of what is fit, and not. Forsake thy cage,
        Thy rope of sands,
Which pettie thoughts have made, and made to thee
    Good cable, to enforce and draw,
        And be thy law,
    While thou didst wink and wouldst not see.
        Away; take heed:
        I will abroad.
Call in thy deaths head there: tie up thy fears.
        He that forbears
    To suit and serve his need,
        Deserves his load.
But as I rav'd and grew more fierce and wilde
        At every word,
    Me thoughts I heard one calling, *Child*!
        And I reply'd, *My Lord*.

Among the common characteristics of those poets who have been too indiscriminately labelled as 'metaphysical' this dramatic quality is perhaps more obvious and more striking than either scholastic argumentation or subtle analogies and comparisons. And this dramatic quality, which is equally apparent in those two so spiritually differing poems by Donne and by Herbert, ought perhaps to be regarded as an aspect, a consequence, of that new attitude to literature which has been so tersely and so illuminatingly described by Professor F. P. Wilson. 'To the new age', he writes,

> so often sceptical, tentative, and self-conscious in its exploration of hidden motives, a new style was necessary, a style that could express the mind as it was in movement, could record the thought at the moment it arose in the mind. The amplifications and formal figures of Elizabethan rhetoric were as unsuitable for their purposes as the roundness of the Ciceronian period wheeling its way to a long foreseen conclusion. The new style appears in the fifteen-nineties in the poetry of Chapman, Donne, Raleigh, and others, in the prose of Bacon, in the plays of Shakespeare and Jonson. It is the style of 'So, so, break off this last lamenting kiss', of 'Cover her face; mine eyes dazzle; she died young'. A loosening of rhythm, a closer approximation to the diction of common life that is not incompatible with magnificence, a rejection of copiousness and elaborate word-schemes—these make possible the concentration of Donne's love poems and of Bacon's prose, and the tragic vision of Shakespeare, Webster, and Middleton.[1]

It was, I suppose, the felt need for a style which could, in Professor Wilson's words, 'express the mind as it was in movement' that led, often at any rate, to the introduction into lyrical poetry of qualities characteristic of dramatic verse, and gave to many seventeenth-century lyrics something of the quality of dramatic dialogue or soliloquy. Donne seems to have been the first to introduce into lyrical verse those natural speech-rhythms, which require not lines but sentences, paragraphs or stanzas for their completion, that colloquial diction, and that approximation to the language—heightened, it is true—of impassioned colloquial speech which Shakespeare and his

[1] *Elizabethan and Jacobean*, 26.

fellows introduced into dramatic verse, and which Shakespeare and
Sidney, here almost alone, achieved also in the sonnet:

> Then, eu'n of fellowship, O Moone, tell me
> Is constant *Loue* deem'd there but want of wit?
> Are Beauties there as proud as here they be?
> Do they aboue loue to be lou'd, and yet
> Those Louers scorne whom that *Loue* doth possesse?
> Do they call *Vertue* there vngratefulnesse?[1]

> I do forgiue thy robb'rie, gentle thiefe,
> Although thou steale thee all my pouerty.[2]

> How can it? O how can loues eye be true,
> That is so vext with watching and with teares?[3]

Even single lines from the poems of Donne and his successors often
seem more specifically dramatic than specifically lyrical:

> I wonder by my troth, what thou, and I
> Did, till we lov'd?

> If yet I have not all thy love,
> Deare, I shall never have it all.

> I saw Eternity the other night.

It is difficult to isolate and compartmentalize the various elements in Donne's poetry and genius, and I may perhaps seem to
have wandered a little from my immediate purpose, which was to
analyse the wit in some of the more outrageous of the *Songs and
Sonets* and to decide how far it was necessary to regard them as
records of actual experiences and as expressions of actual convictions. In insisting upon the elements of paradox, exaggeration and
dramatization in these poems, it has been impossible to avoid

[1] *Astrophel and Stella*, xxxi (1598).
[2] Sonnet 40.
[3] Sonnet 148.

discussing incidentally certain qualities of style which are equally characteristic of many poems written in a different mood, both by Donne and by his successors. To these qualities of style it may often be necessary to recur; meanwhile, I hope I have sufficiently proved my main contention, which is, that the poems we have been considering are to be regarded rather as evidence of Donne's wit than of his actual principles and practice. If, however, any reader is still unconvinced, I would ask him how seriously he is prepared to take what in its day seems to have been one of the most admired of all the *Songs and Sonets*, which in the second edition of Donne's Poems (1635) was placed at the beginning of that section of the book, and which was the first of nineteen poems translated by the Dutch poet Constantine Huyghens, a member of the Dutch embassy in London and a great admirer of Donne's poems. Indeed, some of Huyghens's Dutch correspondents selected this poem for special commendation.

The Flea

Marke but this flea, and marke in this,
How little that which thou deny'st me is;
It suck'd me first, and now sucks thee,
And in this flea, our two bloods mingled bee;
Though know'st that this cannot be said
A sinne, nor shame, nor losse of maidenhead,
   Yet this enjoyes before it wooe,
    And pamper'd swells with one blood made of two,
    And this, alas, is more than wee would doe.

Oh stay, three lives in one flea spare,
Where wee almost, yea more then maryed are.
This flea is you and I, and this
Our mariage bed, and mariage temple is;
Though parents grudge, and you, w'are met,
And cloysterd in these living walls of Jet.
   Though use make you apt to kill mee,
    Let not to that, selfe murder added bee,
    And sacrilege, three sinnes in killing three.

Cruell and sodaine, hast thou since
Purpled thy naile, in blood of innocence?
Wherein could this flea guilty bee,
Except in that drop which it suckt from thee?
Yet thou triumph'st, and saist that thou
Find'st not thy selfe, nor mee the weaker now;
  'Tis true, then learne how false, feares bee;
  Just so much honor, when thou yeeld'st to mee,
  Will wast, as this flea's death tooke life from thee.

Why was this poem so admired? Certainly not for qualities which
many modern critics have taught us to look for and value in poetry
—self-expression, self-revelation, sincerity, and so forth. It was
admired, I take it, for its sheer wit, for the astonishing fact that
Donne had been able to write three stanzas, twenty-seven lines, of
close-knit and consecutive argument on such an apparently un-
promising subject as a flea-bite, and to extract from it such an
ingenious and elaborate simile as that about the flea, in which their
bloods are mingled, being their marriage-bed and marriage-temple,
which if she kills she will be committing first, murder, through
killing him in it, secondly, suicide, through killing herself in it, and,
thirdly, sacrilege, through destroying the temple or church in which
they were married. It was the very triviality of the subject which
made the triumph of Donne's wit seem so astonishing; he had
performed a kind of miracle, had almost succeeded in triumphing
over the laws of nature—had, as it were, made a fire without sticks,
built a house without bricks, created something out of nothing, or
next to nothing. As Nashe, the manifestations of whose wit were
very different from Donne's, but who held nevertheless, a similar
conception of wit, wrote in that passage from the Preface to *Lenten
Stuffe* which I have already quoted:

Euery man can say Bee to a Battledore, and write in prayse
of Vertue and the seuen Liberall Sciences, thresh corne out of the
full sheaues and fetch water out of the Thames; but out of drie
stubble to make an after haruest, and a plentifull croppe without
sowing, and wring iuice out of a flint, thats *Pierce a Gods name*,
and the right tricke of a workman.

Just as Dryden's contemporary the Earl of Roscommon, of the 'unspotted bays', declared in his *Essay of Translated Verse* that although translation might be less 'noble' than original composition, it nevertheless afforded more opportunity for the display of judgment, so Donne's admirers might have declared that although such poetry as *The Flea* might be somewhat deficient in high seriousness, it nevertheless offered unrivalled opportunities for the display of the author's wit.

I have now, perhaps, said enough in support of my contention that the autobiographical element in the *Songs and Sonets* has been greatly exaggerated, and that it is quite unnecessary to assume that even those which are most dramatically convincing were inspired by actual experiences or addressed to real persons. This, I think it will be agreed, is certainly true of the more outrageous and paradoxical ones, but even with the more tender and apparently serious ones we should beware of asserting too positively that they could only have been inspired by a particular experience or a particular person. It is, as a matter of fact, almost certain that many of them were partly inspired by Donne's experience of marriage, but the only poem which, if we accept Walton's testimony, there is any external evidence that he actually addressed to his wife is *A Valediction: forbidding mourning*. We must try to keep hypothesis and conjecture, however probable, in its place, and not allow it to distract us from the poetry itself or to influence too greatly our analysis and interpretation of it. What is really important is to attend carefully to the tone of voice, the inner vibration: that, ultimately, is the only means of determining the degree to which what I may call Donne himself is present in any poem. It is with effects, not with causes, that we are primarily concerned, and too much speculation about possible causes may easily distract us from our proper business, which is to appreciate and estimate effects.

Here we encounter something like a paradox. The most dramatically convincing poems are, on the one hand, some of the outrageous and paradoxical ones, which are almost wholly unserious and imaginary, and, on the other hand, many of the more tender and serious ones, which were probably written after his marriage. That is to say, the degree of dramatic convincingness, the degree in which willing suspension of disbelief is produced, has little or nothing to do with the seriousness or unseriousness of the poems, with the extent to which Donne's real self is present, or with the actuality of what is described or expressed. It is, I think, those poems which, on the whole, seem to a modern reader least dramatically convincing and most artificial which positively require, in order to explain their very existence, the hypothesis that they were inspired by a particular relationship and addressed to real persons. I refer to certain rather wire-drawn, hyperbolical poems, similar in tone and spirit to some of Donne's verse-letters to the Countess of Bedford and the Countess of Huntingdon, and which, like them, were probably written between 1607 and 1612, that is to say, a good deal later than most of the *Songs and Sonets*—poems in which Donne either celebrates his Platonic affection for a woman or else complains that such affection is all she will give him. The fact that five of these poems—*The Funerall*, *The Blossome*, *The Primrose*, *The Relique*, and *The Dampe*—occur so frequently together in the manuscripts suggested to Grierson[1] that they had a common origin; and the fact that in the second (1635) edition of Donne's poems the title of *The Primrose* carried the addition *being at Montgomery Castle, upon the hill, on which it is situate* further suggested to him that *The Primrose*, together with the other poems commonly found with it in the manuscripts, was addressed to Mrs. Herbert. In that poem Donne describes himself as seeking for a 'true love' among the primroses, as rejecting the common five-petalled ones around him as 'mere women', and then as recoiling from the choice between one with four petals (*i.e.* less than a woman) or one with six petals (*i.e.* more than a woman):

> should she
> Be more then woman, shee would get above
> All thought of sexe, and thinke to move
> My heart to study her, and not to love.

In *The Blossome*, where he purports to be in love with a woman who does not respond, he says he will leave his heart behind with her, but tells it to meet him in London twenty days hence:

> I would give you
> There, to another friend, whom wee shall finde
> As glad to have my body, as my minde.

[1] II, xxiv.

It would not, I think, be too wildly improbable to suppose that the
'other friend' is his wife, that the lady who cares only for his mind
is Mrs. Herbert, and that all that is said, or intended, is within the
limits of courtly compliment. Indeed, if we assume, as I think we
must, that this and other poems that resemble it were written during
what we may roughly call the Mitcham period, when Donne was
no longer the brilliant Inns of Court man, campaigner, and Secretary, whom his old friend Sir Richard Baker remembered as 'a great
frequenter of Playes' and 'a great visiter of Ladies', I think that is
how we must interpret those lines. What, in spite of the less than
half-serious argument, is characteristic of these poems is a certain
tender playfulness, or playful tenderness, which differs, on the one
hand, from that sheer wit and deliberate outrageousness, and, on
the other, from that celebration of contented love, which, as regards
spirit and content, are the two chief characteristics of the earlier and
more numerous *Songs and Sonets*. 'Well then,' he says to his heart,
in *The Blossome*,

> Well then, stay here; but know,
>   When thou hast stayd and done thy most;
> A naked thinking heart, that makes no show,
> Is to a woman, but a kinde of Ghost;
> How shall shee know my heart; or having none,
>   Know thee for one?
> Practise may make her know some other part,
> But take my word, shee doth not know a Heart.

Not, perhaps, precisely how one might have supposed Donne would
have addressed her whom Walton calls his Paula, but not, surely,
in that respect, less astonishing than *The Autumnall*, which Walton
does not seem to have found astonishing, and which we have
already examined so carefully.

A similar tenderness, conveyed by rhythm and emphasis and
accentuated by the flimsiness and trumperiness of the logic, or
pretended logic, pervades those two companion poems, *The
Funerall* and *The Relique*, in both of which the subject is a 'subtile
wreath of haire', 'a bracelet of bright haire', around his arm, which
is to be buried with him, and which was given to him by a woman
capable only of Platonic love. In *The Funerall*, after some very

elaborate speculations as to what she might have meant by her gift, he tells his friends to bury it with him, since he is love's martyr, and since this relic, if it fell into other hands, might cause idolatry. He will have displayed, he declares, some humility in having attributed to it the power of a soul, preserving his body from putrefaction, and some pride in having buried some of her who would save none of him. In *The Relique* he declares that when his grave is reopened the bracelet of bright hair will make the discoverers suppose that the bones are those of some loving couple who hoped thereby to make their souls meet for a moment at the last day. If it is a time of superstition they will be adored as relics, and since at such times miracles are looked for, he will tell what miracles they two performed:

> First, we lov'd well and faithfully,
> Yet knew not what wee lov'd, nor why,
> Difference of sex no more wee knew,
> Then our Guardian Angells doe;
> Comming and going, wee
> Perchance might kisse, but not between those meales;[1]
> Our hands ne'r toucht the seales,
> Which nature, injur'd by late law, sets free:[2]
> These miracles wee did; but now alas,
> All measure, and all language, I should passe,
> Should I tell what a miracle shee was.

Is it necessary to spend time in insisting that this celebration of Platonic, of almost sexless, love was not addressed to Ann More, either before or after their marriage? Is it even necessary to insist that it was not written by the impudent young man who began the Eighteenth Elegy, *Loves Progress*, with the words:

---

[1] *i.e.*, not between the kisses of salutation and parting.

[2] This obscure line derives, as Sir Herbert Grierson has pointed out (*Criticism and Creation*, 1950, 104), from Ovid's *Metamorphoses*, X, 329–31, where Myrrha, in defence of her incestuous passion for her father, appeals to the example of the animals:

> *Felices quibus ista licent! Humana malignas*
> *Cura dedit leges et quod natura remittit*
> *Inuida iura negant.*

'Happy the creatures to whom these things are permitted! Human scrupulosity has promulgated wicked laws, and what nature allows jealous decrees deny.' An unexpected and rather disconcerting re-emergence of 'the silenc'd tales o' th' Metamorphoses' into Donne's poetry!

> Who ever loves, if he do not propose
> The right true end of love, he's one that goes
> To sea for nothing but to make him sick?

Mr. Garrod, it is true, both in his article on *Donne and Mrs. Herbert* in the *Review of English Studies* for July 1945 and in the notes to his selection from Donne's poetry and prose in the Clarendon Press Series, will not have it that any of these poems were addressed to Mrs. Herbert, because, apparently, he finds their tone and content incompatible with what Walton, in his *Life* of George Herbert, has told us about the 'amity' and the 'many sacred Indearments betwixt these two excellent persons'. 'This Amity', says Walton,

> was not an *Amity* that polluted their Souls; but an *Amity* made up of a chain of sutable inclinations and vertues; an *Amity*, like that of St. *Chrysostoms* to his dear and vertuous *Olimpias*; whom, in his Letters, he calls his *Saint*: Or, an *Amity* indeed more like that of St. *Hierom* to his *Paula*; whose affection to her was such, that he turn'd Poet in his old Age.[1]

Nevertheless, as I have already spent some time in insisting, *The Autumnall*, which we know on Walton's own authority to have been addressed to Mrs. Herbert, contains much that, to a modern reader, seems strangely incongruous with the 'amity' Walton has described. Is it, after all, so hard to believe that Donne, after his marriage, and although he always deeply loved his wife, could also have come to love another, and perhaps more intellectually equal, woman, even though innocently and platonically, or that he should sometimes have addressed her in the tenderly playful, the courtly and hyperbolical, strain of the poems we have been considering, now celebrating the innocence of their affection, now adopting the pose of an ardent lover languishing in thraldom to an enchanting but unresponsive mistress, who will not take him seriously as a lover, and who cares only for his mind? Knowing Donne as we do, knowing his poetry as we do, is it really possible to conceive how these poems, except at this time of his life and under these circumstances, should ever have been written at all? They are the only poems among the *Songs and Sonets* which seem

[1] *World's Classics* ed., 265.

to me positively to require the hypothesis of some special kind of personal relationship as their inspiration and cause. The more cynical and outrageous poems can be sufficiently explained by the assumption that he was either getting at the sugared sonneteers and their admirers or just displaying his wit. Many of the more serious and tender poems were probably inspired by his wife, although, if we had no independent evidence about the nature of Donne's love for his wife, I do not think we should find it absolutely necessary to assume that these poems could *only* have been inspired by a particular personal relationship, as distinct from a relationship which Donne, growing weary of mere wit, had imagined, and had found pleasure in imagining. But is it really possible to suppose that Donne, at any period of his life, should have imagined, purely for his own pleasure, the kind of relationship which the courtly and Platonic poems imply—those poems in which he either celebrates an affection in which

> not the bodies marry, but the mindes

or adopts the pose of an ardent lover languishing in thraldom to an enchanting but unresponsive mistress who will not take his passion seriously? In fact, I find it necessary to assume that the attitude which Donne here adopts was one which he adopted, and could only have adopted, not primarily in order to please himself, but under the influence of a rather special kind of relationship and in order to please a particular person or particular persons. These poems were not written by Donne the snook-cocker and coat-trailer, and they were not written by Donne the ardent lover; they were written, I cannot but suppose, by the Donne who wrote *The Autumnall*, the Donne of the Mitcham period, and the kind of relationship which they rather hyperbolically and artificially celebrate seems to me essentially similar to the kind of relationship which, as we may infer from Walton and from *The Autumnall*, existed between Donne and Mrs. Herbert, or which we may imagine to have existed between Donne and those other Muses, or, as he professes to regard them in some of his verse-letters, those divinities, of his middle years, the Countess of Bedford and the Countess of Huntingdon.

The last of that group of poems which are commonly found

together in the manuscripts and which there are some grounds for connecting with Mrs. Herbert is *The Dampe*, which, although it is a good deal less tender and respectful than the others, and a good deal more impudent, still has certain obvious affinities with them, the most obvious being the idea of 'after my death', which is the mainspring of *The Funerall* and *The Relique*. You think, he declares, that when I am dead and being dissected and your picture is found in my heart a sudden damp (that is to say, a sudden stupor or trance) of love will affect the bystanders as it affected me, and that your original murder will thus become a massacre. If, though, you would gain a really notable victory, first kill the giant Disdain and the enchantress Honour, and deface all the records of your triumphs over others, and kill me then. And so he goes on. It is curious to find Donne, who in his younger days had so deliberately and contemptuously rejected the Courtly and Petrarchan tradition, now, in his middle years, playing with such conceptions as those of murder and massacre, of the giant Disdain and the enchantress Honour, remote as his use of such conceptions may be from that of the tradition to which they properly belong.

There are at least three other poems which presuppose a similar relationship, and which, like those we have been considering, were almost certainly written during Donne's middle years. There is *The Will*, more light-hearted than the rest, though one of the most elaborately logical, or pseudo-logical, of Donne's poems, in which he declares that his inappropriately and unresponsively bestowed love has taught him to bequeath his other qualities with equal inappropriateness: his eyes to Argus, his constancy to the wandering planets, his faith to Catholics and his good works to the brethren of Amsterdam, and so on:

> To him for whom the passing bell next tolls,
> I give my physick bookes; my writen rowles
> Of Morall counsels, I to Bedlam give;
> My brazen medals, unto them which live
> In want of bread; To them which passe among
>   All forrainers, mine English tongue.
>   Thou, Love, by making mee love one
> Who thinkes her friendship a fit portion
> For yonger lovers, dost my gifts thus disproportion.

It is not unlikely, I think, that the last three lines were playfully addressed to Mrs. Herbert, since Donne's two other muses or divinities, the Countess of Bedford and the Countess of Huntingdon, were both younger, not older, than himself. On the other hand, *The undertaking*, which in at least four manuscripts is entitled *Platonique Love*, and in which Donne declares that he has done a braver thing than all the worthies did, that is to say, has loved virtue attired in a woman and forgotten the he and she—this poem may well have been addressed to either of his two younger patronesses; for the stanza

> If, as I have, you also doe
>   Vertue'attir'd in woman see,
> And dare love that, and say so too,
>   And forget the Hee and Shee

recalls both the following passage from that elaborate verse-letter to the Countess of Huntingdon, which we have already considered:

> In woman so perchance milde innocence
>   A seldome comet is, but active good
> A miracle, which reason scapes, and sense;
>   For, Art and Nature this in them withstood[1]

and the following passage from one of the verse-letters to the Countess of Bedford:

> for you are here
> The first good Angell, since the worlds frame stood,
> That ever did in womans shape appeare.[2]

The poem entitled *Twicknam Garden* was certainly written for the Countess of Bedford, since Twickenham Park was her residence from 1608 until 1617. It begins

> Blasted with sighs, and surrounded with teares,
>   Hither I come to seeke the spring

[1] Grierson, I, 201, ll. 9-12.
[2] Grierson, I, 190, ll. 30-2.

and concludes

> O perverse sexe, where none is true but shee,
>   Who's therefore true, because her truth kills mee;

and its ostensible subject is Donne's unrequited love for the Countess, which, he declares, is able to convert manna to gall and to prevent the beauty of the place that surrounds him from bringing him any refreshment. This, I say, is the poem's ostensible subject, although I think one cannot but feel that its real subject is that mood of dejection and emptiness and unrelatedness which we find expressed in some of Donne's letters to his friend Sir Henry Goodyer. This, too, one feels, is the real subject of *A nocturnall upon S. Lucies day*, of which the ostensible subject is the death, actual or imagined, of a mistress, whom Grierson, chiefly, it would seem, because her name was also that of the saint, suggested to have been Lucy, Countess of Bedford, who, although she did not as a matter of fact die until 1627, when Donne had been for six years Dean of St. Paul's and had long ceased to write secular poetry, was seriously ill in 1612. I had already noticed, when I observed that Mr. Garrod, in his volume of selections from Donne in the Clarendon Press Series, had noticed too, a certain affinity between the *Nocturnall* and another poem, *The Dissolution*, in which Donne also laments the actual or imagined death of a mistress, who, as Mr. Garrod remarks, may be plausibly conjectured to have been the same person whose actual or imagined death is lamented in the *Nocturnall*. She's dead, declares Donne, in that rather wire-drawn poem *The Dissolution*; she's dead, resolved into her first elements, and, since we were part of one another, my elements are decomposing too. Her death has revived in me those elements which love requited had almost abolished: my fire of passion, my sighs of air, my tears of water, my earthen despair. I shall therefore die more violently than she died, and my soul will outstrip hers as a second bullet, with more powder behind it, may overtake a first. It will be observed that in these two poems, unlike those we have just been considering, the theme is not the celebration of a Platonic relationship or the elaborately, never very seriously, and often almost playfully maintained fiction of an unrequited love, but a lament for the loss of one who had loved him even as he had loved her. Grierson, indeed, at the same time as he tentatively connected the *Nocturnall* with the Countess of Bedford, asked whether perhaps the third stanza of that poem did not speak 'a stronger language than that of Petrachian adoration'[1]:

> Oft a flood
> Have wee too wept, and so
> Drownd the whole world, us two; oft did we grow
> To be two Chaosses, when we did show
> Care to ought else; and often absences
> Withdrew our soules, and made us carcasses.

What, though, so far as I am aware, neither Grierson nor any other commentator has noticed is the remarkable similarity between the image, or 'conceit', in this stanza and the one in that fiendishly ingenious poem *A Valediction: of weeping*. My tears, Donne there declares, reflect your image, and are thus both fruits of present grief and symbols of grief to come; for, just as your image perishes in each tear of mine as it falls, even so we two shall be nothing when separated. Just as a ball, which was nothing, can be made into a world, which is everything, each tear of mine which bears your image becomes a world, until you weep too, and you, my dissolving heaven, inundate this world. Do not, like a moon, draw up my sea-like tears in order to shed them again and drown me in your embrace, thus teaching the sea and the wind to do what of their own accord they may do all too soon.

> O more then Moone,
> Draw not up seas to drowne me in thy spheare,
> Weepe me not dead, in thine armes, but forbeare
> To teach the sea, what it may doe too soone;
> Let not the winde
> Example finde,
> To doe me more harme, then it purposeth;
> Since thou and I sigh one anothers breath,
> Who e'r sighes most, is cruellest, and hasts the others death—

of which Professor Crofts remarks: 'Thus the brain-sick fancies are piled up, twaddle upon twaddle, until the whole thing explodes with

[1] II, 10.

a passionate outcry and a familiar image'.[1] It is natural, and, I think,
legitimate to assume that this poem, like several others in which he
speaks of her and of himself as forming two hemispheres, or one
perfect world, was written out of his experience of marriage; and
the reference to parting and to a sea-voyage suggests that it may
even have been written on the same occasion as the famous *Valediction: forbidding mourning*, which, as Walton has told us, Donne
wrote before setting out for Paris with Sir Robert Drury in 1611.
Now *A Valediction: of weeping*, surely to some extent inspired by his
wife, has, I think it will be agreed, both in imagery, and, in its last
stanza, in accent, a distinct affinity with that third stanza of the
Nocturnall in which Grierson seemed to find what he called 'a
stronger language than that of Petrarchian adoration'.[2] Indeed, in
the Introduction to his large edition of Donne,[3] though not in the
Commentary, he declared, repelling Gosse's suggestion that the
Nocturnall was a bitter poem, that 'it *might* have been written to
Ann More'.

But although in both the *Nocturnall* and *The Dissolution* Donne
speaks of a woman, not as he does in the Platonic or Courtly
poems, but as he only does in those where we may assume his wife
is at least partly present, the woman celebrated in the *Nocturnall*
and *The Dissolution* is either actually or anticipatedly dead. Since
it is almost impossible to suppose that Donne wrote these two poems
after the actual death of his wife in 1617, when he had been two
years in orders, and when, as Walton tells us, he became finally
'crucified to the world', is it possible to suppose that he may have
written them during some grave illness of hers, anticipating, as it
were, what his life would be without her? And, if so, is it possible
that he may have written at any rate the *Nocturnall* during his
visit to the Continent with Sir Robert Drury, when he parted very
unwillingly from his wife, who was then expecting a child, and was
in great anxiety about her until news of her safety finally reached
him in Paris? Since Donne and the Drurys left England in Novem-
ber 1611 and stayed for some considerable time in Paris, it may just
conceivably have been there on St. Lucy's Day 1611, that is to say,
according to the Julian Calendar, which Donne used, on 13th

[1] *Essays and Studies*, 1936, 142–3.
[2] II, 10.
[3] II, xxii.

December, that he wrote the *Nocturnall*. Except for Herrick's on his 'Prew',[1] the only other possible example I know of what may be called the anticipatory epitaph is the poem beginning

> Let the bird of lowdest lay

with its sequel entitled *Threnos*, beginning

> Beautie, Truth, and Raritie,
> Grace in all simplicitie,
> Here enclosde, in cinders lie

which Shakespeare contributed to those other poems on the subject of the Turtle and Phoenix which were appended to Robert Chester's allegorical poem *Loves Martyr*, published in 1601. A possible example, I say, because the late Bernard Newdigate's discovery of one of the four poems which Ben Jonson contributed to that volume, the *Ode ἐνθουσιαστική*, with the heading 'To L: C: of: B:', makes it just possible to suppose that the Phoenix and the Turtle there celebrated were the Countess of Bedford and her husband, both of whom were still alive.

I have spent some time on this question of the person celebrated and lamented in the *Nocturnall*, because those who insist on connecting this poem with the Countess of Bedford, and on including it among what I have called the Platonic or Courtly poems, tend to weaken, through this poem's unlikeness to them, our sense of the essential similarity of those poems, and to strengthen the contention of Mr. Garrod, and of any others who may follow him, that *The Primrose* and the rest were not addressed to Mrs. Herbert (even Mr. Garrod, I may remark in passing, is not prepared to deny that *Twicknam Garden* was addressed to the Countess of Bedford).

I have dwelt upon what I call the paradox of these Courtly and Platonic poems in some detail, because I think that a consideration of it should help us to put the autobiographical element in the

---

[1] *Upon* Prew *his Maid.*
In this little Urne is laid
Prewdence Baldwin (once my maid)
From whose happy spark here let
Spring the purple Violet.
Prudence survived her master by four years.

Songs and Sonets in its proper place. The fact that those poems which alone imperatively require the assumption of an actual personal relationship in order to explain how they ever came to be written at all are neither the most dramatically convincing nor the most serious should make us beware of assuming as a matter of course that, where Donne seems to us to have 'done best', he must needs have had 'most truth', most actual or factual truth, for his subjects. What is really important is to attempt to classify the *Songs and Sonets* according to their moods and attitudes and degrees of seriousness, and to use our biographical knowledge, if we use it at all, merely in order to test or confirm conclusions we have reached by methods that can entirely dispense with it.

At this point it may perhaps be as well to offer a rough statistical survey of the whole collection. It consists of fifty-five poems, one of which, 'He that cannot chuse but love', in which a woman rejects, for different reasons, every possible lover, and decides to love herself, occurs in only two of the various manuscripts Grierson examined, was first printed in the Appendix to the 1650 edition of Donne's Poems, and seems to me rather unlikely to be his. The remaining fifty-four poems may be roughly classified as follows:

(1) Ten deliberately outrageous, paradoxical or cynical poems, in which, I am sure, Donne is mainly concerned to excite admiration and astonishment by a display of wit: 'Goe and catche a falling starre', *Womans Constancy, The Indifferent, Loves Vsury, Communitie, Confined Love, Loves Alchymie, The Curse, The Apparition, Loves Diet.* About most of these poems there is something so energetic and dramatically convincing that many, perhaps most, modern readers have been taken in by them.

(2) Five merely witty and ingenious poems about love, not outrageous or cynical or bitter, but far more exclusively cerebral, far less spirited and energetic, than those I have mentioned: *The Flea, A Ieat Ring Sent, The triple Fool, A Valediction: of my name in the window, Witchcraft by a picture.*

(3) Four songs, three of which (the first three I shall mention) are given in one group of MSS. as 'Songs which were made to certain ayres which were made before', and which, tender and impassioned as are some of their phrases, may perhaps be regarded (if I may be allowed to make a rather crude distinction) as literary rather than occasional: *The Baite,* 'Swetest love, I do not goe',

The Message ('Send home my long strayd eyes to mee'), *Break of day*.

(4) Eight poems almost certainly written during Donne's middle years and perhaps addressed to Mrs. Herbert or the Countess of Bedford: *The undertaking, The Will, the Funerall, The Blossome, The Primrose, The Relique, The Dampe, Twicknam Garden*.

(5) Three poems which, though witty rather than impassioned, and although two of them return to that theme of woman's inconstancy which plays so great a part in the more outrageous poems, are nevertheless tender and playful rather than cynical, and which ought possibly to be included in the next group: *The Legacie, Loves Deitie, Loves exchange*.

(6) Twenty poems, including the problematical *Nocturnall*, and *The Dissolution*, which, although the relationship between wit and passion, intellect and feeling, is by no means uniform, are nevertheless, as a group, more serious, more impassioned, more tender, and, one cannot but feel, more personal and less detached than the rest, and of which it is tempting to suppose (how justifiably I shall proceed to consider) that some were at least partly inspired by Ann More: *The good-morrow, The Sunne Rising, The Canonization, Lovers infiniteness, A Feaver, Aire and Angels, The Anniversarie, A Valediction: of the booke, The Dreame, A Valediction: of weeping, A Nocturnall upon S. Lucies day, The broken heart, A Valediction: forbidding mourning, The Dissolution, The Prohibition, The Expiration, The Computation, The Paradox, A Lecture upon the Shadow*, and (although I greatly doubt whether it is by Donne) *The Token*.

(7) Finally, there are four poems which may be described as serious analyses of love, as distinct from merely witty or paradoxical generalizations upon it: *Farewell to Love*, the earliest, probably, and written in a rather bitter and disenchanted mood; *Negative Love, Loves Growth, The Extasie*.

It is very necessary to attempt some such classification of the *Songs and Sonets* as that which I have provisionally offered, for although there are, no doubt, many limiting cases, there are certain broad and obvious differences in tone and seriousness, and those who overlook them may easily fall into generalizations not really applicable to the collection as a whole. It was, I think, such a failure to distinguish that was primarily responsible for the misunderstandings in Mr. C. S. Lewis's essay on *Donne and Love Poetry in the*

Seventeenth Century,[1] one of the less happy excursions of that distinguished scholar and critic, as also for some similar misunderstandings in the essay of Professor Crofts in *Essays and Studies*: failure to distinguish between what I have called the deliberately outrageous poems and the more serious ones, and also, I think, failure to recognize the element of sheer wit and paradox, one might almost say, of sheer fun, in the outrageous poems. This, I think, has led Mr. Lewis and Professor Crofts to take the outrageous poems too seriously and the more serious poems too lightly: as Mrs. Bennett, who herself tends, perhaps, to take the outrageous poems too seriously, remarks in a postcript to her reply to Mr. Lewis, *The Love Poetry of John Donne*,[2] both Mr. Lewis and Professor Crofts 'are unable to believe that a poet so brilliantly cynical is to be taken seriously when he is reverent or tender'. And this reverence and tenderness, of which the fact is so much more important than the possible or probable cause, is apparent, not so much in the choice of words or images or even arguments, as in rhythms and cadences, in the tone of the poet's voice. As Mrs. Bennett insists, in her reply to Mr. Lewis, unless readers 'can hear the difference between quick and slow movements, or between smooth and staccato, and unless they can submit to the rhythm sufficiently to throw the emphasis precisely where Donne has arranged for it to fall, they cannot understand his poetry'. Consider, for example, the contrast between what Mrs. Bennett calls 'the bored, flippant tone' of

> Will no other vice content you?
> Will it not serve your turn to do, as did your mothers?
> Or have you all old vices spent, and now would finde
>   out others?
> Or doth a feare, that men are true, torment you?
> Oh, we are not, be not you so,
> Let mee, and doe you, twenty know;

the contrast between what she calls the 'tone of angry scorn', in

>   Must I alas
> Frame and enamell Plate, and drinke in Glasse?

---

[1] In *Seventeenth-Century Studies presented to Sir Herbert Grierson*, 1938, 64 ff.
[2] *Op. cit.*, 85 ff.

Chafe waxe for others seales? breake a colts force
And leave him then, being made a ready horse?—

consider the contrast between the tone of these passages and that of

The Anniversarie

All Kings, and all their favorites,
    All glory of honors, beauties, wits,
The Sun it selfe, which makes times, as they passe,
Is elder by a year, now, then it was
When thou and I first one another saw;
All other things, to their destruction draw,
    Only our love hath no decay;
This, no to morrow hath, nor yesterday,
Running it never runs from us away,
But truly keepes his first, last, everlasting day.

Two graves must hide thine and my coarse,
    If one might, death were no divorce.
Alas, as well as other Princes, wee,
(Who Prince enough in one another bee,)
Must leave at last in death, these eyes, and eares,
Oft fed with true oathes, and with sweet salt teares;
    But soules where nothing dwells but love
(All other thoughts being inmates) then shall prove
This, or a love increased there above,
When bodies to their graves, soules from their graves remove.[1]

And then wee shall be throughly blest,
    But wee no more, then all the rest;
Here upon earth, we'are Kings, and none but wee
Can be such Kings, nor of such subjects bee.
Who is so safe as wee? where none can doe
Treason to us, except one of us two.
    True and false feares let us refraine,
Let us love nobly, and live, and adde againe
Yeares and yeares unto yeares, till we attaine
To write threescore: this is the second of our raigne.

[1] The body is the grave of the soul.

It is, then, important to attempt some kind of classification of the
Songs and Sonets and to recognize that some of them are more
serious, or, as we might be inclined to say, more 'sincere', than
others: that, for example, while *The Flea* and *The Anniversarie*
are both love-poems, and are both constructed with characteristic
logic and sequaciousness, they are nevertheless, as regards their
degrees of seriousness, poles asunder. It should, of course, be possible
to distinguish the serious from the less serious poems, the reverent
and tender from the merely or mainly witty, simply by attending to
the tone of Donne's voice, by responding appropriately to the varied
rhythms and cadences of his verse. It would seem, though, that by
no means all readers, not even all intelligent readers, are capable of
such immediate responsiveness and discrimination. What first
impresses them is the brilliance of the wit, especially in the deliberately outrageous poems, whose rhythm, although far less subtle
than in the more serious ones, is so splendidly dramatic and rhetorical, has such *brio* and attack, that, for some readers at any rate,
it tends, as it were, to polarize the whole collection. Because in these
outrageous poems Donne is so often shouting at the top of his
voice, readers whose metrical and emotional responses are perhaps
a little crude and undeveloped may tend to assume that there he is
speaking from his heart, while in the more serious poems, which
to them appear simply less vivid, less excited and less exciting, he is
speaking more or less with his tongue in his cheek. It is chiefly in
order to help such readers to perceive what is really there that it is
worth while to spend a little time in trying to show that it is very
likely that in these more serious and tender poems Donne had more
truth for his subject than in the others, and that they were at least
partly inspired by his experience of marriage. This is not a view that
has commended itself only to the more superficial and fanciful
critics of Donne's poetry: Mrs. Bennett, one of the shrewdest of
them, declares that

There are a number of poems which celebrate that rarer love
in which the senses are but vehicles and mating is a 'marriage of
true minds'. There is still no certain means of judging to whom
any given poem was addressed; but we know that his relation to
Anne More was of this character. Thirteen years after his marriage
to her he could write: 'We had not one another at so cheap a

rate as that we should ever be weary of one another.' The sentence
strikes the same note of security as distinguishes his most mature
love poetry.[1]

Is there—as distinct from what seems to some of us, as the result
of considering Donne's life and poetry as a whole, the general
probability—is there, in the poems themselves, any kind of *factual*
evidence in favour of this hypothesis? The only poem there is some
evidence that he actually addressed to his wife is *A Valediction: forbidding mourning*, which Walton tells us that Donne wrote before
setting out for Paris with Sir Robert Drury in 1611. There are
though at least four other of the *Songs and Sonets* which contain
some kind of factual evidence either as to the date when they were
composed or the person who at least partly inspired them: namely,
The Sunne Rising, *The Canonization*, *A Valediction: of the booke*, and
The Anniversarie. In the seventh line of *The Sunne Rising* Donne bids
the sun, among other things,

> Goe tell Court-huntsmen, that the King will ride.

Here we have a definite *terminus a quo*: this line, I think we can say
with certainty, was written, not only after Donne's marriage in
December 1601, not only after the death of Elizabeth on 24th March.
1603, but after James I had been on the throne long enough for his
passion for hunting to have become, as it did, a topic of both private
conversation and public satire. As Sir Edmund Chambers has remarked:

> He disliked London, and at all times of the year, and where
> ever the Court might be, he was constantly leaving the greater
> part of it behind, referring the transaction of business to the Privy
> Council, and betaking himself with the Master of the Horse and
> Sir Thomas Lake, a clerk of the signet who acted as his private
> secretary, to Theobalds or Royston, or some other hunting box,
> at which his favourite pursuit might be conveniently enjoyed.
> From thence he would hurry back, often for a day or two only,
> when some office of state or Court ceremony urgently demanded
> his attendance. There is abundant evidence that this abnormal

[1] *Four Metaphysical Poets*, 1934, 21–2.

passion for the chase had much to do with the early unpopularity of James. It led to neglect of business, the grave inconvenience of ministers, excessive purveyance, and the trampling of crops; and the popular discontent soon found vent in libels on the stage and elsewhere. But James said that he could not lead a sedentary life and must study his health above all things.[1]

The first stanza of *The Canonization* is as follows:

> For Godsake hold your tongue, and let me love,
> Or chide my palsie, or my gout,
> My five gray haires, or ruin'd fortune flout,
> With wealth your state, your minde with Arts improve,
> Take you a course, get you a place,
> Observe his honour, or his grace,
> Or the Kings reall, or his stamped face
> Contemplate, what you will, approve,
> So you will let me love.

This, again I think one can say quite definitely, was written not only after Donne's marriage, since it was his marriage that ruined his fortune, but also after the accession of James, since otherwise Donne would have written of the Queen's, not of the King's, 'reall or stamped face'.[2] Here, then, are two poems written at least eighteen months or two years after Donne's marriage, and in which it seems impossible to suppose that the love celebrated could be other than that for his wife; for, however dangerous it may be to assert too positively what Donne, at any time of his life, could or could not have been capable of, I must admit that, in view of all we know of Donne's love for Ann More from his letters, from Walton, and from the sonnet written after her death, in which he declared that it was the admiring her which had first whetted his mind to seek for God, I find it difficult to suppose that at any time after his marriage Donne could have written tender and impassioned, as distinct from playful and hyperbolical, poems (such as *The Autumnall*

---

[1] *The Elizabethan Stage*, I, 21-2, a passage which as early as 1925 had already been referred to by Mario Praz as evidence for the date of Donne's poem, *Secentismo e Marinismo in Inghilterra*, 117, note.

[2] Similarly, a *terminus ante quem* for the date of the Second Part of *The Return from Parnassus* is provided by allusions in that play to 'the Queenes day', 'the Queenes law', 'the Queenes peace', and 'the Queenes friends'.

and its companions) about anyone else. In the other two poems I have mentioned the factual element is more capable of a fictitious interpretation, and may, by readers who have not perceived those differences of tone which this factual evidence is being cited in order to confirm and to interpret, be dismissed as merely imaginary fact. *A Valediction: of the booke* seems, as I shall suggest, to be presenting a manuscript volume of love-poems, there hyperbolically described as 'our manuscripts' and as 'those myriades of letters', which, even if their presentation was only imaginary, can hardly have been imagined as other than those of the *Songs and Sonets* (there may, of course, have been other poems now lost) which had been at least partly inspired by his wife. *The Anniversarie* begins:

> All Kings, and all their favorites,
> All glory of honors, beauties, wits,
> The Sun it selfe, which makes times, as they passe,
> Is elder by a yeare, now, then it was
> When thou and I first one another saw.

If, as seems probable, the plurals in the first line were intended to include King James and *his* favourites, the poem must have been written some considerable time after the King's accession, and certainly more than a year after Donne and his future wife 'first one another saw'. And the first two lines of the second stanza,

> Two graves must hide thine and my coarse,
> If one might, death were no divorce,

seem to prove that the person addressed is imagined, not as a wife, whom, together with her husband, *one* grave would eventually 'hide', but as a mistress. And in most of these poems celebrating a love which Donne seems first to have experienced in marriage, the person addressed is more easily imaginable as a mistress than as a wife. If they were largely inspired by his wife, they have not the appearance of being addressed to her.

In fact, although it is certain that at least some of the *Songs and Sonets* were written after Donne's marriage, and although there is a strong probability that many of them were inspired by his wife, that dramatic element in his genius on which I have so often insisted

should make us beware of asserting too positively that any particular
poem could not possibly have been written at a particular time, or
that it must have been, or that it could not possibly have been,
inspired by a particular experience or a particular person. Let us
recall how, in considering the more dramatic Elegies and noticing
the great differences between Donne's cynical and contemptuous
attitude to the women in the First Elegy (*Iealosie*) and in the Seventh
(*Natures lay Ideot*), his occasionally cynical but by no means contemptuous attitude towards the young girl in the high-spirited
Fourth Elegy (*The Perfume*), and his genuine tenderness both
towards the woman in the Twelfth Elegy (*His Parting from her*)
and, in the Sixteenth Elegy, towards the youthful mistress who
would have gone with him as his page—let us recall how, in
noticing these differences in tone and attitude, the suggestion arose
that it did not seem necessary to assume that whenever Donne was
writing tenderly rather than merely wittily, cynically and impudently, whenever he was, as it were, expressing himself Shakespeareanly rather than Ovidianly, he must necessarily have been
writing out of actual experience, not just out of his imagination,
and whether we should not assume that, now and then, if only
for the sake of variety, he chose to dramatize other moods of his
very diverse and volatile self than that of mere outrageousness. In
none of Donne's Elegies, in few, perhaps, of all his poems, is the
dramatic illusion more complete than in that Sixteenth Elegy, *On
his Mistriss* ('By our first strange and fatall interview'), which in
the Bridgewater MS. has the title *His wife would have gone as his
page*, but which, I think we can say with certainty, was not addressed to Ann More after their marriage, nor even occasioned by
any particular incident before it, although as I have remarked, it is
possible that at some time during their courtship Donne may have
imagined a situation in which Ann, who was only seventeen when
he married her in 1601, wished to accompany him on a foreign
journey disguised as his page. Similarly, while I think it probable
that Ann More, or the image of her, or the idea of her, was somehow associated with all or most of those twenty poems which I
have grouped together, partly because of their tone and partly
because of two continually recurring themes, that of the all-sufficiency of their love and that of absence as a kind of death, I admit
that it is not really possible to demonstrate this. Moreover, although

it is certain that some of these poems were written after their marriage, it is possible that some may have been written during their courtship, that they were, so to speak, anticipations rather than recollections or celebrations, and that here, even as in the Elegies, Donne's dramatic imagination, though here with more truth for its subject, was playing a considerable part.

Consider, for example, *The Dreame*, which begins

> Deare love, for nothing lesse then thee
> Would I have broke this happy dreame,
>   It was a theame
> For reason, much too strong for phantasie,
> Therefore thou wakd'st me wisely; yet
> My Dreame thou brok'st not, but continued'st it,
> Thou art so truth, that thoughts of thee suffice,
> To make dreames truths; and fables histories;
> Enter these armes, for since thou thoughtst it best,
> Not to dreame all my dreame, let's act the rest

and in which Donne proceeds to declare that although at first sight he thought she was an angel, her more than angelic knowledge of the moment when excess of joy would wake him proved that it could only have been her more than angelic self; and that now her departing makes him doubt whether it was really herself after all—unless, indeed, she came only to render him inflammable and will return to set him alight. This is dramatically convincing, but I think it is more likely to have been all dream than, as it professes to be, half dream and half fact—that, indeed, although very different in tone, it is just as purely dramatic and imaginary as the Fourth Elegy, *The Perfume*, with its 'Hydroptique father', its 'immortall mother', its 'grim eight-foot-high iron-bound serving-man', and

> Thy little brethren, which like Faiery Sprights
> Oft skipt into our chamber, those sweet nights.

Mrs. Joan Bennett, partly, perhaps, because she is inclined to take this poem more literally than I do, and partly, perhaps, because it seems to her more light-hearted and less deeply impassioned than some of the others, seems to assume that it must have been inspired by some woman whom Donne had loved before Ann More entered his life. Tending, as I think, in her illuminating study of Donne,[1] to take what I have called the deliberately outrageous poems too seriously, and trying, as it were, to find some not too abrupt transition from what seems to her the bitterness and cynicism and disenchantment there expressed to Donne's transforming love for Ann, Mrs. Bennett speaks of a set of poems which 'record the poignant delight of mutual love-making, without reference to outside interference, and with no hint of inadequacy in the beloved',[2] which, she suggests, may have been written before he fell in love with Ann and during the same years as what I have called the deliberately outrageous poems. Of this 'set of poems', as she calls them, Mrs. Bennett mentions only three, *The Dreame*, *The Sunne Rising*, and the *Breake of day*, a kind of *aubade* spoken by a woman. Now although *The Dreame* contains no internal evidence of its date of composition, *The Sunne Rising* must, as we have seen, because of its allusion to James I's passion for hunting, have been written at least eighteen months or two years after Donne's marriage, and it seems therefore legitimate to suppose that if Donne had any particular woman in mind when he wrote it, that woman was his wife. Let us examine this poem. If in *The Dreame* there is a considerable element of dramatic imagination, in *The Sunne Rising* there is a considerable element of what one might be tempted to call literary inspiration. On the one hand, though more light-hearted, perhaps, less deeply impassioned, than some other poems on the recurring theme of the all-sufficiency of two lovers and the recurring image that together they form one world, it nevertheless contains that theme and that image, and, if we are to group Donne's poems at all, clearly belongs to the group in which that theme and image occur. On the other hand, though we may say with probability that it was inspired by Ann More, or by the idea of her, we can say with certainty that it was partly inspired by the thirteenth elegy of the First Book of Ovid's *Amores*, and that, in spite of the characteristic differences between them, Ovid's impudent address to Aurora, telling her not to be in such a hurry, suggested Donne's impudent address to the sun. Ovid's

[1] In *Four Metaphysical Poets*, 1934.
[2] *Op. cit.*, 20.

poem, needless to say, is much less sequacious, much less strictly and continuously argumentative, than Donne's, and consists mainly of a list of the many different persons whom Aurora contrives to annoy—sailors, travellers, soldiers, farm labourers, draught-oxen, schoolboys (who may well have suggested Donne's 'late schoole boyes, and sowre prentices'). All this leads up to the couplet

Omnia perpeterer; sed surgere mane puellas,
  Quis, nisi cui non est ulla puella, ferat?

All this I could put up with; but to make girls rise at dawn,
  who but one with no girl of his own could endure this?

If, Ovid continues, your son Memnon was black, it was because your heart was so. You are ready enough to leave Tithonus (who, if he could say what he knew, would show us that there is not a worse woman in Heaven), but if you were in the arms of Cephalus you would say *lente currite, Noctis equi*. Why should I suffer because you have an old husband—was it on my advice that you married him? And so on, to the concluding couplet: 'I had done with my reproaches; you might have supposed she had heard; she blushed; yet no later than usual came the dawn.'

There can be no doubt, I think, that it was Ovid's impudent address to Aurora which suggested Donne's impudent address to the sun, and which led him, with characteristic contempt for the elegances of poetic diction, to call him whom Spenser and others had so often addressed as 'the golden eye of heaven', 'Hyperion', 'the glorious planet Sol', and the like, 'Busie old foole' and 'Sawcy pendantique wretch'. But Donne has combined with this impudence, or, if you will, with this anti-Spenserianism, the more serious and tender theme of the all-sufficiency of two lovers.

> Busie old foole, unruly Sunne,
>   Why dost thou thus,
> Through windowes, and through curtaines call on us?
> Must to thy motions lovers seasons run?
>   Sawcy pedantique wretch, goe chide
>   Late schoole boyes, and sowre prentices,
> Goe tell Court-huntsmen, that the King will ride,
> Call countrey ants to harvest offices;

Love, all alike, no season knowes, nor clyme,
Nor houres, dayes, moneths, which are the rags of time.

    Thy beames, so reverend, and strong
      Why shouldst thou thinke?
I could eclipse and cloud them with a winke,
But that I would not lose her sight so long:
    If her eyes have not blinded thine,
      Looke, and to morrow late, tell mee,
  Whether both the' India's of spice and Myne
  Be where thou leftst them, or lie here with mee.
Aske for those Kings whom thou saw'st yesterday,
And thou shalt heare, All here in one bed lay.

    She'is all States, and all Princes, I,
      Nothing else is.
Princes doe but play us; compar'd to this,
All honor's mimique; All wealth alchimie.
    Thou sunne art halfe as happy'as wee,
      In that the world's contracted thus;
    Thine age askes ease, and since thy duties bee
    To warme the world, that's done in warming us.
Shine here to us, and thou art every where;
This bed thy center is, these walls, thy spheare.

In the Elegies we have often seen Donne exploiting the situations and, to some extent, the morality, of Ovid's *Amores*, in order to produce novel and perhaps rather shocking effects. Here what one may call the Ovidian element is combined with a genuine tenderness and with an idea, that of the all-sufficiency of two lovers, which are both quite foreign to Ovid. Donne, in fact, is here attempting to do several different things simultaneously: on the one hand, to write an impudent address to the sun in a defiantly colloquial diction which shall, as it were, cock a snook at the Spenserian and Petrarchan conventions, and, on the other hand, to work out the ingenious idea, or conceit (too ingenious for Ovid) that the sun only goes further to fare worse, a conceit which gives structural unity to the poem and which combines naturally with the far profounder, more deeply felt, less merely witty and ingenious idea that he and his beloved are a world in and for themselves. Three strands or strains which in the Elegies and elsewhere we have often observed separately—impudence, witty and ingenious argument, tenderness—are here combined and fused. But who shall say which was the initial impulse? Was it intellectual or was it emotional? Did a mood of tenderness supervene, as it were, upon a desire to write an impudent and witty poem, or did wit and impudence supervene upon a mood of tenderness? Or was it from the beginning inseparably and almost indistinguishably both? And, if this poem stood alone, would it be necessary to assume that it was inspired by Donne's actual tenderness for a particular woman rather than by his tenderness for the idea of a woman? For Donne, like other poets, like other dramatic poets, was quite capable of such uncentred tenderness:

> Twice or thrice had I loved thee,
> Before I knew thy face or name

he wrote at the beginning of *Aire and Angels*.

I have spent some time in considering *The Dreame* and *The Sunne Rising* because they are, as it were, limiting cases. The strong element of dramatic imagination in the one and of literary inspiration in the other, the strong element of wit and invention with which, in both poems, the genuine tenderness is mingled might perhaps lead us, as it led Mrs. Bennett, to assume, on the one hand, that they could not have been inspired by Ann More, and, on the other hand, to invent some hypothetical predecessor of Ann More as the inspirer of their tenderness. Nevertheless, if the two poems stand together (and for Mrs. Bennett they do stand together), and if, since *The Sunne Rising* was certainly written after Donne's marriage, it is reasonable to assume that the tenderness in it was inspired by Ann, it is no less reasonable to suppose that the tenderness in *The Dreame* may also have been inspired by Ann, either before or after their marriage, or else that, before he loved Ann, and at a time when he was not, perhaps, in love with any particular woman, the tenderness which had always been potentially present in Donne there found, as it also found in some of the Elegies, dramatic and imaginative expression. We must, in fact, resist the temptation to multiply hypotheses beyond what is necessary. We must not allow the probable, I might almost say, the certain, hypothesis that Ann More inspired Donne to write at least some poems and that at least some of these poems are among the *Songs and Sonets*—we must not allow this hypothesis to become too rigid and exclusive, so that it begins to play tricks with us, making us suppose that we know exactly which poems were inspired by Ann More, and leading us to invent a long line of former mistresses as the inspirers or addressees of whichever poems seem to us not quite serious, or tender, or reverent enough to have been inspired by Ann. I could not agree more strongly with anyone than I do with Mrs. Bennett in her insistence that it is necessary to distinguish among the *Songs and Sonets* by attending to the poet's rhythms, inflexions and tones of voice, but, while the distinction between the deliberately outrageous poems, the merely witty poems, and those which contain at least some seriousness or reverence or tenderness is absolute and immediately apparent, it seems to me that we should not insist too much on such differences and distinctions as we may detect within this last group. I have indeed ventured to separate off eight poems in a courtly and hyperbolical strain as being similar to and contemporary with *The Autumnall*, but within those twenty poems which I have grouped together as having been probably inspired by Ann More, as well as in others which I have grouped around them and might as well, perhaps, have grouped with them, I am content to recognize and to accept, as entirely characteristic and expected, very considerable variations in seriousness and intensity and in the predominance and interrelationship of various elements: wit, drama, tenderness, reverence, passion, and so on.

What, though, as I have already remarked, seems chiefly to have led Mrs. Bennett to speak of an intermediate group of poems, to assume a kind of intermediate love as the inspirer of them, and to include in that group one poem, *The Sunne Rising*, which a piece of internal evidence she had not noticed proves to have been written after Donne's marriage—what seems chiefly to have led her to this hypothesis was the fact that she had, as it seems to me, taken the deliberately outrageous poems too seriously and therefore felt the need for some kind of transition from what seemed to her their bitterness and cynicism to that sense of happiness and security breathed by the later poems. 'To Donne', she declares, 'this experience was like awakening from a nightmare: he cries

And now good morrow to our waking soules,
Which watch not one another out of feare;

or he asserts that, after their death, he and his mistress will be thought
of as

You, to whom love was peace, that now is rage.

This welcome to serenity is the counterpart of his former distrust,
both of his own and of his mistress' constancy.'[1] Here, I think, Mrs.
Bennett, like others, is taking the deliberately outrageous poems too
seriously, too autobiographically, and discovering in them more
actual bitterness and cynicism and disenchantment than is really
there. It is sufficient simply to recognize the existence of the greater
seriousness, the happiness and the sense of security, in the poems
she mentions, without attempting to explain it as being partly or
largely a reaction from various kinds of deep unhappiness which
had gone before: sufficient to recognize the existence of these new
qualities and of what, however sceptical one may be about the
possibility of autobiographical interpretation, one cannot but
regard as a development or a progress, or avoid explaining to some
extent in terms of the entrance into Donne's life of Ann More. Here
I would differ from Mrs. Bennett only in so far as I should prefer
to regard that experience as the more continuous actualization in
Donne, the more habitual sway in him (to borrow a phrase of
Wordsworth's), of potentialities which he had hitherto only
occasionally experienced and expressed, rather than (more dramatically, or melodramatically) as the reformation of a rake, or the
restoration of an unhappy and distempered spirit. I admit, though,
that the precise extent to which Donne may have been, as the
Groupers say, 'changed' by his love for Ann More must remain a
matter of conjecture. What is really important is to recognize and
distinguish among the *Songs and Sonets* these very different attitudes
and very different tones of voice.

It is chiefly in order to sensitize readers not immediately sensitive
to such differences in tone and attitude that it is worth while trying
to demonstrate the probability that in many at least of the more
serious and tender poems (or, more strictly speaking, in poems where

[1] *Four Metaphysical Poets*, 22.

one wants such readers to perceive the seriousness and the tenderness)
Donne had more truth for his subject than in the others. You will
agree, we may say to such readers, that Donne's love for Ann More
was one of the most important events in his life. You will remember
that in the seventeenth of the *Holy Sonnets*, written after her death,
when he had become, as Walton says, crucified to the world and
had left trifles and trifling behind him, he declared:

> Since she whom I lov'd hath payd her last debt
> To Nature, and to hers, and my good is dead,
> And her Soule early into heaven ravished,
> Wholly on heavenly things my mind is sett.
> Here the admyring her my mind did whett
> To seeke thee God; so streames do shew their head.

Now, without trying to describe too precisely just what Donne
may have been before he loved Ann More, is it not reasonable to
suppose that in that 'admiring' which, as he declared after he had
lost her, had whetted his mind to seek God, there was a progress, a
development, a process, in the course of which he discovered much
about love, much about life, much about himself which he had not
known before? All we ask of you is to consider certain of the
Songs and Sonets as records of such discoveries, and to see whether,
if you consider them in this way, they will not come to mean far
more to you than they did before, and whether you will not come
to perceive in them a tone, an attitude, a fundamental seriousness
quite different from anything in those other, and, as we think,
earlier poems which have hitherto so impressed you and in which
you have taught yourself to recognize what you call the real Donne.
Nevertheless, although the biographical, or autobiographical,
approach may thus come to serve a useful purpose, it is not as
autobiography, as records of actual experience, but as works of art,
as distillations and shapings of experiences which may have been
partly actual and partly imaginary, that these poems, like all other
good poems, ultimately concern us; true though it be that anything
which may illuminate either the way in which great poetry has
been written or the psychology of such a fascinating character as
Donne is a very legitimate subject of curiosity and investigation.

As an aid to deciding which of Donne's poems Ann may have

inspired, or, at any rate, as an aid to establishing some kind of interrelationship between his more serious love-poems, not enough attention has been given to the poem entitled *A Valediction: of the booke*. In spite of a certain playful tenderness and a certain hyperbole, it is a serious poem, that is to say, it is not a mere exercise in ingenuity. It is true that, Donne's dramatic imagination being what it was, we can easily over-estimate the factual, or apparently factual, element in his poetry, and it is quite conceivable that this poem may be about an imaginary gift and an imaginary parting; nevertheless, whether or no, like a more famous Valediction, it was actually addressed to his wife, it seems to be at least imagined as accompanying a manuscript volume of love-poems, and it is hard not to suppose that the statements (hyperbolical as some of them are) which Donne there makes about the nature of these poems apply to those of the *Songs and Sonets* which evoke the figure of that wife-mistress, or mistress-wife, who must surely have been at least partly inspired by Ann More.

> I'll tell thee now (dear Love) what thou shalt doe
>   To anger destiny, as she doth us,
>   How I shall stay, though she Esloygne[1] me thus
> And how posterity shall know it too.

'Study our manuscripts,' he continues,

> Study our manuscripts, those Myriades
>   Of letters, which have past twixt thee and mee,
>   Thence write our Annals, and in them will bee
> To all whom loves subliming fire invades,
>   Rule and example found.

Much is obscure; however, since it would seem to be from *his* book, mentioned in the title, that she is to compose *hers*, it seems reasonable, in view of the hyperbolical tone and style of the poem, to assume that the 'myriades of letters' he is inviting her to study in order that she may compose the annals of their love are the poems he has transcribed for her as a parting gift. The book, the annals, she is to compile therefrom, written in a style significant only to

---

[1] *m'éloigne*, removes me to a distance.

those who, like themselves, are learned in love ('Wee for loves clergie only'are instruments') would, he declares, preserve the substance of present learning from a second invasion of the Goths and Vandals; and then, in a stanza which, I think, should help us to decide which of the *Songs and Sonets* were inspired by Ann More, he describes what *would be* the two most fundamental qualities or aspects of these imaginary annals, and therewith, I think one may reasonably assume, what *were*, for him, the two most fundamental qualities of the actual poems from which the imaginary annals were to be compiled:

> Here Loves Divines (since all Divinity
>   Is love or wonder) may finde all they seeke,
>   Whether abstract spirituall love they like,
> Their Soules exhal'd with what they do not see,
>   Or, loth so to amuze[1]
>   Faiths infirmitie, they chuse
>   Something which they may see and use;
>   For, though minde be the heaven, where love doth sit,
> Beauty a convenient type may be to figure it.

'Abstract spirituall love' and something that may be seen and used, heavenly beauty and earthly beauty, mind and body—it is the combination of these antithetical but complementary qualities that will distinguish, so Donne declares, the annals of their love, and it was these qualities which, I think we may infer, did for him in fact distinguish the actual poems from which those imaginary annals were to be compiled. Now it is precisely this combination of qualities that distinguishes certain of the *Songs and Sonets*, and it is these, I think we may assume, that were at least partly inspired, some perhaps before, some after their marriage, by his wife, the admiring whom, as he was to declare later, had whetted his mind to seek God. And these antithetical but complementary qualities do not exist separately in separate poems; they co-exist inseparably and almost indistinguishably in all those love-poems which I believe Donne took, and which we should take, seriously, and which we may assume to have been inspired by Ann. It is perhaps only in *A Valediction: forbidding mourning* that what Donne calls 'abstract spiritual

[1] *i.e.* to bemuse, to puzzle.

love' predominates, although even in that poem it does so only because Donne is there concentrating his attention upon that aspect of their love which can make it endure absence:

> Dull sublunary lovers love
>   (Whose soule is sense) cannot admit
> Absence, because it doth remove
>   Those things which elemented it.
>
> But we by a love, so much refin'd,
>   That our selves know not what it is,
> Inter-assured of the mind,
>   Care lesse, eyes, lips, and hands to misse.

When I call these love-poems serious I do not mean that they are solemn; many, perhaps most of them, are bathed in that serious gaiety, that sacred mirth, which many seventeenth-century poets understood better than we do, and which was probably one of the things Mr. Eliot had in mind when he spoke of a dissociation of sensibility. The distinction I am making is one which I think Donne himself was making when, in a fragmentary passage in a letter to his friend Sir Henry Goodyer, written in 1609 or 1610, and in reply, presumably, to some opinion which Goodyer had expressed about one of his more unregenerate songs, he declared: 'I doe not condemn in my self, that I have given my wit such evaporations, as those, if they be free from prophaneness, or obscene provocations.'[1] Donne, I think we may say with certainty, would no more have called *The Anniversarie*, or *The good-morrow*, or *Lovers infiniteness* 'evaporations' than he would have called the *Valediction: forbidding mourning*, written a year or two after that letter to Goodyer, an evaporation. By his 'evaporations' he meant, I am sure, what I have called the deliberately outrageous poems—*Goe and catch a falling starre*, *The Indifferent*, *Loves Vsury*, *Loves Alchymie*, and the rest.

> I can love her, and her, and you and you,
> I can love any, so she be not true.
>
> Will no other vice content you?
> Will it not serve your turn to do, as did your mothers? . . .

[1] 1651, 36; Gosse, I, 197.

> Let mee thinke any rivalls letter mine,
> >   And at next nine
> Keep midnights promise; mistake by the way
> The maid, and tell the Lady of that delay . . .

> Our ease, our thrift, our honor, and our day,
> Shall we, for this vaine Bubles shadow pay?
> >   Ends love in this, that my man,
> Can be as happy'as I can; If he can
> Endure the short scorne of a Bridegroomes play?

Such evaporations were not, we may be sure, associated in Donne's mind with those 'Myriades of letters', those many poems, from which, in playful but splendid hyperbole, he suggested to his partner that she should compile their annals, that book where Love's divines should discover all they sought. The evaporations, though often splendidly vital and dramatic, are (to borrow Arnold's useful if over-rigid distinction) poetry conceived in the wits, whereas Donne's serious love-poems are conceived in the soul as well as in the wits.

> *Al cor gentil ripara sempre amore*
> *Com'a la selva augello in la verdura,*
> *Nè fe'amore avanti gentil core*
> *Nè gentil cor avanti amor natura*

wrote Guido Guinizelli, one of the predecessors of Dante: 'Love keeps repairing to the gentle heart as does a bird to the greenness of the wood; nor did Nature make love before gentle heart, nor gentle heart before love'. Guido and his companions would probably have regarded Donne's evaporations as the utterances of what they would have called a *cor vile*, and that, if you persist in taking them seriously, is what they become; but of course they are not to be taken seriously, and are to be regarded as expressions of Donne's wit rather than of his heart, a wit of which an assumed or reactionary heartlessness is one of the essential characterisitics. Donne's serious love-poems, though, are as much the expression of a *cor gentil* as those of Guido or of Dante himself. I have said that we cannot really pretend to know how far Donne was changed by his love for Ann, but that I myself preferred to regard that experience rather as the actualization of potentialities hitherto only occasionally experienced and expressed than as the reformation of a rake, or the restoration of a distempered spirit, or, if you will, as the transformation of a *cor vile* into a *cor gentil*. Guido, who declared that Nature neither made love before gentle heart nor gentle heart before love, would probably have regarded such questions as idle and ignorant, as perhaps they are. The important thing is to recognize, to hear, to overhear, the differences between the evaporations and the more serious poems.

When, in that rather misunderstanding essay to which I have already referred, Mr. C. S. Lewis declares that 'when we have once mastered a poem by Donne there is nothing more to do with it', his remark, though grotesquely untrue of the more serious poems, is, to some extent, true of the evaporations, for these poems contain in themselves no seed or principle of development, nothing that can, as it were, grow up with us or within us. They were written, one cannot but think, partly because Donne liked writing and partly for the astonishment and admiration of young wits and templars. One can imagine them being read aloud in taverns or convivial gatherings. The more serious poems, on the other hand, are far more intimate and far less public. The *Valediction: forbidding mourning*, which, so Izaak Walton tells us, was written for Donne's wife on a particular occasion, is perhaps a limiting case, but most of these poems, I cannot but think, were written in the first place for his own pleasure and perhaps for hers, and then, like Dante's Canzoni, for the initiated, for those *che hanno intelletto d'Amore*, rather than for casual hearers and readers. By which I do not mean to suggest—the evidence of the manuscript collections, if nothing else, is against it—that those who enjoyed the evaporations could not enjoy the more serious poems, or that those who enjoyed the more serious poems could not enjoy the evaporations. One may be sure that such a friend as Sir Henry Wotton enjoyed both, although I think it probable that the man who was to write *You meaner beauties of the night* and to praise the 'Doric delicacy' of the songs in *Comus* was perhaps more discriminating in his admiration than most of Donne's readers, and certainly more discriminating than Huyghens and his Dutch friends, to whom *The Flea* seemed almost miraculous.

A recurring theme in these poems is, as I have said, that of the all-sufficiency of their love, and a recurring image that of themselves as a world in and for themselves.

> Thine age askes ease, and since thy duties bee
> To warme the world, that's done in warming us

we have heard him exclaim, perhaps more wittily than passionately, in *The Sunne Rising*, and in *The Anniversarie*, more deeply ·and tenderly,

> Here upon earth, we'are Kings, and none but wee
> Can be such Kings, nor of such subjects bee.
> Who is so safe as wee? where none can doe
> Treason to us, except one of us two.

And in *The good-morrow* the dramatic and colloquial opening lines lead, quite naturally and without any sense of straining or exaggeration, to a comparison, a suggested, fleeting, insinuated comparison, of her to that Platonic archetype of which all earthly beauties are but dim reflections, and then of her and himself, first to two perfect hemispheres, and then to one simple substance, indestructible because irreducible to anything less primary and elemental than it already is.

> I wonder by my troth, what thou, and I
> Did, till we lov'd? were we not wean'd till then?
> But suck'd on countrey pleasures, childishly?
> Or snorted we in the seaven sleepers[1] den?
> T'was so; But this, all pleasures fancies bee.
> If ever any beauty I did see,
> Which I desir'd, and got, t'was but a dreame of thee.
>
> And now good morrow to our waking soules,
> Which watch not one another out of feare;

[1] Seven noble brothers of Ephesus, who, to escape the persecution of Christians by the Emperor Decius in 251, hid in a cave, whose entrance was blocked up, but where they were said to have slept for nearly 200 years and then to have emerged, still youths, in the reign of the younger Theodosius: see Gibbon, *Decline and Fall*, ed. Bury, III, 412–15.

For love, all love of other sights controules,
And makes one little roome, an every where.
Let sea-discoverers to new worlds have gone,
Let Maps to other, worlds on worlds have showne,
Let us possesse one world, each hath one, and is one.

My face in thine eye, thine in mine appeares,
And true plaine hearts doe in the faces rest,
Where can we finde two better hemispheares
Without sharp North, without declining West?
What ever dyes, was not mixt equally;
If our two loves be one, or, thou and I
Love so alike, that none doe slacken, none can die.

Another recurring theme is that of absence and parting as a death, or
kind of death. The whole of that short and very concentrated poem
The Expiration turns upon it:

So, so, breake off this last lamenting kisse,
　　Which sucks two soules, and vapors Both away,
Turne thou ghost that way, and let mee turne this,
　　And let our selves benight our happiest day,
We ask'd none leave to love; nor will we owe
　　Any, so cheape a death, as saying, Goe;

Goe; and if that word have not quite kil'd thee,
　　Ease mee with death, by bidding mee goe too.
Oh, if it have, let my word worke on mee,
　　And a just office on a murderer doe.
Except it be too late, to kill me so,
　　Being double dead, going, and bidding, goe.

I might almost have reserved this poem until I came to examine
more closely the formal structure of the *Songs and Sonets*, for it
is a particularly good example of the way in which Donne's
close-packed, almost imageless logic can yet be so interpenetrated
with feeling and so poetically alive. There is not a single visual
image, except the merely suggested, generalized, and, as it were,
stylized one of the parting kiss and the turning away, and yet

nothing thereby seems to be lost. Indeed, poem after poem of Donne's is a refutation of the widely held modern view that poetry consists essentially in the arrangement—or should I rather say the collocation?—of visual images. The meaning of Donne's poems lies far more in the interplay between their logical structure and their rhythm and cadences than in their occasional illustrative imagery; it is, as Bradley said in some connection of Shakespeare, a resonant meaning and a meaning resonance. The very next poem in the collection, *The Computation*, is a more playful variation on the same theme. It is also a good example of the way in which Donne will develop the logical implications of a familiar paradox or hyperbole. That time, as a lover experiences it, cannot be measured by the clock, that in moments of happiness hours can seem minutes and that during absence from his mistress days can seem weeks, is an experience which scores of poets and sonneteers had described. Donne, though, treats it in his own characteristic fashion:

> For the first twenty yeares, since yesterday,
>   I scarce beleev'd, thou could'st be gone away,
> For forty more, I fed on favours past,
>   And forty'on hopes, that thou would'st, they might last.
> Tears drown'd one hundred, and sighes blew out two,
>   A thousand, I did neither thinke, nor doe,
>   Or not divide, all being one thought of you;
>   Or in a thousand more, forgot that too.
> Yet call not this long life; But thinke that I
> Am, by being dead, Immortall; Can ghosts die?

It is because these two themes and two images, that of themselves as a world and that of parting and absence as a kind of death, occur together in the third stanza of *A nocturnall upon S. Lucies day* that, as I have said, I find it difficult to suppose that that poem is about the Countess of Bedford, and have suggested that it ought perhaps to be regarded as a kind of anticipatory elegy upon his wife, an attempt to imagine the nothingness of life without her:

>   Oft a flood
>   Have wee two wept, and so
> Drownd the whole world, us two; oft did we grow

To be two Chaosses, when we did show
Care to ought else; and often absences
Withdrew our soules, and made us carcasses.

Because it is in Donne's more serious, more impassioned, more
tender love-poems that these images occur, may one assume that
all the poems in which they occur were inspired by his wife? A
kind of limiting case, perhaps, is *The Legacie*: here, too, occurs
the image of parting as a kind of death, but, although there is real
tenderness in the rhythms and cadences of this poem, there is not
only a more playful, less serious wit than in *The Anniversarie*,
The good-morrow, and the rest, but also, in the last stanza, an
accusation, or half-accusation, of inconstancy—that feminine inconstancy so habitually assumed and so wittily, not to say boisterously,
exploited in the evaporations. In order that the reader may sur-
render himself as completely as possible to the rhythm and tone of
this poem, I will prefix to it a brief analysis of its logical structure.
When I last died (that is to say, when I was last absent from you), I
appointed myself my own executor and legacy. I told myself to
send you my heart, but when I looked for it I could not find it. I
found indeed something like a heart, which I meant to send instead,
but no one could hold it, for it was yours.

The Legacie

When I dyed last, and, Deare, I dye
   As often as from thee I goe,
   Though it be but an houre agoe,
And Lovers houres be full eternity,
I can remember yet, that I
   Something did say, and something did bestow;
Though I be dead, which sent mee, I should be
Mine owne executor and Legacie.

I heard mee say, Tell her anon,
   That my selfe (that is you, not I,)
   Did kill me, and when I felt mee dye,
I bid mee send my heart, when I was gone,

But I alas could there finde none,
  When I had ripp'd me,'and search'd where hearts did lye;
It kill'd mee againe, that I who still was true,
In life, in my last Will should cozen you.

Yet I found something like a heart,
  But colours it, and corners had,
  It was not good, it was not bad,
It was intire to none, and few had part.
As good as could be made by art
  It seem'd; and therefore for our losses sad,
I meant to send this heart in stead of mine,
But oh, no man could hold it, for twas thine.

Must we assume, as I suppose Mrs. Bennett would, that such a poem is not sufficiently serious and impassioned to have been inspired by Donne's love for Ann, and that it was probably inspired by some lesser and earlier love? If we do, if we insist too much on what seems to us its unlikeness, then I think, as I have already indicated, that we shall be allowing our hypothesis (which, after all, however probable, remains an hypothesis) to become too rigid, so that it begins to hinder us rather than help us, and to prevent us from seeing and feeling what it was intended to make us see and feel more clearly. What seems to me important is to recognize that the difference between such a poem as *The Legacie* and the more serious love-poems is one of degree, while the difference between those poems and the evaporations is one of kind. And these differences of degree and of kind are perceptible only, or almost only, in rhythm and cadence. In the opening lines of *The Legacie*,

> When I dyed last, and, Deare, I dye
> As often as from thee I goe

we have essentially the same basic feeling, or combination of thought and feeling, as in the opening lines of *The good-morrow*:

> I wonder by my troth, what thou, and I
> Did, till we lov'd?

or as in the last stanza of *The Anniversarie*:

> Who is so safe as wee? where none can doe
> Treason to us, except one of us two.

The later expression, at any rate, can be felt and regarded as a
natural development of the earlier, just as even the

> Yet I found something like a heart

in the last stanza of *The Legacie* is separated only by difference of
degree, not of kind, from the

> If yet I have not all thy love,
> Deare, I shall never have it all

of *Lovers infiniteness*. Between poems such as *The Legacie* and the
more consistently serious and impassioned ones there are all
manner of gradations and connections; the graver and later poems
may be regarded as intensifications, as further realizations, of what
is present, more or less potentially present, if you like, in the lighter
and earlier. But between the evaporations and the graver love-
poems there are no such gradations and connections. The boisterously assumed cynicism of, for example,

> If thou findst one, let mee know,
>   Such a Pilgrimage were sweet;
> Yet doe not, I would not goe,
>   Though at next doore wee might meet,
> Though shee were true, when you met her,
> And last, till you write your letter,
>   Yet shee
>   Will bee
> False, ere I come, to two, or three

—this is splendid fun, but, as I have said, it is poetry conceived in
the wits, not in the soul, and contains in itself no principle of development; it could not possibly be regarded, as could many things in such
poems as *The Legacie*, as a stage in the progress of that 'admiring'

which inspired *The good-morrow*, *The Anniversarie*, the *Valediction: forbidding mourning*, and which, as Donne said, ultimately whetted his mind to seek God. Even in those twenty poems which I have suggested were inspired by his wife, as well as in others which I have grouped around them, and which I might as well, perhaps, have grouped with them, there are considerable variations in seriousness and intensity and in the predominance and interrelationship of various elements. Nevertheless, while it is impossible to decide just what was the chief inspiration of each of these poems, it is certainly possible, by attending to their rhythms and cadences, to perceive that they differ among themselves only in degree, not in kind; and this fundamental identity among the poems themselves is far more important than the identity of the person to whom they were addressed or by whom they were inspired. Take, as another limiting case, that rather unjustly neglected poem

The broken heart

He is starke mad, who ever sayes,
   That he hath beene in love an houre.
Yet not that love so soone decayes,
   But that it can tenne in lesse space devour;
Who will beleeve mee, if I sweare
That I have had the plague a yeare?
   Who would not laugh at mee, if I should say,
   I saw a flaske of *powder burne a day*?

Ah, what a trifle is a heart,
   If once into loves hands it come!
All other griefes allow a part
   To other griefes, and aske themselves but some;
They come to us, but us Love draws,
Hee swallows us, and never chawes:
   By him, as by chain'd shot, whole rankes doe dye,
   He is the tyran Pike, our hearts the Frye.

If'twere not so, what did become
   Of my heart, when I first saw thee?
I brought a heart into the roome,
   But from the roome, I carried none with mee:

If it had gone to thee, I know
Mine would have taught thine heart to show
  More pitty unto mee: but Love, alas,
  At one first blow did shiver it as glasse.

Yet nothing can to nothing fall,
  Nor any place be empty quite,
Therefore I thinke my breast hath all
  Those peeces still, though they be not unite;
And now as broken glasses show
A hundred lesser faces, so
  My ragges of heart can like, wish, and adore,
  But after one such love, can love no more.

This is obviously much lighter and slighter than *The Anniversarie* or *The good-morrow*, or even than *The Dreame* or *The Sunne Rising:* on the other hand, while it differs from those poems only in degree, it differs in kind from such poems as *The Indifferent*, *Loves Vsury*, *Loves Alchymie*, *Loves Diet*, or even, I should be inclined to say, from such a sheerly witty poem as *The Flea.* For *The broken heart*, though mainly witty, is not merely witty, and contains the seed, the potentiality, of the fuller and graver poems. By all means, if it helps you, assume that all the poems in which there is tenderness as well as wit were inspired by Ann More. Assume, if you like, that such poems as *The Legacie* and *The broken heart* were written in the early stages of their courtship, when that 'admiring' which was to lead Donne so far had only just begun. Even in that temple, as one might have supposed, of pure music, the Mozarteum at Salzburg, I have held in my hand a programme which sought to prepare our minds for, if I remember rightly, the first movement of Mozart's D minor Quartet by suggesting that we should imagine ourselves gazing upon a spacious meadow. I did not myself find this line of approach helpful, and I think that if Mozart himself had been gazing upon anything in particular when inspiration came to him, it was rather more likely to have been a spacious billiard table than a spacious meadow. However, if such associations really help people to get more inside a piece of music I can see no objection to them. Similarly, you may adopt whatever hypothesis you please if it helps you to perceive the fundamental identity underlying and unifying the differences of these love-poems, and if it helps you to respond more completely to their inflexions, cadences, and rhythms. The important thing is to perceive that a fundamental tenderness and seriousness can be combined in all manner of ways and degrees with a certain playfulness and wit. The chief value, I think, of a careful study of the *Songs and Sonets* is to become aware of this great flexibility of thought and feeling, this possibility of the widest gradation, of the utmost subtlety and variety, in the response to a particular kind of experience. It was, as I have already suggested, chiefly of this that Mr. Eliot was thinking when he spoke of a dissociation of sensibility and professed to find much of our later poetry crude and, as it were, one-noted in comparison with the best seventeenth-century verse.

II. The 'Songs and Sonets' as Love-Poetry

I have now, perhaps, sufficiently insisted on the variety of the *Songs and Sonets*, and on the necessity of attending carefully to their rhythms and cadences in order to distinguish between the evaporations and the more serious poems. I hope at least that I have removed any unwillingness the reader may have had to believe, as Mrs. Bennett expresses it, 'that a poet so brilliantly cynical is to be taken seriously when he is reverent or tender'. There remains, though, a further objection to be considered and disposed of: namely, that these poems, however serious they may be, are horribly egotistical and analytical and introspective, and so unlike real love-poems, or what certain of Donne's critics regard as real love-poems, that some special category must be found for them. This objection is closely connected with another objection, sometimes made by the same critics, to that comparative lack of visual imagery of which I spoke incidentally in connection with *The Expiration* and which, both formally and substantially, is one of the most remarkable characteristics of these poems. Dr. Johnson, in his account of the so-called metaphysical poets in his *Life of Cowley*, complained that 'in forming descriptions, they looked out not for images, but for conceits'; and of Cowley himself he wrote: 'One of the great sources of poetical delight is description, or the power of presenting pictures to the mind. Cowley gives inferences instead of images, and shews not what may be supposed to have been seen, but what thoughts

the sight might have suggested.' The last sentence, which occurs
in the course of a severe but not unjust criticism of Cowley's
Davideis, is, as a matter of fact, as concise and accurate a description
of Donne's best poetry as it would be possible to devise. How, for
example—to take one of Donne's most brilliant, if not, perhaps,
one of his most serious poems—how could one better describe the
difference (already noticed by Mrs. Bennett) between Donne's
Nineteenth Elegy, *Going to Bed*, and Carew's *Rapture*, than by saying
that Donne 'shews not what may be supposed to have been seen,
but what thoughts the sight might have suggested'?

> Soft were my numbers; who could take offence
> While pure description held the place of sense?

wrote Pope in the *Epistle to Arbuthnot*, referring to his youthful
Pastorals and *Windsor Forest*. Pope later

> Stooped to truth and moralised his song

but the notion that pure description was one of the chief ingredients
of poetry, and that poetry which lacked it was scarcely poetry at all,
long persisted. Perhaps it was the common repetition and misunderstanding, out of its context, of Horace's *ut pictura poesis* which led
to that commonplace of Renaissance criticism that a poem should
be like a picture, should be, as Sidney said, a speaking picture, and
to the notion that whatever subject could be well treated by a
painter could be equally well treated by a poet, a notion which
Lessing, in his *Laokoon*, was the first critic to oppose. And even
since Lessing there has persisted an obstinate conviction that what
Dr. Johnson called 'the power of presenting pictures to the mind' is
not merely what Johnson was content to call 'one of the great
sources of poetical delight', but the very essence of poetry. An old
lady to whom Pope had been reading Spenser told him that he had
been showing her a gallery of pictures, and, although we have lately
been much rebuked for our inability to find more than this in the
Faerie Queene, Donne has been rebuked for giving us no portrait
gallery of his mistresses, not even a miniature of Ann More.
'Throughout his life,' says Professor Crofts, in that essay to which I
have so often referred,

Throughout his life he was a man self-haunted, unable to escape from his own drama, unable to find any window that would not give him back the image of himself. Even the mistress of his most passionate love-verses, who must (one supposes) have been a real person, remains for him a mere abstraction of sex: a thing given. He cannot see her—does not apparently want to see her; for it is not of her that he writes, but of his relation to her; not of love, but of himself loving.[1]

I must confess that I find most of this passage both astonishing and difficult to comprehend: the implied demand that a love-poet should write of his mistress, as distinct from his relationship to his mistress, and should describe her so that we can see her, and the implied statement that if he writes of himself loving he is not writing of love.

Let us consider first the demand that love-poetry should be descriptive—descriptive not of the poet's emotions, but of their object. This demand has, I suppose, been most completely fulfilled by Spenser in the *Epithalamion:* consider the following stanza:

> Loe where she comes along with portly pace,
> Lyke Phoebe from her chamber of the East,
> Arysing forth to run her mighty race,
> Clad all in white, that seemes a virgin best.
> So well it her beseemes that ye would weene
> Some angell she had beene.
> Her long loose yellow locks lyke golden wyre,
> Sprinckled with perle, and perling flowres a tweene,
> Doe lyke a golden mantle her attyre,
> And being crowned with a girland greene,
> Seeme lyke some mayden Queene.
> Her modest eyes abashed to behold
> So many gazers, as on her do stare,
> Vpon the lowly ground affixed are.
> Ne dare lift vp her countenance too bold,
> But blush to heare her prayses sung so loud,
> So farre from being proud.

[1] *Essays and Studies*, 1936, 133–4.

Nathlesse doe ye still loud her prayses sing,
That all the woods may answer and your eccho ring.

Like Phoebe, like some angel, like some maiden queen; clad all in
white, yellow locks, modest eyes, blushes—you can, of course,
read into the stanza whatever emotions you are able, at any particular
time, to associate with these things, but, if you did not know
already, it would not really tell you any more about what it is like
to be in love than it would tell an imaginative child. Whatever
experiences may have gone into it, the experience that emerges
from it, as distinct from experiences we ourselves may associate
with it, is that of visual beauty, graced by some tremulous shimmer
of Christian and Platonic idealism. This love of visual beauty was
Spenser's deepest and most permanent experience, and, when he
was in love, he associated beautiful things with his mistress and his
mistress with beautiful things. And that is what many, though by
no means all, poets have done: they have told us, or tried to tell us,
what their beloved was like: like an angel, like a maiden queen, like
a red, red rose that's newly sprung in June; but, in so doing, they
have not really told us any more about love than we knew before,
or than a child could imagine. They have simply provided us with
various beautiful images which we may either contemplate with
disinterested aestheticism, or around which we may allow our own
ardours, aspirations, anticipations or recollections to cluster as they
please.

I must admit, as I have said, that I am very puzzled by this
demand that what we should expect from a love-poet is first and
foremost a pictorial, Spenserian description of his mistress, or, at
least, a description of various beautiful things which she is 'like', or
which the poet associates with her. This is not what Donne gives us:
he tells us, not what his mistress is like, but what it is like to be in
love with her, knowing that she loves him in return. Professor
Crofts complains that Donne does not see her, or even, apparently,
want to see her; but—to return to that unintentionally admirable
description of Dr. Johnson's—Donne is interested, not primarily in
what he sees, but in the thoughts and feelings which the sight, the
company, the existence of his beloved inspire in him. I am puzzled,
too, by the criticism that he writes not of love but of himself loving,
for most of the more serious and impassioned poems are about

mutual love, and I cannot understand how the person addressed in such lines as

> I wonder by my troth what thou and I
> Did, till we lov'd?

or

> Who is so safe as we? where none can doe
> Treason to use, except one of us two

or

> T'were prophanation of our joyes
> To tell the layetie our love

can be dismissed as 'a mere abstraction of sex'. What—to take a more generally acceptable love-poet—what, from the *Vita Nuova*, the *Canzoniere* and the *Divine Comedy*, do we chiefly remember of Beatrice, whom Dante, when asked who she was, called 'the source of my song'? Not, I think, pictorial descriptions and visual images, but rather an impression, one might almost say an experience, of all she had come to mean to Dante, as a symbol around which revolved all his aspirations and beliefs about the way in which man might make himself immortal, as a love which, beginning on earth and for earthly beauty, had led him up the mount of Purgatory and through the spheres of Paradise to the love which moves the sun and the other stars. But Donne, although he was later to declare that

> Here the admyring her my mind did whett
> To seeke thee God; so streames do shew their head,

never, in the *Songs and Sonets*, dwells upon what he calls 'abstract spirituall love' as distinct from what may be seen and used. His serious love-poems are neither ideal like Dante's nor unideal like those of the Roman lyrists. Consider *Negative Love*, a serious poem, not an 'evaporation', but written, one may assume, before he had found what he was seeking:

I never stoop'd so low, as they
Which on an eye, cheeke, lip, can prey,
    Seldome to them, which soare no higher
    Then vertue or the minde to'admire,
For sense, and understanding may
    Know, what gives fuell to their fire:
My love, though silly, is more brave,
For may I misse, when ere I crave,
If I know yet, what I would have.

If that be simply perfectest
Which can by no way be exprest
    But *Negatives*, my love is so.
    To All, which all love, I say nc
If any who deciphers best,
    What we know not, our selves, can know,
Let him teach mee that nothing; This
As yet my ease, and comfort is,
Though I speed not, I cannot misse.

What he was seeking was neither merely visible beauty nor merely 'vertue or the minde', but something in which both were somehow inseparably and almost indistinguishably one, and in poems such as *The good-morrow* and *The Anniversarie* he describes, or celebrates, the discovery, the enjoying, the experiencing of what he has been seeking. What, I suppose, puzzled and still puzzles some of Donne's readers and critics is why he should describe this experience, in all its gradations and interrelationships, so subtly and so seriously without ever, apparently, wanting to pass beyond it. They can understand a delighted description of visible beauty such as Spenser's, and they can understand an idealistic and philosophic description of a love which has immeasurably transcended its original object, or immeasurably sublimated and universalized that object, such as Dante's, or to some extent, Petrarch's, but with Donne, apparently, they cannot understand why a love-poetry so rooted in the senses should be so unpictorial, and why a love-poetry so unpictorial and analytic should be so untranscendental and unphilosophic. Here I should almost be inclined to venture the paradox that Donne is doing precisely what Professor Crofts say he is not doing, namely, writing about love, and that this is why some readers have been unable to understand what he is talking about. Spenser writes of love as visible beauty, or as the intensification of visible beauty; Dante writes of the sublimation of human love into the love of wisdom and the love of God; Ovid and some other of the Ancients, Dryden and some of his contemporaries, write of love as a kind of pleasure or as a kind of sport: but Donne writes of the mutual love of a man and a woman not as one pleasure among other pleasures, or as one experience among other experiences, or as an experience that intensifies other experiences, or as a starting point for voyages into unknown modes of being, but as of something complete and sufficient in and for itself.

> She'is all States, and all Princes, I,
> Nothing else is

he wrote in *The Sunne Rising*: the expression is hyperbolical, no doubt, but not, I think, so hyperbolical as one might suppose. For what distinguishes Donne's serious love-poetry is not merely its seriousness but its single-mindedness. 'Nothing else is'. Everything except their love for one another is shadowy and unsubstantial: everything else, one might almost say, exists for him only in so far as it can be related to this, can be made to illustrate this, to throw light upon this. He does not use this experience as a mere starting-point, as a means for investigating and interpreting other experiences: all other experiences, all other universes of discourse, all his ingenious analogies, all his so-called metaphysics, are valuable to him only in so far as they help him to feel and comprehend more clearly and more intensely the essential this-ness of this experience. I do not, as I have so often insisted, care to multiply hypotheses, but, if we may assume that many or most of Donne's serious love poems were written after his marriage, when his prospects had been ruined, and when he, who would seem always to have been as much a spectator as a participator of life, found himself more than ever detached from it, it would be possible to offer some psychological and biographical explanation, or partial explanation, of their peculiarity. *The Canonization* was certainly written after his marriage, for he there speaks of his ruined fortune, and it was his marriage that had ruined it. Let us consider the first and the two last stanzas:

For Godsake hold your tongue, and let me love,
  Or chide my palsie, or my gout,
My five gray haires, or ruin'd fortune flout,
    With wealth your state, your minde with Arts improve,
      Take you a course, get you a place,
      Observe his honour, or his grace,
Or the Kings reall, or his stamped face
  Contemplate, what you will, approve,
  So you will let me love . . .

Wee can dye by it, if not live by love,
  And if unfit for tombes and hearse
Our legend bee, it will be fit for verse;
    And if no peece of Chronicle wee prove,
      We'll build in sonnets pretty roomes;
      As well a well wrought urne becomes
The greatest ashes, as halfe-acre tombes,
  And by these hymnes, all shall approve
  Us *Canoniz'd* for Love:

And thus invoke us; You whom reverend love
  Made one anothers hermitage;
You, to whom love was peace, that now is rage;
    Who did the whole worlds soule contract, and drove
      Into the glasses of your eyes
      (So made such mirrors, and such spies,
That they did all to you epitomize,)
  Countries, Townes, Courts: Beg from above
  A patterne of your love!

These continual assertions that he and she are a world, are *the* world, are an epitome of everything, are not merely hyperbolical. 'Nothing else is': other things only seem to be.

      All other things, to their destruction draw,
        Only our love hath no decay.

Only in and through their mutual love could he, as it were, establish contact with reality, could he endow with meaning a life and a

world both of which had grown more than ever shadowy and
unsubstantial. I do not know whether the reader will agree with
me, but I cannot help associating those two last stanzas of *The
Canonization* with the last lucid words of punished, purged and
pardoned Lear to Cordelia:

> No, no, no, no: come let's away to prison,
> We two alone will sing like Birds i' th' Cage:
> When thou dost aske me blessing, Ile kneele downe
> And aske of thee forgiuenesse: So wee'l liue,
> And pray, and sing, and tell old tales, and laugh
> At gilded Butterflies: and heere poor Rogues
> Talke of Court newes, and wee'l talke with them too,
> Who looses, and who wins; who's in, who's out;
> And take vpon's the mystery of things,
> As if we were Gods spies: And wee'l weare out
> In a wall'd prison, packs and sects of great ones,
> That ebbe and flow by th'Moone.[1]

For Lear, too, nothing else was, princes did but play them, and all
other things to their destruction drew. This—if I may be forgiven
my continual hammering at a point which seems to have eluded so
many readers and critics—this, as regards their content, is what
distinguishes Donne's serious love-poems from almost all others:
this self-enclosedness and self-inclusiveness. Love is not, as in so
many other love-poems, presented against a background of normal
life and activity which it heightens and intensifies: love is life—
or rather, as I feel almost compelled to say, in spite of my warning
against hypotheses—Donne's relationship with his wife, all that
was left to him after the ruin of his fortune, that alone is real,
nothing else is. To this he clings as to a wave-swept rock; this
is his shelter from the storm, his hermitage, his light in darkness—
as much Donne's light in darkness as the light Vaughan celebrated
was for him. Here, although I have so often disagreed with him, I
think that Professor Crofts, at the conclusion of his essay on Donne,
is very near the truth when, after a description of Donne's poetic
technique which I cannot wholly accept, he declares:

---

[1] V, iii, 8–19.

But it is surely not the technique of a philosophical poet. It suggests rather a man who felt that in the last resort the structures of the intellect were useless, and that contact with ultimate reality could be found only in passion: the passion of love, or the passion of faith.

I doubt whether passion is quite the right word, since it suggests rather a series of intense moments than a continuous experience, and it is above all a continuous, though intense, experience that is the subject of Donne's serious love-poems. Also, as I shall try to show later, I think that in Donne's religious poetry there is perhaps more of the drama than of the passion of faith. If, though, Professor Crofts would allow me to re-write his last sentence somewhat as follows, I should entirely agree with him: 'a man to whom in the last resort the structures of the intellect were useless, and for whom contact with ultimate reality could be achieved only in and through some intensely personal, some almost dramatic, experience: the intensely personal drama of his relationship with a woman, or the intensely personal drama of his relationship with God'.

Leaving aside, as being almost beyond the reach of argument, those who demand that a love-poem should be above all pictorial, we may say that the intense personal drama of Donne's love-poetry has seemed incomprehensible to two kinds of critic: to those whom we may call the idealists, because the experience described does not seem to be leading anywhere or pointing to anything beyond itself; and to those whom we may call the materialists, because it all seems to be much ado about nothing. The materialists, it is true, have not often expressed themselves on this subject: indeed, I rather think their first and last spokesman has been Dryden, who, it will be remembered, addressing the Earl of Dorset in his *Discourse concerning the Original and Progress of Satire*, expressed himself as follows:

You equal Donne in the variety, multiplicity, and choice of thoughts; you excel him in the manner and the words. I read you both with the same admiration, but not with the same delight. He affects the metaphysics, not only in his satires, but in his amorous verses, where nature only should reign; and perplexes the minds of the fair sex with nice speculations of philosophy,

when he should engage their hearts, and entertain them with the
softnesses of love.[1]

Dryden, it is clear, could make nothing of Donne's love-poetry.
Love for him, as for many of his contemporaries, was a diversion, a
kind of sport, an entertainment, and it was the business of a love-
poet to be entertaining, and not to take either love or those whom
Dryden calls the fair sex too seriously. By 'nature' and by 'the softnesses of love' he means, I suppose, those

> Gentle Murmurs, sweet Complaining,
>   Sighs that blow the Fire of Love;
> Soft Repulses, kind Disdaining

of which he makes Venus sing in his and Purcell's *King Arthur*.
His notions both of love as entertainment and of the fair sex may be
gathered from a rapid reading of the collected songs from his plays.
There is often a smirk in them and sometimes a leer, and many of
them suggest an hilarious and slightly tipsy chorus of men of wit
and pleasure singing in unison. Take, as an example, this from
Troilus and Cressida:

> Can Life be a Blessing,
>   Or worth the possessing,
> Can Life be a blessing if Love were away?
>   Ah no! though our Love all Night keep us waking,
> And though he torment us with Cares all the Day,
>   Yet he sweetens, he sweetens our Pains in the taking,
> There's an Hour at the last, there's an Hour to repay.

> 2

> In ev'ry possessing
>   The ravishing Blessing,
> In ev'ry possessing the Fruit of our Pain,
>   Poor Lovers forget long Ages of Anguish,
> What e're they have suffer'd and done to obtain;
>   'Tis a Pleasure, a Pleasure to sigh and to languish,
> When we hope, when we hope to be happy again.

[1] *Essays*, ed. Ker, II, 19.

Dryden's love-poetry is at least always entertaining, and was presumably found so by those of the fair sex who attended his plays.
In these songs, though, he seems to be more concerned with entertaining than with what he calls 'engaging the heart', and he was
probably not so stupid as to overlook the fact that most of Donne's
love-poems were addressed, or, what amounts to the same thing,
had the appearance of being addressed, to a particular woman, and
that such poems should be essentially more intimate in tone than
songs intended for the stage. But even so, he cannot for the life of
him understand what Donne is doing. Donne, he seems to assume,
is courting a mistress, trying to engage her heart, but, instead of
gently murmuring and softly complaining, he keeps a dreadful
pudder o'er her head about angels and hemispheres and simple
substances, perplexing her with what Dryden calls metaphysics.
The fact is, of course, that in these poems Donne is not courting a
mistress, but is trying to make clear both to himself and to a kind
of wife-mistress or mistress-wife precisely what their relationship
means to him; and, as I have insisted, it means everything to him:
it alone is completely real, in comparison with it 'nothing else is'.
'It is not of her that he writes, but of his relation to her', complains
Professor Crofts—a complaint which, in view of the fact that Donne
declares over and over again that his relationship to her means
everything to him, seems to me incomprehensible, implying, as it
does, a charge of egotism, self-centredness, and what Professor
Crofts calls 'self-hauntedness'. Is the hypothesis that these poems
were inspired by his wife after all indispensable? Will that hypothesis alone prevent readers from deploring with Professor Crofts
Donne's silence about things he can take for granted? For in these
poems Donne is not courting a woman, or professing his affection
for her, or trying to establish a relationship with her; he is writing
about a relationship already established. He does not need to assure
her of his love, for he knows that she is as sure of that as he is of
hers; what he is trying to do is to make the nature and meaning of
this love, of this relationship, clearer both to her and to himself.
Has even Professor Crofts tended, to some extent, to assume, with
Dryden, that these are poems of courtship, and is he complaining
that they are not what one might have expected such poems to be?
For that, I am sure, is how Dryden is looking at the matter: here,
he says in effect, is a poet trying to engage the heart of a woman,

and what does he do? Why, instead of telling her how he is raging, melting and burning for the blessing of possessing her, he perplexes her with philosophical speculations. Dr. Johnson, too, in a generalization which lumps together Donne's serious love-poems with Cowley's superficial imitations of them in *The Mistress*, said of those whom he called the metaphysical poets that 'their courtship was void of fondness', betraying thereby, it is true, an unresponsiveness, in which he has had many successors, to Donne's rhythms and inflections, but assuming, apparently, with Dryden, that Donne's love-poems, like other love-poems, were essentially poems of courtship, and that as such, as expressions of what he called 'fondness', they were to be judged. Even had the true nature of Donne's poems been pointed out to him, he would still, one may be fairly certain, have refused to admire them, or even to sympathize with them. Such isolation, such a detachment from all the ordinary concerns of life, as left a man able to feel reality, to feel that he was completely alive, only in and through his relationship with his wife, would have seemed to Johnson something not far removed from insanity. One remembers that passage in the Preface to his edition of Shakespeare where he speaks so contemptuously of the universal agency of love in the plays of other dramatists and of the 'hyperbolical joy and outrageous sorrow' with which they fill the mouths of their characters—a passage leading to the conclusion that

> love is only one of many passions; and as it has no great influence upon the sum of life, it has little operation in the dramas of a poet, who caught his ideas from the living world, and exhibited only what he saw before him. He knew, that any other passion, as it was regular or exorbitant, was a cause of happiness or calamity.

To a critic who believed that love had not, or ought not to have, any 'great influence upon the sum of life', Donne's love-poems, even had he been able to see them for what they really were, could not have seemed other than morbid and extravagant. And so, together with the life out of which they were written, in a sense they are. But only in the sense in which many of the supreme achievements in art and thought, when measured by the criterion of an imaginable but unattainable ideal of completeness, seem in various ways unbalanced, one-sided, extravagant or extreme. For the choice before finite man is more often between extremism and mediocrity than between extremism and completeness. And that, I think, is what Aristotle had in mind when he profoundly observed that although virtue or excellence, if we regarded its essence and its definition, was a mean between two extremes, it was also, if we regarded it in relation to the best and the highest, itself an extreme. Indeed, it is perhaps an awareness and a dislike of this undeniable element of extravagance and extremism in Donne and in his poetry—an extremism which, unlike that of Blake, shall we say, or Shelley, or Hölderlin, does not appear as a sacrifice of the actual to the ideal, of the finite to the infinite, but rather—although Donne later declared that it was this 'admiring' that whetted his mind to seek for God—as an attempt to achieve completeness within incompleteness, as a renunciation of the world, not in favour of other-worldliness, but in favour of a kind of private world where 'nothing else is'—it is perhaps an awareness of this element of extremism, of untranscendental extremism, which is at the bottom of that occasionally nagging dissatisfaction that pervades Professor Crofts's essay. But I must return from this digression, which is leading us into rather deep waters, to my remark that Dr. Johnson, like Dryden, seems to have supposed that Donne's love-poems were poems of courtship. Even Mr. Lewis, whom one scarcely expects to find in agreement with Dryden, seems to have made the same mistake, for he wrote of The Extasie: 'What any sensible woman would make of such a wooing it is difficult to imagine'. His challenge was accepted by Mrs. Joan Bennett, who, presenting herself in the role of a sensible woman, replied, very sensibly as I think, that Donne's serious love-poems were not about love-making but about being in love, the state, or rather states, of which he dramatizes and analyses and illustrates by a wealth of analogy.

It is possible that into my criticisms of the objections of Dryden and of Dr. Johnson to Donne's love-poetry there may have stolen some appearance of injustice, or even of animosity, towards those two great writers, and I will admit that it is not entirely fair to represent Dryden's love-poetry merely by that song I quoted from Troilus and Cressida. The fact remains, though, that you cannot really see what a thing is until you have also seen what it is not, and that the confrontation of some more typically English writers with that 'super-subtle Venetian' the younger Donne does often rather sharply reveal the presence of a certain half-exasperatingly, half-endearingly *bovine* quality in the English mind—a certain lack of subtlety, a tendency to pervert distinctions into antitheses, an incapacity to reconcile or, at any rate, to accept contradictions—in a word, a lack of that 'negative capability' which Keats praised in Shakespeare. If in recent times there has been a tendency to overpraise the poetry of Donne and of some of his contemporaries at the expense of Milton's, there has also been a tendency to overpraise Johnson's literary criticism, once so unjustly neglected, and perhaps to insist overmuch, and with overmuch satisfaction, upon Johnson's tremendous Englishness. In literary criticism—if not always in life, where a certain pragmatic insistence upon those qualities which seem to have most 'survival value' is perhaps indispensable—in literary criticism we should try to keep continually before our minds some ideal of totality, of perfection, and try to make ourselves no less habitually aware of the limitations than of the virtues in those writers we most admire. And the great means to this end is the continual exercise of analysis and comparison. The literary critic should resist invitations to become 'committed' or 'engaged', to emulate the pulpit or the platform, and should try rather to retain and to exercise something of the disinterested curiosity and freedom of the dramatist—often, perhaps, if he can, of the great comic dramatist, and, while admiring wholeheartedly all that is most admirable in, let us say, Wordsworth, should be very willing to imagine a dialogue between Wordsworth and Goethe, in whom Wordsworth could see no more than a 'heartless sensualist'. In the end such a disinterested and detached procedure may have as much to contribute to morality, or even to religion, as more impatiently didactic methods: for by steadily contemplating, on the one hand, an ideal of totality, of perfection, and, on the other hand, the impossibility of achieving it, we shall become, perhaps, not less human, but less 'humanist'.

We have now, I think, sufficiently considered various objections to Donne's serious love-poems and various misunderstandings of them; and perhaps in attempting to show what they are not I may have helped the reader to see more clearly what they are. They are not pictorial, like Spenser's *Epithalamion*; they are not sensual and heartless, like Ovid and Dryden, but neither, on the other hand, are they ideal and transcendental like Dante and Petrarch. They are not poems of courtship, but are addressed to a woman whom Donne has already courted and won. They are not about her as an individual nor (in spite of Professor Crofts's complaint about self-hauntedness) are they about Donne as an individual: they are about the oneness of two persons, or about two persons who have become one, about what this oneness feels like, how it has been achieved, how it may be preserved. And Donne's preoccupation with this oneness, with this whole greater than the sum of its parts, with this new world which he and she have created, was probably, as I have suggested, intensified by the fact that, after the ruin of his fortune and his prospects, it was, in a sense, the only world left to him.

> His desolation had begun to make
> A better life.

Sir Thomas Browne wrote in his *Religio Medici*: 'The world that I regard is my self; it is the Microcosm of my own frame that I cast mine eye on; for the other (he means the Macrocosm, the great world), I use it but like my Globe, and turn it round sometimes for my recreation.' Similarly, the world which Donne regards in these poems is the microcosm which they two have created. Visual or pictorial imagery could scarcely have helped him to make clearer to himself and others the nature of this world, this oneness, this relationship. What was it like? Not like a red, red rose, or Phoebe, or a virgin queen—no, but like two hemispheres, like a hermitage, like some primal and undecomposable substance: like something that could be thought or felt, but not, with some few rare exceptions, like anything that could be seen.

Professor Crofts has complained that the subject of these verses is a mere abstraction of sex. The real subject, as I have said, is not a person, but a relationship between two persons, and only in the sense that a relationship is in some sort an abstract thing and can only be made an object of contemplation by means of an act of abstract thought—only in this sense can either the subject of Donne's poems or the poems themselves be called abstract. Nevertheless, in his attempts to express that obscure dissatisfaction which he has not sufficiently analysed, Professor Crofts is continually stumbling against the truth. Donne is being somehow abstract, Donne is writing about his relationship with a woman rather than about a woman, Donne is writing about sex—all this is perfectly true, but (just why I cannot pretend to know) it so repels Professor Crofts that he cannot bring himself to look at it steadily.

To say that the subject of these poems is a mere abstraction of sex is a confused telescoping of two facts—namely, that Donne is writing about his relationship with a woman rather than about a woman, and that in trying to describe and analyse this relationship he is often writing about that abstraction which we call sex. Which we call sex. For if the Oxford Dictionary is correct, and there is every reason to suppose that it is, Donne was the first writer to use the word in this modern sense. Earlier writers had spoken of the male sex and the female sex, of the sex of animals and plants, and, deferentially, jocularly or poetically, of the fair sex, the weaker sex, and even of the sex, but no writer before Donne had used the word in the much more abstract and complex sense of the physiological differences between men and women and their various implications, physiological and psychological. In *The Relique*, one of those later, those courtly, Platonic and Petrarchan poems, which, as I have suggested, were perhaps written for Mrs. Herbert, he declared:

> Difference of sex no more wee knew,
> Then our Guardian Angells doe.

Even that, for its time, is rather remarkable, and indicates, like the

> And forget the Hee and Shee

of that other Platonic poem *The undertaking*, a very considerable progress in abstraction and reflection. But in yet another of these courtly, Platonic or Petrarchan poems, in *The Primrose*, Donne uses the word sex, in a passage quoted by the Oxford Dictionary as its earliest example of this use of the word, in a sense in which it had never, probably, been used before:

> should she
> Be more then woman, shee would get above
> All thought of sexe, and thinke to move
> My heart to study her, and not to love.

Donne had already used the word in this sense in a more serious, and, as I think, earlier poem, contemporary with *The Anniversarie* and its companions—in *The Extasie*, the longest of the *Songs and Sonets* and the most analytic, conceptual, and, in a sense, philosophic of Donne's love-poems: his most elaborate attempt to describe that something that was neither merely visible beauty nor merely 'vertue or the minde', which he had declared in *Negative Love* that he was searching for, and which he had now found:[1]

> This Extasie doth unperplex
>   (We said) and tell us what we love,
> We see by this, it was not sexe,
> We see, we saw not what did move.

I have said that the word *sex* as Donne here uses it is both more complex and more abstract than it had ever been before. And Donne did not reach this conception merely through immediate experience, but as the result of a process of abstraction, as the result of a careful analysis of the elements in immediate experience. Donne, in fact, has differentiated, distinguished and interpenetrated with thought a whole area of experience which had hitherto remained undifferentiated and unexplored.

III. *Logical Structure in the 'Songs and Sonets'*

I will conclude what I have to say about the *Songs and Sonets* with a more detailed examination of some of their more purely formal characteristics. I need scarcely say anything more about the colloquial vigour of their diction and their rejection of traditional ornaments, but I will ask the reader to attend rather more closely to something which I have often incidentally mentioned—namely, to that untransposability of lines and stanzas which is the chief formal characteristic of so much of the best seventeenth-century poetry, and of which I remarked that, while Ben Jonson achieved it by imitating something of the methods of Roman lyric, Donne achieved it by applying to poetry something of the formal and syllogistic logic of theological argument and academic debate.

[1] From which the reader may rightly conclude that I do not agree with Professor Pierre Legouis in regarding *The Extasie* as a kind of solemn and elaborate joke, a dramatic lyric in which Donne has chosen to represent himself as a hypocritically philosophical Don Juan: *Donne the Craftsman*, 61 ff.

There is scarcely one of Donne's poems of which a clear prose analysis could not be given; in almost every one of them there is some kind of argument, an argument which is sometimes conducted in almost rigidly syllogistic form. These arguments, as we have seen, are sometimes deliberately outrageous and paradoxical, sometimes merely ingenious, sometimes playful, sometimes mainly or wholly serious. And these different kinds of argument are combined in all manner of ways with different kinds and gradations of feeling, the feeling being mainly perceptible in and through the rhythms and inflections of the verse, in the interaction between these and the logical structure. We may, if we like, thinking of the medieval Schoolmen with whose writings and methods he was so familiar, call this logical argumentation the medieval element in Donne's poetry, and we may also, if we like, call the intensely individual defiances and floutings, experiences and sensations, to which he applies this logic, the Renaissance element. We must remember, though, that such neat antitheses often appear to tell us a great deal more than they really do. Although it is probably true to say that Donne's best poems are ultimately concerned with sensations rather than with thoughts, it is equally true that, although these poems cannot be properly understood until they have been felt, they cannot be properly felt until they have been understood. Many readers to-day prefer a poetry which they can never completely understand, feeling, as they do, that what can be completely understood has been, as it were, exhausted; and it was partly for this reason, and partly as a reaction against rhetoric and clichés and what Yeats called the world of the newspapers, that Mallarmé and the Symbolists rejected logic and meaning and argument as impurities, and tried to make poetry approximate to the condition of music. In Donne's best poetry there is always a balance of elements: an intellectual or logical structure which could be clearly and completely conveyed by a prose analysis, and a content or substance of experience, passion, feeling, sensibility, or whatever we prefer to call it, which could not be so conveyed, and which is perceptible only in and through rhythm and cadence. Perhaps between Mallarmé or some other Symbolist at his most meaningless, or most speechless, and Donne at his most merely ingenious there may not be much to choose. But what of the difference between *The Anniversarie*, or *A nocturnall upon S*. Lucies *day*, or *A Valediction: forbidding mourning*, or *The Extasie* and, let us say, Mallarmé's *L'Après-midi d'un Faune*, or Valéry's *La Jeune Parque*, poems of which almost no two interpretations agree and several have almost nothing in common? Is the intelligibility of Donne's poems an advantage or a disadvantage? Is their argumentative logic, their analysability into prose, an impurity and a defect? Has their undeniable shapeliness and continuity been too dearly bought? Do we prefer the fleeting and tantalizing glimpses afforded by what has been called 'pure poetry'? How much poetry is compatible with logic, or how much logic is compatible with the highest poetical pleasure? These, like that of the importance or unimportance of visual imagery, are some of the many interesting questions about poetry in general which are raised by a careful and comparative study of Donne's. Leaving the reader to answer them for himself, I will proceed to an examination of what I have called the more formal elements of the *Songs and Sonets*. Let us, to begin with, turn once again to

The Dreame

Deare love, for nothing lesse then thee
Would I have broke this happy dreame,
    It was a theame
For reason, much too strong for phantasie,
Therefore thou wakd'st me wisely; yet
My Dreame thou brok'st not, but continued'st it,
Thou art so truth, that thoughts of thee suffice,
To make dreames truths; and fables histories;
Enter these armes, for since thou thoughtst it best,
Not to dreame all my dreame, let's act the rest.

As lightning, or a Tapers light,
Thine eyes, and not thy noise wak'd mee;
    Yet I thought thee
(For thou lovest truth) an Angell, at first sight,
But when I saw thou sawest my heart,
And knew'st my thoughts, beyond an Angels art,
When thou knew'st what I dreamt, when thou knew'st when
Excesse of joy would wake me, and cam'st then,
I must confesse, it could not chuse but bee
Prophane, to thinke thee any thing but thee.

Comming and staying show'd thee, thee,
But rising makes me doubt, that now,
      Thou art not thou.
That love is weake, where feare's as strong as hee;
'Tis not all spirit, pure, and brave,
If mixture it of *Feare, Shame, Honor*, have.
Perchance as torches which must ready bee,
Men light and put out, so thou deal'st with mee,
Thou cam'st to kindle, goest to come; Then I
Will dreame that hope againe, but else would die.

In a sense, this is a very abstract and intellectual poem, and yet I think it will be agreed that the *effect* of it is anything but abstract in the pejorative sense. It is an absolutely consecutive and continuous piece of argument from the first line to the last, and each simile, whether phenomenal (lightning, taper, torches) or intellectual (angels, simple and compound substances) is almost inseparable from the thought it illustrates and expresses. The pictorial element, if present at all, is at a minimum: what is described is not a sight, but (to borrow those depreciating words of Dr. Johnson's about Cowley's *Davideis*, which, as I have said, contain such an admirably, though unconsciously, accurate account of Donne's poetry at its best) such thoughts, and, one must add, such feelings, as the sight might be supposed to have suggested. The diction is precise and almost scientific, and the words are completely uncharged with associations not strictly relevant. In comparison with the typical Elizabethan or the typical Romantic lyric the poem might be called abstract and intellectual, but, as I have said, its effect is anything but abstract in the pejorative sense. There is as much of drama, imagination, feeling, sensation, experience (whether actual or imaginary is no matter) as of intellect and logic, and this sensational or experiential element is conveyed, not by a choice of words rich in association, but by speech-rhythm, inflexion, cadence. Every line, in fact, is intensely alive. Observe how, in the following passage, there is not one superfluous word, how every word demands precisely the right emphasis, and how even such words as 'beyond', 'what', 'when', 'then', contribute an almost measurable quantity of energy towards the total effect:

But when I saw thou sawest my heart,
And knew'st my thoughts, *beyond* an Angels art,
When thou knew'st *what* I dreamt, when thou knew'st *when*
Excesse of joy would wake me, and cam'st *then*,
I must confesse, it could not chuse but bee
Prophane, to thinke thee *any* thing but thee.

We are confined, though, to the particular experience, the particular
bit of personal drama, which Donne is describing; we do not feel
that it is in any way symbolic of something else, or that it melts and
merges into something else, as we so often do when reading Romantic poetry, or, for that matter, Shakespeare's Sonnets. I have already,
while examining Donne's love-poetry with attention rather to its
substance than to its form, insisted upon a certain enclosedness and
inclusiveness, as one of its most remarkable characteristics: this,
though, is no less characteristic of its manner than of its matter, the
two things being indeed, as in all good poetry, ultimately inseparable. It is also one of the most remarkable characteristics of the best
poetry of other so-called metaphysical poets: not only is the language strictly denotative—the subject, the experience, is also precise,
defined and delimited. The difference between Donne's religious
poetry and Herbert's, as the expressions of two different kinds of
religious experience, has often been insisted upon, and is, indeed
very obvious, but the resemblances between Donne's serious
love-poetry and Herbert's religious poetry, as what may be
called dialectical expressions of personal drama, have too often
been overlooked. We have already, with attention directed chiefly
upon their dramatic qualities, compared Donne's *The Apparition*
with Herbert's *The Collar*: let us now, with an eye to more
detailed resemblances, compare Donne's *The Dreame* with Herbert's
Dialogue:

> Sweetest Saviour, if my soul
>   Were but worth the having,
> Quickly should I then controll
>   Any thought of waving.
> But when all my care and pains
> Cannot give the name of gains
> To thy wretch so full of stains,
> What delight or hope remains?

What, Child, is the ballance thine,
  Thine the poise and measure?
If I say, Thou shalt be mine;
  Finger not my treasure.
What the gains in having thee
Do amount to, onely he,
Who for man was sold, can see;
That transferr'd th'accounts to me.

But as I can see no merit,
  Leading to this favour:
So the way to fit me for it
  Is beyond my savour.
As the reason then is thine;
So the way is none of mine:
I disclaim the whole designe:
Sinne disclaims and I resigne.

That is all, if that I could
  Get without repining;
And my clay, my creature, would
  Follow my resigning:
That as I did freely part
With my glorie and desert,
Left all joyes to feel all smart— —
  Ah! no more: thou break'st my heart.

The resemblances between this poem of Herbert's and Donne's *The Dreame*, in style and expression though not in substance, are very striking. First, like Donne's poem, Herbert's is a continuous argument, or argument and counter-argument, from the first line to the last, although Herbert's arguments are not ingenious and scholastic like Donne's, and are not illustrated and supported by ingenious analogies. Secondly, as in Donne's poem, the language is precise, strictly denotative, uncharged with romantic associations, and the subject, the experience, is strictly delimited and particular. Thirdly, Herbert's poem is, in a sense, even more abstract than Donne's: not only is there no decoration or ornament, there is not a single visual image, and the only metaphors, very subordinate

ones, are those of the balance and the transferred accounts in the
second stanza. Finally, in spite of so much plainness, in spite of the
rejection of so many of what had been and have been regarded as
indispensable constituents of poetry, in spite of this limitation to
what one might almost call bare argument, the effect of Herbert's
poem, as of Donne's, is anything but bare or bleak or abstract. It
is, on the contrary, intensely dramatic, and this excitingly dramatic
effect is produced, as in Donne's poem, by an exquisite interaction
between logical structure and speech-rhythm, every word receiving
precisely the right emphasis and performing the maximum amount
of work, every word being, as Herbert himself said of the true
country parson's sermon, 'heart-deep'. In such poetry 'all the
charm of all the Muses' can flower in the humblest monosyllables:

> What, Child, is the ballance *thine*,
> > *Thine* the poise and measure?
> If I say, Thou *shalt* be mine;
> > Finger not my treasure.
> *What* the gains in having *thee*
> Do amount to, onely *hc*,
> Who for man was sold, can see;
> That transferr'd th'accounts to me.

How very similar, as a poetic method, as a way of saying something
in metre, how very similar this is—if one may say so without
irreverence—to Donne's method and manner in *The Dreame:*

> But when I saw thou sawest my heart,
> And knew'st my thoughts, *beyond* an Angels art,
> When thou knew'st *what* I dreamt, when thou knew'st *when*
> Excesse of joy would wake me, and cam'st *then*,
> I must confesse, it would not chuse but bee
> Prophane, to thinke thee *any* thing but thee.

It is in this dialectical expression of personal drama that Herbert,
like Donne, excels; and, in trying to describe and analyse what
seems to me most characteristic in these two poems, I have also
described what seem to me the most important stylistic qualities
which Donne, Herbert and some other seventeenth-century poets

have in common, which distinguish them from the poets of the School of Jonson, and which justify us, to some extent, at any rate, in speaking of a School of Donne or of a Dialectical School.

The strictly delimited subject and the strictly denotative style of such a poem as *The Dreame* differs entirely from the substance and style of Shakespeare's Sonnets, where the language is deeply coloured and charged with all manner of associations, so that it sets up nfinite vibrations, 'awakening all the cells where memory slept'.

> O how shall summers hunny breath hold out
> Against the wrackfull siedge of battering dayes
> When rocks impregnable are not so stoute,
> Nor gates of steele so strong but time decayes?

This, like so much else in Shakespeare's Sonnets, is not really pictorial, although here as elsewhere there is a suggestion of some vast allegory, some unsubstantial pageant, unrolling itself on this huge stage on which the stars in secret influence comment. But although Shakespeare's language is not predominantly pictorial, it is much less precisely denotative, much more highly charged with complex associations, than Donne's, and Shakespeare's Sonnets are much less seif-enclosed than Donne's Songs. And I should not be disposed to quarrel with anyone who should insist that they are much more inexhaustible. You can classify Shakespeare's Sonnets to some extent, but it would be rather absurd to attempt detailed prose analyses of them. In a sense, they are really all variations on the same great theme, that of Mutability and Time, destroyers of youth and beauty and glory, and of everything except, perhaps, of love. That same unsubstantial pageant is for ever fading and re-forming: Beauty is pleading with action no stronger than a flower, or stealing away as imperceptibly as a dial-hand from its figure; Time is transfixing the flourish set on youth, the once-foiled famous victor is being razed from the book of honour, captive Good is attending Captain Ill. *Ibant obscuri*. What we have are not so much points and arguments and demonstrations as broodings and meditations, *suspiria de profundis, lacrimae rerum*. But Donne's poems are nearly always argumentative rather than meditative, and he confines himself to the development and illustration of some very definite point, however tender or impassioned or excited his argument may be.

This does not mean that we always or chiefly remember Donne's poems as arguments; neither, although the logical structure is always there, is it always equally apparent, or, as it were, obtrusive. The logical structure of *The Anniversarie* might be briefly exhibited as follows:

(1) Everything passes and decays except our love.
(2) Even after death it will be increased rather than diminished.
(3) But whereas then we shall be no more blest than the other spirits, here on earth we are kings.

When one tries to recall this poem one tends, as with some other of the *Songs and Sonets*, to forget the argument, the logical structure, and to remember only the superb dramatic expression:

> All other things, to their destruction draw,
>   Only our love hath no decay;
> This, no to morrow hath, nor yesterday,
> Running it never runs from us away,
> But truly keepes his first, last, everlasting day.

In this poem the argumentative structure, the logical skeleton, is comparatively unobtrusive. On the other hand, in *A Valediction: forbidding mourning* the argument is closer and less general and far more essentially and inseparably blended with the substance of the poem. The poem is also a good example of one of Donne's favourite methods or formulas—that of a proposition supported by arguments from analogy. In the first three stanzas the proposition, let our parting be peaceful, is stated, and amplified by two similes or analogies: let it be as peaceful as the deaths of virtuous men and as inconspicuous as the supposed trepidation, or oscillation, of the crystalline sphere. Then an argument is advanced in support of this proposition: our love is independent of the senses, and cannot therefore be affected by absence; and this argument is illustrated by two analogies: our two-fold soul will not be broken by absence, but merely expanded by it, like gold beaten into leaf; or, if we have two souls, they are like the two legs of a compass.

> As virtuous men passe mildly away,
>   And whisper to their soules, to goe,

Whilst some of their sad friends doe say,
   The breath goes now, and some say, no:

So let us melt, and make no noise,
   No teare-floods, nor sigh-tempests, move,
T'were prophanation of our joyes
   To tell the layetie our love.[1]

Moving[2] of th'earth brings harmes and feares,
   Men reckon what it did and meant,
But trepidation of the spheares,[3]
   Though greater farre, is innocent.

Dull sublunary lovers love
   (Whose soule is sense) cannot admit
Absence, because it doth remove
   Those things which elemented it.

But we by a love, so much refin'd,
   That our selves know not what it is,
Inter-assured of the mind,
   Care lesse, eyes, lips, and hands to misse.

Our two soules therefore, which are one,
   Though I must goe, endure not yet
A breach, but an expansion,
   Like gold to ayery thinnesse beate.

If they be two, they are two so
   As stiffe twin compasses are two,
Thy soule the fixt foot, makes no show
   To move, but doth, if the'other doe.

And though it in the center sit,
   Yet when the other far doth rome,
It leanes, and hearkens after it,
   And grows erect, as that comes home.

[1] Despite Walton's testimony, some may find it hard to believe that Donne could have thus addressed the woman to whom he had been for many years publicly married.

[2] Quaking.

[3] The notion of a trepidation, or oscillation, of the ninth, the crystalline, sphere was introduced by an Arab into the Ptolemaic astronomy in order to account for certain phenomena really due to the motion of the earth's axis.

Such wilt thou be to mee, who must
Like th'other foot, obliquely runne;
They firmnes makes my circle just,
And makes me end, where I begunne.

The poem, in fact, is both a close and continuous argument, and,
at the same time, continuously poetical; and although, by means
of a prose analysis, you can separate the argument from the poetry,
you cannot separate the poetry from the argument, as you can, to
some extent, in *The Anniversarie*. In a sense, it is an abstract poem
about abstract ideas. The only visual image is that of the compass,
which is really a geometrical image, and although, as it were,
accidentally visual, as essentially conceptual as the famous one in
Marvell's *Definition of Love*:

As Lines so Loves *oblique* may well
Themselves in every Angle greet:
But our so truly *Paralel*,
Though infinite can never meet.

That compass image, as Professor Wilson has recently pointed out,
had already been used by Joseph Hall in his *Epistles*, which were
printed three years before Donne wrote his poem, and it would not
have appeared to their contemporaries either so striking or so ingenious as it does to us.[1] Nevertheless, in spite of the closeness of the
argument, the abstractness of the ideas, the absence of visual imagery,
and the strictly denotative use of words, the effect of the poem is
no more abstract in the pejorative sense than that of *The Dreame*.

In *A Valediction: forbidding mourning* argument, logical structure,
and what we may roughly call substance are really inseparable. But
while, on the one hand, in such a poem as *The Anniversarie* the

---

[1] *Elizabethan and Jacobean*, p. 30. Mario Praz (*Secentismo e Marinismo in Inghilterra*,
1925, 109, note) had already noticed that the same image had been used by Guarini in
madrigal xcvi (*Rime*, Venice, 1958), a departing lover's reply to the preceding madrigal,
in which his mistress had expressed the fear that during his travels he might forsake
her: 'I am ever with you, moved about but fixed; and if I steal from you the lesser I
leave you the greater. I am like the compass in that I fix one foot in you as in my
centre, while the other suffers all the turns of fortune, but cannot do other than turn
around yourself.' Since the contexts are identical, it is difficult not to suppose that
Donne had this well-known madrigal in mind. A free verse translation of it appeared
in *Wits Recreations*, 1641 (Hotten reprint, p. 315) and *Westminster Drollery* (1st part),
1671, and is ascribed in several MSS to Carew (*Poems*, ed. Dunlap, p. 131).

substance is to some extent independent of the logical structure, or
at least, rememberable apart from it, there are several poems, more
witty than impassioned, where structure and pattern are almost
everything, and where the experiential or emotive content is
almost negligible. One of the most elaborate of such poems is *The
Will*, where the logical pattern of each stanza is as rigidly prescribed
in advance as the verse-pattern itself. Each stanza, in fact, is a compressed syllogism, the conclusion and the minor premiss being
combined or telescoped and stated first, and the major premiss
being reserved, as a kind of surprise, until the end.

> Before I sigh my last gaspe, let me breath,
> Great love, some Legacies; Here I bequeath
> Mine eyes to *Argus*, if mine eyes can see,
> If they be blinde, then Love, I give them thee;
> My tongue to Fame; to'Embassadours mine eares;
>   To women or the sea, my teares.
> Thou, Love, hast taught mee heretofore
> By making mee serve her who'had twenty more,
> That I should give to none, but such, as had too much before.

If the argument here were reduced to strict syllogistic form, it
would run as follows:

Major Premiss: Gifts should be given only to those who have too
                much of the gift already.
Minor Premiss: Argus has too many eyes.
Conclusion: Therefore I give my eyes to Argus.

Donne continues:

> My constancie I to the planets give;
> My truth to them, who at the Court doe live;
> Mine ingenuity and opennesse,
> To Jesuites; to Buffones my pensivenesse;
> My silence to'any, who abroad hath beene;
>   My money to a Capuchin.
> Thou Love taught'st me, by appointing mee
> To love there, where no love receiv'd can be,
> Onely to give to such as have an incapacitie.

My faith I give to Roman Catholiques;
All my good works unto the Schismaticks
Of Amsterdam; my best civility
And Courtship, to an Universitie;
My modesty I give to souldiers bare;
   My patience let gamesters share.
Thou Love taughtst mee, by making mee
  Love her that holds my love disparity,
Onely to give to those that count my gifts indignity.

I give my reputation to those
Which were my friends; Mine industrie to foes;
To Schoolemen I bequeath my doubtfulness;
My sicknesse to Physitians, or excesse;
To Nature, all that I in Ryme have writ;
   And to my company my wit.
Thou Love, by making mee adore
  Her, who begot this love in mee before,
Taughtst me to make, as though I gave, when I did but restore.

To him for whom the passing bell next tolls,
I give my physick bookes; my writen rowles
Of Morall counsels, I to Bedlam give;
My brazen medals, unto them which live
In want of bread; To them which passe among
   All forrainers, mine English tongue.
Thou, Love, by making mee love one
  Who thinkes her friendship a fit portion
For yonger lovers, dost my gifts thus disproportion.

Therefore I'll give no more; But I'll undoe
The world by dying; because love dies too.
Then all your beauties will bee no more worth
Then gold in Mines, where none doth draw it forth;
And all your graces no more use shall have
   Then a Sun dyall in a grave.

Thou Love taughtst mee, by making mee
Love her, who doth neglect both mee and thee,
To'invent, and practise this one way, to'annihilate all three.

This, although formally very characteristic, and an astonishing example of that prodigious wit which Donne's contemporaries so admired, is not, I need scarcely insist, a very serious poem, or even a very important one. There is here little or nothing of that interaction between logical structure and experiential or emotional content, between intellect and feeling, argument and passion or tenderness, which we have noticed in *The Dreame* and in *A Valediction: forbidding mourning*. This, though, is not to say that the poem is merely mechanical, that the metre is merely (in Wordsworth's phrase) 'superadded', or that it in any way resembles those many versified anecdotes in which that occasionally very great poet Thomas Hardy amused himself by working out the possible permutations and combinations produced in the relationships of A, B and C by the operations of X, The Blind Will. Even here—although it would perhaps require a really gifted reader or reciter to reveal it—Donne's exploitation of the resources of metre and rhythm is scarcely less remarkable than his ingenuity and wit. Consider, for example, the ironical self-depreciation, the Chaucerian swiftness (too swift for dull or inattentive readers), of

To Nature all that I in Ryme have writ;
And to my company my wit,

and the superb and unexpected change of pattern and, as it were, of key in the last stanza.

I remarked that the logical pattern of each stanza was as rigidly prescribed in advance as the verse-pattern itself. Over and over again in the *Songs and Sonets* we find Donne not merely choosing but *inventing* the appropriate stanza-form for the poem he wants to write. Professor Pierre Legouis has calculated that of the forty-nine poems which are in stanzas no less that forty-four are in stanza forms which are not exactly repeated. In respect of this extreme metrical originality, the only other seventeenth-century poet who can be compared with Donne is George Herbert, in whose *Temple*, out of 164 poems, 116 are in metrical forms which are not repeated.

Professor Pierre Legouis entitled his short study of Donne's poetry *Donne the Craftsman*: here, indeed, is yet one more paradox in a paradoxical career—the fact that Donne, who did not write for publication, and who never regarded his poetry as the serious business of his life, evidently bestowed more care and pains upon his poems than many poets for whom poetry has been a whole-time occupation. Perhaps one may say of him what Rilke made his Malte Laurids Brigge say of Félix Arvers: *Er war ein Dichter und hasste das Ungefähre* ('He was a poet and hated the more-or-less').

Let us consider yet another kind of relationship or interaction between form and content. In some of the courtly or Petrarchan poems written during Donne's middle years, notably in *The Funerall*, the argumentative element is as unserious, one might even say, as trivial, as in *The Will*, but this trivial argument is here combined with real feeling and tenderness. Indeed, here the very flimsiness and trumperiness of the logic does but accentuate the tenderness, which, as always with Donne, is perceptible only in and through inflection and cadence. A mere prose analysis of *The Funerall* might well suggest that it was a poem as merely witty and ingenious as *The Will*. This subtle wreath of hair about my arm is my out-ward soul, which will preserve my body from putrefaction. For if the hair-like nerves that descend from my brain can reunite all my members, these hairs which ascended from a far better head can do it far better—unless, indeed, she was merely fettering me like a condemned prisoner. Whatever she meant, bury it with me, for I am love's martyr, and if this relic should fall into other hands it might cause idolatry. I shall at least have displayed both humility in having attributed to it the power of a soul, and some pride in having buried some of her who would save none of me. Never-theless, the effect of the poem is very different from the drooling and doodling stuff which this analysis might have led one to expect:

The Funerall

Who ever comes to shroud me, do not harme
  Nor question much
That subtile wreath of haire, which crowns my arme;

The mystery, the signe you must not touch,
   For 'tis my outward Soule,
Viceroy to that, which then to heaven being gone,
   Will leave this to controule,
And keepe these limbes, her Provinces, from dissolution.

For if the sinewie thread my braine lets fall
   Through every part,
Can tye those parts, and make mee one of all;
These haires which upward grew, and strength and art
   Have from a better braine,
Can better do'it; Except she meant that I
   By this should know my pain,
As prisoners then are manacled, when they'are condemn'd to die.

What ere shee meant by'it, bury it with me,
   For since I am
Loves martyr, it might breed idolatrie,
If into other hands these Reliques came;
   As 'twas humility
To afford to it all that a Soule can doe,
   So, 'tis some bravery,
That since you would save none of mee, I bury some of you.

   And here, with this brief account of some of their more formal characteristics, we must leave the *Songs and Sonets*. Our long examination of them has, I hope, enabled us to perceive more clearly some of the constituent elements of poetry and the different ways in which they may be combined. We have learnt, at any rate, that wit, argument and logic are not incompatible with the finest poetry, and that a firm logical structure and a continuous development may, when combined with a certain *quantum* of experiential and emotional substance, offer a very special and peculiar satisfaction. Above all, we have learnt, I hope, that mere visual imagery is not, as is so commonly supposed to-day, an indispensable, or even, perhaps, a very important, constituent of good poetry, and that far more important are things which to-day receive too little attention, namely, rhythm, cadence, inflexion, interacting with a clearly defined verse-pattern and a clearly perceptible logical structure. For although Donne's poems cannot be fully felt until they have been understood, although Ben Jonson said of him that for not keeping of accent he deserved hanging (was Ben, I wonder, thinking of the deliberately jaw-breaking Satires, or was he just being insensitive?), and although to the uninitiated Donne is a harsh, crabbed, abstract and intellectual poet, it is, in the last analysis, their possession of a certain musical quality, a resonant meaning and a meaning resonance, that distinguishes his best from his merely interesting or amusing poems. His best poems, in fact, are those which read best—those into which a reader can put most are those which have most to give. It is a sensitive ear that must pronounce the final verdict upon them and enable us to arrange them in order of merit. And at the top of the list will be those which communicate the greatest range and complexity and subtlety of inner vibration.

5

THE DIVINE POEMS

THE transition from Donne's secular to his religious poetry may be conveniently effected by lingering for a little over the two *Anniversaries* which he published in 1611 and 1612 in commemoration of Elizabeth Drury, who died in 1610 at the age of fifteen. Donne had never even seen her, and it is possible that he began to write the *Funerall Elegie*, which he probably presented shortly after her death in 1610, which was printed with the *First Anniversarie* in 1611, and out of which both that poem and its successor seem to have developed, with no loftier motive than that of attracting the attention of her wealthy and ambitious father. Certainly, it was in 1611, the year in which the *First Anniversarie* was published, that Donne accompanied Sir Robert Drury and his wife on a journey to the Continent, and in the following year that he and his family moved into one of the new houses which Sir Robert had built beside his own mansion in Drury Lane. Nevertheless, even if it was with no very disinterested motive that Donne began to write these poems with the, for him, unusual intention of publishing, that would be only one more example of the fact that you can never really explain anything by a mere description of its origins. For having once started, Donne descended very deep, and the result of much profound and solitary meditation found expression in verse. When, in reply to Ben Jonson's accusations that he had overpraised Elizabeth Drury to the point of blasphemy, he declared that 'he described the idea of a woman, and not as she was', and when, hearing that some of his older and nobler patronesses had been offended by the praises lavished on this slip of a girl, he told correspondents that, since he had received 'so very good testimony of her worthiness', he felt it his duty to say, not what he was sure was just truth, but the very best he could conceive, Donne must have known that he was not really telling the truth either about the poems or about himself. For the hyperbolical praises of Elizabeth Drury, which were pretty

certainly written in order to please her father, are only incidental;
what is essential are the reflexions on the vanity of the world and of
earthly life which rose and called for expression when once Donne
had got to work. In fact, like *Lycidas*, which was also an occasional
poem, Donne's *Anniversaries* immeasurably transcend their immediate occasion, although without that occasion, that external stimulus,
they would never have been composed. The full original titles are
a better description of them than any of Donne's defences. The
first, published in 1611, was entitled *An Anatomie of the World.
Wherein, by occasion of the untimely death of Mistris* ELIZABETH DRVRY
the frailty and the decay of this whole World is represented. In 1612 Donne
re-published this poem with the additional title of *The First Anniversarie*, together with another poem which he called *The Second Anniversarie* but of which the full title was: *Of The Progresse of the Soule.
Wherein: By occasion of The Religious death of Mistris* ELIZABETH
DRVRY, *the incommodities of the Soule in this life, and her exaltation in
the next, are contemplated.*[1]

In these poems, which, although they contain some of the most
splendid verse he ever wrote, are nevertheless, like most of his long
or longish poems, not equally poetical throughout, there is something especially characteristic both of Donne and of his age, or of
part of his age. That comparative detachment from this life and
that longing for the next, which, if we are to believe the Preface to
Biathanatos, seem to have been his even during his brilliant youth,
and that sense of vanity and shadowiness which seems to have been
his even when he seemed most immersed in the pursuit of vanities
and shadows—these characteristics, which had been deepened by
the long period of isolatedness and hope deferred which followed
the ruin of his fortunes, find their completest verse-expression in the
two *Anniversaries*. We may think of them, if we like, as the
Catholic and Medieval, as distinct from the Renaissance, elements
in his mind and make-up; although we too often forget that what
we call the Middle Ages and what we call the Renaissance were not
such enclosed and exclusive periods as we tend to suppose, and that
in all manner of ways they met and mingled. Hence it is that the
Anniversaries contain much that is characteristic of Donne's age as

---

[1] The second anniversary of Elizabeth Drury's death was in December 1612, but
this poem, together with the 2nd ed. of its predecessor, must have been published
before April of that year: see R. C. Bald, *Donne and the Drurys*, 1959, p. 93.

well as of himself. For Donne here expresses something of what one might call the disenchantment of the later Renaissance—the disenchantment of men whose outlook was still half-medieval, but for whom the medieval world-order had been shaken and the medieval world-picture partly antiquated: shaken and partly antiquated, but neither superseded nor replaced. Indeed, for such men certain characteristic medieval conceptions were so far from being abolished by the Renaissance that they were ultimately intensified by it.[1] For example, the medieval moralists loved to dwell on the limitations of man, the depth of his ignorance, the insignificance of his knowledge, and one of the characteristics of the Renaissance was that to many men the boundaries of possible knowledge seemed to have been almost indefinitely extended. There was a 'renovation and new spring of knowledge', as Bacon said. Men applied themselves to learning of every kind with tremendous enthusiasm and persistence, cherishing great hopes. But not all were able to maintain these hopes. In the seventeenth century we can perceive two distinct attitudes to knowledge. The experimental scientists, the practitioners and exponents of 'new philosophy', remain cheerful and confident; but many of the great amateur scholars, the great polymaths, who had been assimilating every possible kind of knowledge in the hope that somehow it would find its place in a great synthesis, began to perceive that of the things which seemed to them really important they knew little more than when they had begun. They became sceptical about the possible attainments of human knowledge, and the new discoveries in astronomy and other sciences merely increased their scepticism. Much of what they had laboriously learnt had been proved to be false: was it not

---

[1] In the third edition (1920) of his *Philosophical Theory of the State* Bernard Bosanquet added to the original Introduction to the second edition a section entitled 'How the Theory stands in 1919', which begins with these words: ' "Then all the old things were true." This is the overwhelming impression which the events of the last five years have left upon my mind. So far as it is possible for facts to affirm ideas, all the simple truths which we learned in our youth are brought home to us afresh to-day. It *is*, then, only spiritual good that is real and stable; earthly and material aims *are* delusive and dangerous, and the root of strife. This is the obvious and simple explanation of what has been happening.' Some modern writers would almost seem to suppose that for Donne and many of his contemporaries the whole fabric of their faith had been shattered by the discoveries of 'new philosophy', and that they, like so many in recent times, had come to feel that they had been building upon sand. But, as Donne might have expressed it, it was 'far from that': for them, no less than for Bosanquet, external happenings merely reinforced their conviction that 'all the old things were true.'

likely that before long the new discoveries would in their turn be
superseded? Were things that were hailed as new discoveries really
anything more than new kinds of error? Where was it all tending?
What was the object of it all? Thus, for many men, the characteristic medieval conception of the insignificance of human knowledge
was ultimately intensified by the Renaissance. This is how Donne,
who often returned to the subject in his sermons, meditates upon it
in the *Second Anniversarie*:

> What hope have wee to know our selves, when wee
> Know not the least things, which for our use be?
> Wee see in Authors, too stiffe to recant,
> A hundred controversies of an Ant;
> And yet one watches, starves, freeses, and sweats,
> To know but Catechismes and Alphabets
> Of unconcerning things, matters of fact;
> How others on our stage their parts did Act;
> What *Cæsar* did, yea, and what *Cicero* said.
> Why grasse is greene, or why our blood is red,
> Are mysteries which none have reach'd unto.
> In this low forme,[1] poore soule, what wilt thou doe?
> When wilt thou shake off this Pedantery,
> Of being taught by sense, and Fantasie?
> Thou look'st through spectacles; small things seeme great
> Below; But up unto the watch-towre get,
> And see all things despoyl'd of fallacies:
> Thou shalt not peepe through lattices of eyes,
> Nor heare through Labyrinths of eares, nor learne
> By circuit, or collections to discerne.
> In heaven thou straight know'st all, concerning it,
> And what concernes it not, shalt straight forget.[2]

Everyone remembers how Donne spoke, in one of his letters to
Sir Henry Goodyer, of his early 'hydroptique immoderate desire of
humane learning and languages': in one of his sermons there is a
passage which has, I cannot but feel, a distinctly autobiographical
flavour, and in which I seem to see him sitting in 'unprofitable

---

[1] Probably='in this low class' (as in a school).
[2] ll. 279–300.

retirednesse' and 'disconsolate melancholy' in the library of what he called 'my hospital at Mitcham'. He is insisting that it is impossible for a man, by any kind of diversion or distraction, to escape from the hand of God:

> If he take up another Comfort, that though health and wealth decay, though he be poore and weake, yet he hath learning, and philosophy, and morall constancy, and he can content himselfe with himselfe, he can make his study a Court, and a few Books shall supply to him the society and the conversation of many friends, there is another worme to devoure this too, the hand of divine Justice shall grow heavy upon him, in a sense of an unprofitable retirednesse, in a disconsolate melancholy, and at last, in a stupidity, tending to desperation.[1]

Another characteristic medieval conception, extending far back into classical antiquity, was that the world was decaying, running down like a clock; that the seasons were becoming more and more unfavourable, and men becoming smaller in stature, weaker in health, more wicked in their ways. For many men, this conception too was intensified, during the seventeenth century, by certain consequences of the Renaissance and of what in many countries was but another aspect of the Renaissance, the Protestant Reformation. All over Europe Protestants were fighting against the established faith, peoples were arming against their rulers, the divine right of kings was being questioned. In England the nation was being divided by religious and economic controversies. The times were out of joint, and to many it seemed obvious that the world was rapidly accelerating in its process of degeneration and decomposition as it approached the end of its course. This theme, to which Donne was also to return later in his sermons, this theme of 'the frailty and decay of this whole world', is almost the whole subject of his *First Anniversarie*.

> Then, as mankinde, so is the worlds whole frame
> Quite out of joynt, almost created lame:
> For, before God had made up all the rest,
> Corruption entred, and deprav'd the best:

[1] *LXXX Sermons*, p. 579.

It seis'd the Angels, and then first of all
The world did in her cradle take a fall,
And turn'd her braines, and tooke a generall maime,
Wronging each joynt of th'universall frame.
The noblest part, man, felt it first; and than
Both beasts and plants, curst in the curse of man.
So did the world from the first houre decay,
That evening was beginning of the day,
And now the Springs and Sommers which we see,
Like sonnes of women after fiftie bee.
And new Philosophy calls all in doubt,
The Element of fire is quite put out;
The Sun is lost, and th'earth, and no mans wit
Can well direct him where to looke for it.
And freely men confesse that this world's spent,
When in the Planets, and the Firmament
They seeke so many new; they see that this
Is crumbled out againe to his Atomies.
'Tis all in peeces, all cohaerence gone;
All just supply, and all Relation:
Prince, Subject, Father, Sonne, are things forgot,
For every man alone thinkes he hath got
To be a Phœnix, and that then can bee
None of that kinde, of which he is, but hee.[1]

Heaven seems farther away now that astrology has been discredited:

What Artist now dares boast that he can bring
Heaven hither, or constellate any thing,
So as the influence of those starres may bee
Imprison'd in an Hearbe, or Charme, or Tree,
And doe by touch, all which those stars could doe?
The art is lost, and correspondence too.[2]

And Donne concludes

[1] ll. 191–218.
[2] ll. 391–6.

> Shee, shee is dead; shee's dead; when thou knowst this,
> Thou knowst how drie a Cinder this world is.
> And learn'st thus much by our Anatomy,
> That 'tis in vaine to dew, or mollifie
> It with thy teares, or sweat, or blood: nothing
> Is worth our travaile, griefe, or perishing,
> But those rich joyes, which did possesse her heart,
> Of which she's now partaker, and a part.[1]

But it is not merely on the insignificance of human knowledge and on the decay of the world that Donne meditates in these poems: the great theme of the *Second Anniversarie* is also the great theme of Donne's Sermons—that of the insignificance of man himself when considered *sub specie temporis*, that of the antithesis between the world and the spirit, the transitoriness and unsatisfactoriness of all earthly enjoyments, the incommodities suffered by the soul in the imprisoning body:

> And what essentiall joy can'st thou expect
> Here upon earth? what permanent effect
> Of transitory causes? Dost thou love
> Beauty? (And beauty worthy'st is to move)
> Poor cousened cousenor, *that* she, and *that* thou,
> Which did begin to love, are neither now;
> You are both fluid, chang'd since yesterday;
> Next day repaires, (but ill) last dayes decay.
> Nor are, (although the river keepe the name)
> Yesterdaies waters, and to daies the same.
> So flowes her face, and thine eyes, neither now
> That Saint, nor Pilgrime, which your loving vow
> Concern'd, remaines; but whil'st you thinke you bee
> Constant, you'are hourely in inconstancie.
> Honour may have pretence unto our love,
> Because that God did live so long above
> Without this Honour, and then lov'd it so,
> That he at last made Creatures to bestow
> Honour on him; not that he needed it,
> But that, to his hands, man might grow more fit.

[1] ll. 427–34.

But since all Honours from inferiours flow,
(For they doe give it; Princes doe but shew
Whom they would have so honor'd) and that this
On such opinions, and capacities
Is built, as rise and fall, to more and lesse:
Alas, 'tis but a casuall happiness.[1]

Thinke further on thy selfe, my Soule, and thinke
How thou at first wast made but in a sinke;
Thinke that it argued some infirmitie,
That those two soules, which then thou foundst in me,
Thou fedst upon, and drewst into thee, both
My second soule, of sense, and first of growth.
Thinke but how poore thou wast, how obnoxious;
Whom a small lumpe of flesh could poyson thus.
This curded milke, this poore unlittered whelpe
My body, could, beyond escape or helpe,
Infect thee with Originall sinne, and thou
Couldst neither then refuse, nor leave it now.
Thinke that no stubborne sullen Anchorit,
Which fixt to a pillar, or a grave, doth sit
Bedded, and bath'd in all his ordures, dwels
So fowly as our Soules in their first-built Cels.
Thinke in how poore a prison thou didst lie
After, enabled but to suck, and crie.
Thinke, when 'twas growne to most, 'twas a poor Inne,
A Province pack'd up in two yards of skinne,
And that usurp'd or threatned with the rage
Of sicknesses, or their true mother, Age.
But thinke that Death hath now enfranchis'd thee,
Thou hast thy'expansion now, and libertie;
Thinke that a rustie Peece, discharg'd, is flowne
In peeces, and the bullet is his owne,
And freely flies: This is to thy Soule allow,
Thinke thy shell broke, thinke thy Soule hatch'd but now.[2]

Donne's meditations in the two *Anniversaries* on the great

[1] ll. 387–412.
[2] ll. 157–84.

general themes of the insignificance of this world in comparison
with the next and of man in comparison with God and the blessed
are more profound and moving than his treatment of more specifically Christian and doctrinal matters in poems written before his ordination in 1615. This, perhaps, is because what Donne is expressing
in the *Anniversaries* has almost as much to do with temperament
and mood, with attitude and outlook, as with specifically Christian
doctrine—is, in fact, as much a matter of feeling and intuition as of
intellect and formulated belief. How close, for example, are those
two passages from the *Second Anniversarie*, on the transience of all
earthly happiness and on the miseries suffered by the soul in the
body, to that speech in *Measure for Measure* in which the Duke,
disguised as a friar, exhorts the condemned Claudio to be 'absolute
for death':

> Be absolute for death: either death or life
> Shall thereby be the sweeter. Reason thus with life:
> If I do loose thee, I do loose a thing
> That none but fooles would keepe: a breath thou art,
> Seruile to all the skyie influences,
> That dost this habitation where thou keepst
> Hourely afflict: Meerely, thou art deaths foole,
> For him thou labourst by thy flight to shun,
> And yet runst toward him still. Thou art not noble,
> For all th'accommodations that thou bearst,
> Are nurst by basenesse: Thou'art by no meanes valiant,
> For thou dost feare the soft and tender forke
> Of a poore worme: thy best of rest is sleepe,
> And that thou oft prouoakst, yet grosselie fearst
> Thy death, which is no more. Thou art not thy selfe,
> For thou exists on manie a thousand graines
> That issue out of dust. Happie thou art not,
> For what thou hast not, still thou striu'st to get,
> And what thou hast forgetst. Thou art not certaine,
> For thy complexion shifts to strange effects,
> After the Moone: If thou art rich, thou'rt poore,
> For like an Asse, whose backe with Ingots bowes,
> Thou bearst thy heauie riches but a iournie,
> And death vnloads thee; Friend hast thou none,

For thine owne bowels which do call thee sire,
The meere effusion of thy proper loines,
Do curse the Gowt, Serpigo, and the Rheume
For ending thee no sooner. Thou hast nor youth, nor age,
But as it were an after-dinners sleepe
Dreaming on both, for all thy blessed youth
Becomes as aged, and doth begge the almes
Of palsied-Eld: and when thou art old, and rich
Thou hast neither heate, affection, limbe, nor beautie
To make thy riches pleasant: what's yet in this
That beares the name of life? Yet in this life
Lie hid moe thousand deaths; yet death we feare
That makes these oddes, all euen.[1]

Here Shakespeare, although probably not consciously or deliberately expounding Christian doctrine, is being at least as specifically
Christian, as medievally Christian, if you like, as Donne in many
similar passages in the *Anniversaries*. This point, which seems to me
a most important one, is very difficult to formulate. On the one
hand, I think I can perceive a distinction, in Donne's sermons and
in his religious poetry, between the temperamental and emotional
and the intellectual and doctrinal elements; on the other hand, I
am not at all sure how far it is legitimate to press this distinction.
Let me take what may seem at first, perhaps, a rather roundabout
way of expressing what I have in mind. In Donne's youthful study,
so earnestly pursued, of the points of controversy between the
Roman and Anglican Churches there was probably, as I have
already suggested, some not inconsiderable element of self-interest;
and when, after the ruin of his fortunes, he turned once more to
theological controversy, assisting Morton and writing *Pseudo-
Martyr*, his intention was probably to attract the notice of the King
and to obtain, through this exploitation of his theological equipment, the secular preferment he hoped for; although the actual
result of his efforts was to convince Morton and the King that he
had in him the makings of a great divine, that secular preferment
should be withheld from him, and that he should be left, as it were,
with only one avenue of escape. Walton professed to see in all this
the hand of Providence, and some modern readers might be tempted

[1] III. i, 5-41.

to see something powerfully ironical. Perhaps, though, Walton was not so very far wrong. In Donne as a young man there seems to have been a, to us, strange mixture of worldliness and other-worldliness, an intense love of life and, at the same time, a certain detachment from life, a certain sense of the shadowiness and vanity of this world and its shows. As the result of his marriage he lost the world, and, although for a time he might try to persuade himself that he and his wife were a world in and for themselves, his letters suggest that he soon began to feel his isolatedness and inactivity, his exclusion from any part on that great stage he had affected to despise. Partly, no doubt, in order to occupy his mind with something, and partly in the hope of obtaining thereby some secular preferment, he applied himself to theological controversy, but—to quote once again what I ventured to call that autobiographical passage in one of his sermons—there was another worm to devour this too, and the hand of divine justice grew heavy upon him, 'in a sense of an unprofitable retiredness, in a disconsolate melancholy, and at last, in a stupidity, tending to desperation'. That certain detachment from life, or non-attachment to it, which he seems to have had even in youth, and which carried with it an undersense of the vanity and shadowiness of things—this mood, this attitude, this response to experience, which isolation and disappointed hopes had deepened, was not, it would seem, something he was intended to escape from, but something he was intended to transform into the great theme of his contemplation and discourse. Thus in two ways Donne was being prepared for the part eventually allotted him: by his long preoccupation with theology and by his deepening sense of the vanity and shadowiness of life on earth and of man considered *sub specie temporis*. And what, after all, is most impressive in Donne's sermons? Not his citation of authorities, not his ingenious and learned exposition of texts and of subtle points of doctrine, but his meditations on the theme that all is vanity and what one might call his exploitation of the dramatic element in the relationship between man and God. In other words, if one regards Donne's sermons as literature, I am inclined to say that the temperamental and experiential element in them is more important than the specifically theological, and the chief characteristic of what I call the experiential element is that deep sense of the vanity and shadowiness of things which Shakespeare too possessed and indulged in certain moments, but which a combination of temperament and circumstances had made almost habitual with Donne.

'As, in looking at a carpet', wrote Thomas Hardy, in one of those fascinating note-book jottings scattered through the two volumes of his wife's Memoir, 'As, in looking at a carpet, by following one colour a certain pattern is suggested, by following another colour, another; so in life the seer should watch that pattern among general things which his idiosyncrasy moves him to observe, and describe that alone.'[1] The pattern which Donne, both by idiosyncrasy and circumstance, was increasingly moved to observe was in many ways akin to that observed by the author of *Ecclesiastes*, by Leopardi, and even by Hardy himself. That deep undersense of vanity, of what Leopardi calls *noia*, by no means incompatible with occasional intense delight in the beauties and pleasures of existence, is one of the eternal moods of the human mind, those moods of which Yeats wrote:

> Time drops in decay
> Like a candle burnt out,
> And the mountains and woods
> Have their day, have their day;
> What one in the rout
> Of the fire-born moods
> Has fallen away?

But while some who have lived habitually in this mood and have habitually perceived this pattern have been content simply to record it, others have been led on, or forced on, to a distinction between appearance and reality, and to a proclamation that, while the things that are seen are temporal, the things that are unseen are eternal. Thus this sensitiveness to the pattern of vanity and *noia* may compel some of those who possess it strongly to search for something they can rest upon, for some ultimate reality that transcends appearances —may compel them, that is to say, either to the formulation of some kind of idealistic philosophy or to the acceptance of some kind of religious faith. What I feel tempted to say is that, while Donne's sensitiveness to the pattern of vanity and *noia* was primary and essential, was one of the eternal moods of the human mind,

[1] *Early Life*, 198.

the particular mode in which he apprehended the ultimate reality
he opposed to it was in a sense secondary, accidental and historically
conditioned. This, I repeat, is what I feel tempted to say; but,
although I feel that this distinction is a real one, I also feel that the
matter is not quite so simple as that, because, after all, we cannot
really imagine Donne without the faith he inherited and which so
permeated the intellectual and moral climate in which he lived; and
we cannot really decide how far, from the beginning, this faith
may have deepened, co-operated with, made both more acute and
more tolerable, his comparative detachment from life, true though
it be that his increasing detachment, his increasing sensitiveness to
the pattern of vanity and *noia*, deepened this faith, or, at any rate,
Donne's conviction of its necessity. Nevertheless, if we try to retain
necessary qualifications and do not make the antithesis too crude, I
think we may usefully distinguish between the temperamental and
emotional and the intellectual and doctrinal elements in Donne's
religious poetry and in his sermons. For is it not the fact that most
modern readers, whatever their beliefs, can accept Donne's statements of what I may call the human situation as they stand and can
respond at once to their power and truth, although they may not
be able to accept at all the consolations which Donne offers, or
may be able to accept them only in a very metaphorical and latitudi-
narian way? Take, for example, this passage from the *Devotions upon
Emergent Occasions*, a little book which Donne composed during a
serious illness in 1623. Prefixed to it are some Latin verses describing
the various stages of his sickness and recovery, and sometimes a
line, sometimes a phrase, from these verses furnishes the text for
each section of the book, these sections, twenty-three in all, consisting of a Meditation followed by what he calls an Expostulation and
then by a Prayer. The text of the thirteenth Meditation does not
at first sight seem very promising: 'The Sicknes declares the infection and malignity thereof by spots'. We can't expect much from
this, you might say. Nevertheless, Donne ingeniously extracts from
it one of his finest and most characteristic meditations. The physi-
cians try to comfort him by saying that, although it is now clear
that he is dangerously ill, they have at last discovered the nature of
his disease, and know how to proceed. Small comfort, this! thinks
Donne; I may die before they are able to help me. They give me a
gleam of hope, but at the same time they increase my anxiety—an

apt symbol of the relationship between human happiness and human misery!

> Wee say, that the world is made of *sea*, & *land*, as though they were equal; but we know that ther is more *sea* in the *Western*, then in the *Eastern Hemisphere*: we say that the *Firmament* is full of *starres*; as though it were equally full; but we know, that there are more *stars* vnder the *Northerne*, then vnder the *Southern Pole*. Wee say, the *Elements* of man are *misery*, and *happinesse*, as though he had an equal proportion of both, and the dayes of man vicissitudinary, as though he had as many *good* days, as *ill*, and that he liued vnder a perpetuall *Equinoctiall*, *night*, and *day* equall, good and ill fortune in the same measure. But it is far from that; he *drinkes misery*, & he *tastes happinesse*; he *mowes misery*, and hee *gleanes happiness*; hee *iournies in misery*, he does but *walke in happiness;* and which is worst, his misery is *positiue*, and *dogmaticall*, his happinesse is but *disputable*, and *problematicall;* All men call *Misery*, *Misery*, but *Happinesse* changes the name, by the taste of man.[1]

As a statement, a rather grim statement, of the human situation, we can respond to this passage, for all its quaint and even fantastic setting and its characteristic wit, as whole-heartedly as to a poem of Leopardi's or a page from, let us say, *The Return of the Native*. But while the two modern writers might make such a statement the basis for an indictment of the cruelty of Nature or the indifference of the Blind Will, Donne dwells upon the miseries of man in this world chiefly in order to magnify his exaltation in the next. As he declared in one of his sermons, where he had been pursuing the same theme: 'But then there is *Pondus Gloriae*, *An exceeding waight of eternall glory*, and that turnes the scale; for as it makes all worldly prosperity as dung, so it makes all worldly adversity as feathers.'[2] We may only be able to accept Donne's *Pondus Gloriae* in a very metaphorical sense, or perhaps not at all, but in his description of what I have called the human situation, both in the meditation I have quoted and in several passages in the two *Anniversaries*, he is following a pattern which at almost all times at least some

[1] 1624, 312–14.
[2] *LXXX Sermons*, 665.

eyes have perceived in the carpet of life, and is expressing one of
the eternal moods of the human mind. And Donne's statement of
the situation, although it leads him to a Christian conclusion, is
not in itself specifically Christian; and in the *Anniversaries* the conclusion itself is expressed in very general, almost conventional,
terms, which, as it were, allow any reader who chooses to substitute
some other conception of the reality behind appearance for the
specifically Christian one:

> Shee, shee is dead; shee's dead; when thou knowst this,
> Thou knowst how drie a Cinder this world is.
> And learn'st thus much by our Anatomy,
> That 'tis in vaine to dew, or mollifie
> It with thy teares, or sweat, or blood: nothing
> Is worth our travaile, griefe, or perishing,
> But those rich joyes, which did possesse her heart,
> Of which she's now partaker, and a part.[1]

It is instructive to compare the very generally religious poetry
of the *Anniversaries* and also of *The Litanie*, a poem composed about
the same time and which I shall mention later, with some of the
more doctrinally religious poems which Donne wrote during the
years before he took orders. The earliest of these poems, the sequence
of seven sonnets entitled *La Corona*, seem to have been written
towards the beginning of Donne's friendship with Mrs. Herbert,
and perhaps under her influence. In a letter quoted by Walton in
his *Life* of George Herbert and dated 'Mitcham, July 11, 1607' (a
date for which Mr. Garrod, forgetting 'O.S.', proposed 'Jany 11')
Donne wrote to her: 'I commit the enclosed *Holy Hymns* and
Sonnets (which for the matter, not the workmanship, have yet
escap'd the fire) to your judgment, and to your protection too, if
you think them worthy of it; and I have appointed this inclosed
Sonnet to usher them to your happy hand.'[2] By calling them '*Holy
Hymns* and *Sonnets*' Donne simply meant that the sonnets were also
hymns of praise, and indeed in the accompanying sonnet, which
Walton also quotes, *To Mrs. Magdalen Herbert: of St. Mary Magdalen*,
Donne requests her to

---

[1] *First Anniversarie*, ll. 427–34.
[2] *World's Classics* ed., 266.

Harbour these *Hymns*, to his dear name addrest.

It is most important to distinguish these seven *La Corona* sonnets from the more famous and far greater *Holy Sonnets*, of which, as Miss Helen Gardner has recently demonstrated, Donne had almost certainly written at least the first six as early as 1609. In the printed texts and in most of the manuscript collections all the sonnets are placed together under the generic title *Holy Sonnets*, but while the first seven are preceded by the sub-title *La Corona*, have individual titles, and are all on the life of Christ, the sonnets that follow them, the *Holy Sonnets* proper, are distinguished merely by numerals.

> *Deigne at my hands this crown of prayer and praise,*
> Weav'd in my low devout melancholie

he exclaims in the introductory sonnet, and in the six that follow, each of which begins with the last line of its predecessor, he meditates on the Annunciation, the Nativity, the appearance in the Temple, the Crucifixion, the Resurrection and the Ascension. Meditates, but intellectually, wittily even, rather than profoundly or passionately, exhibiting and, as it were, underlining, with characteristic ingenuity, some of the paradoxes inherent in Christianity and in the two-fold nature of Christ as God and man. His attitude, whatever it may actually have been, appears in these poems strangely external and detached. He seems, as it were, to be trying to stimulate his faith by means of his intellect, trying to make himself *feel* the reality of these mysteries and paradoxes by displaying them to himself under as many aspects as he can. He has not felt them, one is tempted to say, judging from the evidence of these poems alone, he has not experienced them, anything like so intensely as he has felt and experienced the much more general, and, in a sense, more primary, more fundamental, antithesis between the world and the spirit; they have not become a part of himself to anything like the same degree as has that far more general, less specifically Christian, conviction of the vanity of earthly life so memorably expressed in the *Anniversaries*. 'Yea thou art now', he says to the Virgin in *Annunciation*,

> yea thou art now
> Thy Makers maker, and thy Fathers mother;

Thou'hast light in darke; and shutst in little roome,
Immensity cloystered in thy deare wombe.

In *Temple* he exclaims:

The Word but lately could not speake, and loe,
It sodenly speakes wonders, whence comes it,
That all which was, and all which should be writ,
A shallow seeming child, should deeply know?

And in *Crucifying*:

But Oh! the worst are most, they will and can,
Alas, and do, unto the immaculate,
Whose creature Fate is, now prescribe a Fate

It is substantially the same with the other more doctrinally religious
poems which Donne wrote before his ordination. There is sometimes genuine feeling as well as wit, but wit and intellect predominate. They are essentially religious exercises—Donne is exercising his
faith, whipping it up, trying to make himself feel and experience
what he has apprehended intellectually. Here are the first twenty-
two lines of his poem *Upon the Annunciation and Passion falling upon
one day*, that is to say, on March 25, 1608:

Tamely, fraile body, 'abstaine to day; to day
My soule eates twice, Christ hither and away.
She sees him man, so like God made in this,
That of them both a circle embleme is,
Whose first and last concurre; this doubtfull day
Of feast or fast, Christ came, and went away;
Shee sees him nothing twice at once, who'is all;
Shee sees a Cedar plant it selfe, and fall,
Her Maker put to making, and the head
Of life, at once, not yet alive, and dead;
She sees at once the virgin mother stay
Reclus'd at home, Publique at Golgotha.
Sad and rejoyc'd shee's seen at once, and seen
At almost fiftie, and at scarce fifteene.

At once a Sonne is promis'd her, and gone,
Gabriell gives Christ to her, He her to John;
Not fully a mother, Shee's in Orbitie,
At once receiver and the legacie.
All this, and all betweene, this day hath showne,
Th'Abridgement of Christs story, which makes one
(As in plaine Maps, the furthest West is East)
Of the'Angels *Ave'*, and *Consummatum est*.

Similarly, in *The Crosse* he tries to make that symbol more real to
himself by meditating, in a manner for which there was much
precedent in early Christian writers, on the number of crossed or
cross-like things scattered through the world, and, incidentally,
by punning on the double-sense of *Cross*, as the holy rood and
as vexation, affliction, thwarting:

From mee, no Pulpit nor misgrounded law,
Nor scandall taken, shall this Crosse withdraw,
It shall not, for it cannot; for, the losse
Of this Crosse, were to mee another Crosse;
Better were worse, for, no affliction,
No Crosse is so extreme, as to have none.
Who can blot out the Crosse, which th'instrument
Of God, dew'd on mee in the Sacrament?
Who can deny mee power, and liberty
To stretch mine armes, and mine owne Crosse to be?
Swimme, and at every stroake, thou art thy Crosse,
The Mast and yard make one, where seas do tosse.
Looke downe, thou spiest out Crosses, in small things;
Looke up, thou seest birds rais'd on crossed wings;
All the Globes frame, and spheares, is nothing else
But the Meridians crossing Parallels.

How different from this is *The Litanie*, or a great part of *The
Litanie*, written, probably, in the autumn of 1608, of which he
said in a letter to his friend Sir Henry Goodyer:

Since my imprisonment in my bed, I have made a meditation
in verse, which I call a Litany . . . That by which it will deserve

best acceptation, is, That neither the Roman Church need call it defective, because it abhors not the particular mention of the blessed Triumphers in heaven; nor the Reformed can discreetly accuse it, of attributing more then a rectified devotion ought to doe.[1]

It is a long poem, of twenty-eight stanzas, and is not equally inspired or equally impassioned throughout. Except for the stanzas invoking the various orders of the Church Triumphant, which, in comparison with the rest of the poem, are a little conventional, it is not specifically doctrinal and only very generally Christian. But the stanzas which I am going to quote contain some of the finest religious poetry Donne ever wrote. They are, like all Donne's best religious poetry, intensely personal; and, again like all his best religious poetry, they are less an exposition of Christian doctrine than a passionate and dramatic prayer to be delivered from temptations and distractions, to be made single-hearted, to find in God's will his peace. There was always, as I have insisted, an other-worldly element in Donne, a certain detachment from life, or non-attachment to it; but, although he increasingly felt that the world was vanity, he could never quite liberate himself from it, and in this oscillation between worldliness and other-worldliness, in this increasing longing to make the unworldly element in himself prevail over the worldly, lies the drama of his religious poetry, a poetry which transcends ecclesiastical differences. If we may define religion, in the widest sense, as man's effort to bring his own will into conformity with a transcendent will and purpose which he has apprehended and which he believes to be divine, we may say that Donne's poetry is in this widest sense religious, but only—I feel tempted to add—accidentally or incidentally Christian. Indeed, one of the most beautiful passages in Donne's sermons[2] and several in his letters, where he felt able to express himself more freely, are on those 'things in which all Religions agree'; he speaks to Goodyer of controversialists who 'write for Religion, without it', and he tells Sir Tobie Mathew that he has sometimes been glad to hear that some of his friends have differed from him in religion, since 'It is some degree of an union to be united in a serious meditation of

[1] *Letters* 1651, 32–4; Gosse, I, 195–6.
[2] *LXXX Sermons*, 493.

God, and to make any Religion the rule of our actions.'[1] There is plenty of intellect and wit in these stanzas from *The Litanie*, but Donne employs them, not in trying to make more real to himself specifically Christian doctrines and mysteries and paradoxes, but in analysing dear-bought experience. He is concerned, not with subtleties of doctrine, but with the infinite subtleties of temptation from which he asks to be delivered, with the innumerable wandering by-ways and mazes that would entice him from the straight and narrow path. The religion which gives such passion and plangency to these stanzas is religion in its most primary and fundamental sense: what Donne asks for is purgation, purification, illumination, and, in Rilke's beautiful phrase, a directing of the heart. We are, I think, even more aware of Donne's complex personality in his religious than in his secular poetry, but the religion of this complex personality is ultimately, for all his learnings and his subtlety, very simple. One might almost say that what he longs for is to exchange the complexity of a personality for the singleness and simplicity of a soul.

> Father of Heaven, and him, by whom
> It, and us for it, and all else, for us
> Thou madest, and govern'st ever, come
> And re-create mee, now growne ruinous:
> My heart is by dejection, clay,
> And by selfe-murder, red.
> From this red earth, O Father, purge away
> All vicious tinctures, that new fashioned
> I may rise up from death, before I'am dead . . .
>
> O Holy Ghost, whose temple I
> Am, but of mudde walls, and condensed dust,
> And being sacrilegiously
> Halfe wasted with youths fires, of pride and lust,
> Must with new stormes be weatherbeat;
> Double in my heart thy flame,
> Which let devout sad teares intend; and let
> (Though this glasse lanthorne, flesh, do suffer maime)
> Fire, Sacrifice, Priest, Altar be the same . . .

[1] *Sir T. M.*, 337; Gosse II, 137.

And whil'st this universall Quire,
That Church in triumph, this in warfare here,
　　Warm'd with one all-partaking fire
Of love, that none be lost, which cost thee deare,
　　　Pray ceaselesly, 'and thou hearken too,
　　　　(Since to be gratious
Our taske is treble, to pray, beare, and doe)
Heare this prayer Lord, O Lord deliver us
From trusting in those prayers, though powr'd out thus.

　　From being anxious, or secure,[1]
Dead clods of sadnesse, or light squibs of mirth,
　　From thinking, that great courts immure
All, or no happinesse, or that this earth
　　　Is only for our prison fram'd,
　　　　Or that thou art covetous
To them whom thou lov'st, or that they are maim'd
From reaching this worlds sweet, who seek thee thus,
With all their might, Good Lord deliver us.

　　From needing danger, to bee good,
From owing thee yesterdaies teares to day,
　　From trusting so much to thy blood,
That in that hope, wee wound our soule away,
　　　From bribing thee with Almes, to excuse
　　　　Some sinne more burdenous,
From light affecting, in religion, newes,
From thinking us all soule, neglecting thus
Our mutuall duties, Lord deliver us . . .

　　Through thy submitting all, to blowes
Thy face, thy clothes to spoile, thy fame to scorne,
　　All waies, which rage, or Justice knowes,
And by which thou could'st shew, that thou wast born,
　　　And through thy gallant humblenesse
　　　　Which thou in death did'st shew,
Dying before thy soule they could expresse,

[1] Over-confident (Latin *securus*, free from care).

Deliver us from death, by dying so,
To this world, ere this world doe bid us goe.

When senses, which thy souldiers are,
Wee arme against thee, and they fight for sinne,
  When want, sent but to tame, doth warre
And worke despaire a breach to enter in,
    When plenty, Gods image, and seale
    Makes us Idolatrous,
And love it, not him, whom it should reveale,
When wee are mov'd to seeme religious
Only to vent wit, Lord deliver us.

In Churches, when the'infirmitie
Of him which speakes, diminishes the Word,
  When Magistrates doe mis-apply
To us, as we judge, lay or ghostly sword,
    When plague, which is thine Angell, raignes,
    Or wars, thy Champions, swaie,
When Heresie, thy second deluge, gaines;
In th'houre of death, the'Eve of last judgement day,
Deliver us from the sinister way.

Heare us, O heare us Lord; to thee
A sinner is more musique, when he prayes,
  Then spheares, or Angels praises bee,
In Panegyrique Allelujaes;
    Heare us, for till thou heare us, Lord,
    We know not what to say.
Thine eare to'our sighes, teares, thoughts gives voice and word.
O Thou who Satan heard'st in Jobs sicke day,
Heare thy self now, for thou in us dost pray . . .

That learning, thine Ambassador,
From thine allegeance wee never tempt,
  That beauty, paradises flower
For physicke made, from poyson be exempt,
    That wit, borne apt high good to doe,
    By dwelling lazily

On Natures nothing, be not nothing too,
That our affections kill us not, nor dye,
Heare us, weake ecchoes, O thou eare, and cry.

These stanzas were probably written sometime in 1608. In 1615, all other schemes and ambitions having failed, Donne finally submitted to the King's wish and took Orders, and preferment followed rapidly. In 1617 his wife died, and during the long period of solitary grief that followed Donne became, as Walton tells us, 'Crucified to the World, and all those vanities, those imaginary pleasures that are daily acted on that restless stage; and they were as perfectly crucified to him'.

It is necessary to insist that the *Divine Poems* alone are a very insufficient basis on which to erect generalizations about the nature of Donne's religious experience and theological position, for of most of them it can be said, either with certainty or with some approach to certainty, that they were written before he took Orders, and that they reflect the self-imposed and deliberately practised meditations and exercises of the layman (or even, in a sense, of the neophyte), and suggest only a little of the full range and depth and complexity of the finally committed preacher of God's Word. Only the three *Hymns*, the three sonnets in the Westmoreland Manuscript, the lines *To Mr. Tilman after he had taken Orders* and *Upon the translation of the Psalmes* by Sir Philip Sidney and his sister, together with the paraphrased *Lamentations of Jeremy*, can be said with any certainty to have been written after his ordination. What George Herbert's Christianity meant to him is sufficiently revealed in *The Temple*, but for anything like a proper understanding of what his Christianity meant to Donne we must turn to his sermons.

In most of the *Divine Poems* written before his ordination Donne is making considerable and often original use of that techinque of religious meditation which had been systematized by St. Ignatius Loyola in his *Spiritual Exercises* (1548).[1] This explains the presence of a strong element of dramatization and even, to some extent, of exaggeration, which should not be regarded as the expression of an habitual attitude or mood; for Donne is often deliberately raising to the highest pitch of drama (sometimes, one might almost be tempted to say, of melodrama) what theology tells him is the reality of his

[1] See Helen Gardner's edition of the *Divine Poems*, 1952 Introd., pp. l ff.

situation, in order, as it were, to convince himself, or re-convince
himself, of that reality, in order to achieve the completest possible
imaginative realization of it. He has to stimulate his awareness of God
by dwelling on the awfulness of God, has to exaggerate the sins of his
youth in order to bring home to himself the need for repentance, has
to underline the urgency for repentance by dwelling on the terrors of
death and the possibility of perishing, as he later expressed it, on the
shore. There is something of the vast and terrible drama of the *Dies
Irae* about it all:

> *Tuba mirum spargens sonum*
> *Per sepulcra regionum*
> *Coget omnes ante thronum* . . .

At the round earths imagin'd corners, blow
Your trumpets, Angells, and arise, arise
From death, you numberlesse infinities
Of soules, and to your scattred bodies goe,
All whom the flood did, and fire shall o'erthrow,
All whom warre, dearth, age, agues, tyrannies,
Despaire, law, chance, hath slaine, and you whose eyes
Shall behold God, and never tast deaths woe.[1]
But let them sleepe, Lord, and mee mourne a space,
For, if above all these, my sinnes abound,
Tis late to aske abundance of thy grace,
When wee are there; here on this lowly ground,
Teach mee how to repent; for that's as good
As if thou'hadst seal'd my pardon, with thy blood.

It is as though, in order to convince himself, or sufficiently convince
himself, of the need for repentance here and now, Donne had first
to fill his imagination with the sound and spectacle of the Last
Judgment, when repentance would be too late:

> *Quid sum miser tunc dicturus.*
> *Quem patronum rogaturus,*
> *Cum vix justus sit securus?*
> *Rex tremendae majestatis*
> *Qui salvandos salvas gratis,*
> *Salva me, fons pietatis.*

---

[1] Who shall be alive on the Day of Judgment: *I Cor.*, xvi. 51.

A Hymne to God the Father

I

Wilt thou forgive that sinne where I begunne,
  Which is my sin, though it were done before?
Wilt thou forgive those sinnes through which I runne,
  And doe them still: though still I doe deplore?
    When thou hast done, thou hast not done,[1]
      For, I have more.

II

Wilt thou forgive that sinne by which I wonne
  Others to sinne? and, made my sinne their doore?
Wilt thou forgive that sinne which I did shunne
  A yeare, or two: but wallowed in, a score?
    When thou hast done, thou hast not done,
      For, I have more.

III

I have a sinne of feare, that when I have spunne
  My last thred, I shall perish on the shore;
Sweare by thy selfe, that at my death thy Sunne
  Shall shine as he[2] shines now, and heretofore;
    And, having done that, Thou hast done,
      I have no more.

This hymn, which Donne composed during a serious illness, which
he had set to music and often sung in St. Paul's, and of which,
according to Walton, he said to a friend that it had restored the
same thoughts of joy that possessed his soul when he composed it,—
this hymn ends on a note of peace and security that is scarcely found
in his earlier religious poetry, where the more usual note is that
of the agonized striving of the Fourteenth of the *Holy Sonnets*:

[1] Donne's pun on his own name, on which the poem turns, is brought out by the
spelling in some of the manuscripts.

[2] I am convinced that the true reading of this and the preceding line is to be found
partly in the MSS ('Sunne', not 'sonne') and partly in *1633* ('he', not 'it'). This makes
the intended pun, which occurs so often in the Sermons, much clearer.

Batter my heart, three person'd God; for, you
As yet but knocke, breathe, shine, and seeke to mend;
That I may rise, and stand, o'erthrow mee,' and bend
Your force, to breake, blowe, burn and make me new.
I, like an usurpt towne, to'another due,
Labour to'admit you, but Oh, to no end,
Reason your viceroy in mee, mee should defend,
But is captiv'd, and proves weake or untrue.

Or (even though probably written after his ordination) that of the
Nineteenth, where, watching himself with a kind of sad humour as
he plays his difficult part, he recognizes the continuity between Jack
Donne and Dr. Donne:

Oh, to vex me, contraryes meete in one:
Inconstancy unnaturally hath begott
A constant habit; that when I would not
I change in vowes, and in devotione.
As humorous is my contritione
As my prophane Love, and as soone forgott:
As ridlingly distemper'd, cold and hott,
As praying, as mute; as infinite, as none.
I durst not view heaven yesterday; and to day
In prayers, and flattering speaches I court God:
To morrow I quake with true feare of his rod.
So my devout fitts come and go away
Like a fantastique Ague: save that here
Those are my best dayes, when I shake with feare.

There is indeed a continuity between Jack Donne and Dr.
Donne, although in recent times it has been rather over- than
under-emphasized, and there has been some tendency to dismiss
as a mere rhetorical flourish Walton's words about that final crucifixion to the world. 'We agree', wrote Mr. Eliot in 1931, 'that it
is one and the same man in both early and later life.'[1] We agree,
perhaps, too easily and too superficially, and we tend to suppose
that both in his earlier and in his later years Donne was more typical,
more conventional, than he really was. Throughout this study I

[1] *A Garland for John Donne*, 9.

have been at pains to insist upon that strong element of other-worldliness which seems to have been his even during his wildest days, and upon the fact that even Jack Donne was more like Hamlet than like one of Fletcher's 'wild gallants'. For although, both in his religious poetry and in his sermons, Donne often refers to the sinfulness and 'irregularity' of his youth, there is in all that we can learn of him no trace of anything that can be regarded as a moral or religious crisis or conversion. What, on the other hand, is most strikingly apparent, from the time of his dismissal from Egerton's service until his ordination, is a continuous deepening, a continuous progress in seriousness, and even in devotional religiousness, co-existing, in a manner that many modern readers may find baffling and even, at times, disconcerting, with an unregenerate wit and worldliness and willingness to flatter the great. In 1607 he sent the seven *La Corona* sonnets to Mrs. Herbert; the sonnet *To E. of D. with six holy Sonnets* suggests that two years later, in 1609, he sent six of them to the Earl of Dorset, who had just succeeded to the title, pretending that his Lordship's own muse had inspired them; and in that same year he certainly wrote at least the first six[1] of his Holy Sonnets, certainly, that is to say (of those that I have quoted), *At the round earths imagin'd corners*, and possibly *Batter my heart* as well. *O, to vex me, contraryes meete in one*, which, together with the sonnet on the death of his wife and *Show me deare Christ, thy spouse*, occurs only in the Westmoreland Manuscript, was almost certainly written after his ordination. In it, as I have said, he seems to recognize with a kind of sad humour the continuity between Jack Donne and Dr. Donne. This does not mean, though, as Mr. Eliot once suggested, that he had merely exchanged a conventional rakishness for a conventional religiousness: it means (and this was his great strength as a preacher) that he was peculiarly able to understand, and to help others to understand, just what St. Paul meant when he described himself as the chief of sinners. Two of the great themes of his sermons are, first, the necessity of recognizing our weakness and wickedness and the depths to which we have fallen, and, secondly, the heights to which, with the help of divine Grace, we may hope to rise. It has happened, though, that the intensely dramatic and imaginative way (often not without some rhetorical

---

[1] The first six of the twelve sonnets contained in the most authoritative manuscript collections and printed, in the same order, in the first edition of his *Poems*, 1633.

exaggeration) in which Donne compels himself and his hearers to recognize the first of these two central and catholic truths has led many modern readers, especially those who have been content merely with selections from his sermons, to neglect, or greatly to underestimate, his insistence on the second, and to dwell too much out of context upon some of his imaginative and rhetorical realizations of that due fear of God which is the beginning of wisdom. Intensely aware of the complexity and paradoxicality both of human nature and of religious truth, Donne has a great fondness for the rhetorical elaboration of antitheses: the result is that many modern readers tend to insist too exclusively upon that antithesis, that half-truth, in the elaboration of which Donne's rhetorical powers have most impressed them. It is thus very easy for a modern reader to misunderstand, or misrepresent, his theological position. Partly because of the richness and complexity of his own experience and the depth of his self-knowledge, and partly, perhaps, because he had himself professed two forms of Christianity, he often expresses a charity towards other Churches, and even, sometimes, towards other faiths, and an unwillingness to circumscribe the possibilities of salvation, which are quite exceptional for his time. This, however, does not mean that he was ever less than whole-hearted in his allegiance to the Church of England, which, for him as for Hooker, was and remained the just *via media* between the 'paintedness' of the Church of Rome and the 'nakedness' of Geneva. Ever since Sir Edmund Gosse's discovery of the Westmoreland Manuscript, which contains it, it has been commonly supposed that the sonnet *Show me deare Christ, thy spouse, so bright and cleare* reveals Donne, now for some years in orders, as still hesitating between the Church of Rome and the various Protestant Churches, and asking to which of them his allegiance is really due. This, as Miss Helen Gardner has recently and convincingly demonstrated, is a complete misapprehension: Donne is here only incidentally concerned with the differences of the visible Christian Churches among themselves; it is rather upon the difference between each and all of them, the triumphant and 'painted' Church of Rome and the Protestant Churches, 'lamenting and mourning', in England no less than in the Empire ('Germany'), the terrible discomfiture their cause had just suffered (29th October, 1620) with the defeat of the Elector Palatine at the Battle of the White Mountain, near

Prague,—it is upon the vast and painful difference between these Churches on earth, whether mourning or rejoicing, and the Spouse of Christ, the promised Bride of the Apocalypse, that he is chiefly insisting.

> Show me deare Christ, thy spouse, so bright and cleare.
> What, is it she, which on the other shore
> Goes richly painted? or which rob'd and tore
> Laments and mournes in Germany and here?
> Sleepes she a thousand, then peepes up one yeare?
> Is she selfe truth and errs? now new, now outwore?
> Doth she, 'and did she, and shall she evermore
> On one, on seaven, or on no hill appeare?
> Dwells she with us, or like adventuring knights
> First travaile we to seeke and then make love?
> Betray kind husband thy spouse to our sights,
> And let myne amorous soule court thy mild Dove,
> Who is most trew, and pleasing to thee, then
> When she'is embrac'd and open to most men.

Once again Donne has magnificently dramatized a situation, and perhaps we may not unfitly end, as we began, with the dramatic element in his genius and in his poetry. His stage had now become a pulpit, but I cannot help thinking of that pulpit as a kind of stage which Donne mounted to enact the part of *Homo* in a singularly impressive morality play. How characteristic is the way in which he dramatized his situation in 1619, when he accompanied his friend the Earl of Doncaster on an embassy to Frederic and Elizabeth of Bohemia. First, he preached a beautiful farewell sermon to the Benchers of Lincoln's Inn, where he had himself been a student years ago. After asking them to remember him during his long absence,

> as I shall do you in the eares of that God, to whom the farthest East, and the farthest West are but·as the right and left ear in one of us,

he proceeded, as was his custom, to 'enlarge this meditation', and spoke of another journey and a longer absence:

That if I never meet you again till we have all passed the gate of death, yet in the gates of heaven, I may meet you all, and there say to my Saviour and your Saviour, that which he said to his Father and our Father, *Of those whom thou hast given me, have I not lost one.*[1]

But he had not yet exhausted the dramatic and symbolic significance of this journey and this parting: something still remained to be said, and he said it in verse:

A Hymme to Christ, at the Authors last going into Germany

In what torne ship soever I embarke,
That ship shall be my embleme of thy Arke;
What sea soever swallow mee, that flood
Shall be to mee an embleme of thy blood;
Though thou with clouds of anger do disguise
Thy face; yet through that maske I know those eyes,
   Which, though they turne away sometimes,
     They never will despise.

I sacrifice this Iland unto thee,
And all whom I lov'd there, and who lov'd mee;
When I have put our seas twixt them and mee,
Put thou thy sea betwixt my sinnes and thee.
As the trees sap doth seeke the root below
In winter, in my winter now I goe,
   Where none but thee, th'Eternall root
     Of true Love I may know.

Nor thou nor thy religion dost controule
The amorousnesse of an harmonious Soule,
But thou would'st have that love thy selfe: As thou
Art jealous, Lord, so I am jealous now,
Thou lov'st not, till from loving more, thou free
My soule: Who ever gives, takes libertie:
   O, if thou car'st not whom I love
     Alas, thou lov'st not mee.

[1] *XXVI Sermons,* 1660, 280.

> Seale then this bill of my Divorce to All,
> On whom those fainter beames of love did fall;
> Marry those loves, which in youth scattered bee
> On Fame, Wit, Hopes (false mistresses) to thee.
> Churches are best for Prayer, that have least light:
> To see God only, I goe out of sight:
> And to scape stormy dayes, I chuse
> An Everlasting night.

How dramatic, too, is what was almost certainly the last poem he ever wrote,[1] a poem in which his whole life seems to pass before us: the lover of music and of poetry, who had written songs and sonnets both in the days of what he called his 'Idolatry' and also ('Apollo's first, at last, the true Gods Priest', as Carew said at the close of his *Elegie*) in his 'penitential years'; the lover of curious analogies and resemblances; the traveller, who more than most men had been affected by the implications of the new discoveries of his age, and had found a world of poetry in maps; above all, perhaps, the preacher whose sermon had so often been directed as much to himself as to his congregation: for in the last line of this poem, 'Therfore that he may raise the Lord throws down', he is dwelling for the last of many times on the affinity between his own election and that of the patron saint of his cathedral. Preaching in 1625, on the Sunday after the Conversion of St. Paul, and taking as his text (*Acts*, ix, 4) 'And he fell to the earth, and heard a voice saying unto him, Saul, Saul, why persecutest thou me?', he had elaborated upon a saying of his favourite St. Augustine and had spoken of 'a medicinall falling, a falling under Gods hand, but such a falling under his hand, as he takes not off his hand from him that is falne, but throwes him downe therefore that he may raise him'.[2]

Hymne to God my God, in my sicknesse

> Since I am comming to that Holy roome,
> Where, with thy Quire of Saints for evermore,
> I shall be made thy Musique; As I come
> I tune the Instrument here at the dore,
> And what I must doe then, thinke now before.

[1] For arguments for and against Walton's statement that Donne wrote this poem on his death-bed, see my review of Helen Gardner's edition of the *Divine Poems* in *The Review of English Studies*, January 1954, p.83.

[2] *LXXX Sermons*, no. 46; *Sermons*, ed. Potter and Simpson, VI, 212.

Whilst my Physitians by their love are growne
  Cosmographers, and I their Mapp, who lie
Flat on this bed, that by them may be showne
    That this is my South-west discoverie[1]
    Per fretum febris, by these streights to die,

I joy, that in these straits, I see my West;
  For, though theire currants yeeld returne to none,
What shall my West hurt me? As West and East
    In all flatt Maps (and I am one) are one,
    So death doth touch the Resurrection.

Is the Pacifique Sea my home? Or are
  The Easterne riches? Is *Jerusalem*?[2]
Anyan,[3] and *Magellan*, and *Gibraltare*,
    All streights, and none but streights, are wayes to them,
    Whether where *Japhet* dwelt, or *Cham*, or *Sem*.[4]

We thinke that *Paradise* and *Calvarie*,
  Christs Crosse, and *Adams* tree, stood in one place;[5]
Looke Lord, and finde both *Adams* met in me;
    As the first *Adams* sweat surrounds my face,
    May the last *Adams* blood my soule embrace.

[1] The *North-west* 'discovery' (i.e., voyage of discovery), the long and fruitless attempt to find a North-west Passage from England to China ('Cathay'), was famous enough. Donne, though, must voyage *south-west*: south, because there, like his fever, it is hot; west, because he, like the sun, is setting.

[2] Donne alludes to various opinions about the site of the Garden of Eden, the Earthly here considered as a type, or symbol, of the Heavenly Paradise. Formerly it was supposed to have been situated either in the Pacific Ocean or in the Far East, but in Donne's time it was generally agreed to have been situated in Mesopotamia, in the same region as Jerusalem.

[3] The Behring Strait.

[4] This *seems* to mean: In order to reach by sea either the Pacific or the Far East or Jerusalem from either Europe (the inheritance of Japhet) or from Africa (the inheritance of Ham) or from Asia (the inheritance of Shem), one must pass through straits. This, though, is both geographically inaccurate (the Pacific and the Far East could be reached from Europe by sailing round the Cape of Good Hope) and grammatically difficult ('Whether where' must mean 'Whether from where'). It looks as though Donne's memory had been impaired by his fever.

[5] Not 'on the same spot', but 'in the same part of the world': we *know* that Christ was crucified in Palestine, and we *think* that Paradise (the Garden of Eden) was in Mesopotamia.

So, in his purple wrapp'd receive mee Lord,
By these his thornes give me his other Crowne;
And as to others soules I preach'd thy word,
Be this my Text, my Sermon to mine owne,
Therfore that he may raise the Lord throws down.

I end, then, as I began, with the dramatic element in Donne's life and genius and poetry, for it seems to me that on our response to that, on our attitude to that, our attitude to Donne and to his poetry in general must finally depend. Professor Crofts has spoken of the 'ghastly charade' of his last hours—how he preached his own funeral sermon, had his portrait painted in his shroud and kept it beside his death-bed as an object of meditation. For my own part, I cannot but regard this as a culmination no less fitting and satisfying than that great scene in which Shakespeare's Richard sends for a mirror and, after contemplating it and moralizing upon it for a moment, dashes it to the ground and asks his cousin Bolingbroke to mark 'How soone my Sorrow hath destroy'd my Face'.

To most schoolboys, I suppose, for whom (as for many nine-teenth-century German critics) the moral of Shakespeare's histories and tragedies is that we should admire successful strong men and despise unsuccessful weak ones, the behaviour of Richard, that 'weak king' (so different from Henry V, 'Shakespeare's only hero'), during the deposition scene and elsewhere, is but a silly and sentimental charade. The fact is, though, that for Shakespeare and for those who can follow him the distinction between 'strong men' and 'weak men' has been transcended, that what remains is 'unaccom-modated man', and that the moral or lesson of the deposition scene, though conveyed with incomparably greater poetic and dramatic power, is essentially similar to that of those old moralities which, as Granville-Barker, in some penetrating remarks on the hovel-scene in *King Lear*, memorably reminded us, were 'the infancy of his art'. If we try to realize Donne's actions during his last days and hours imaginatively, in their proper context and against their proper background, we shall see them less and less as a charade and more and more as something in the tradition of the 'sacred representation', the tradition of *Everyman*.

TABLE OF DONNE'S POEMS QUOTED OR DISCUSSED

(The *Elegies*, *Satires*, and *Holy Sonnets* are here listed in their numerical order; the other poems, within their respective groups, in the order in which they are mentioned in the text.)

EPIGRAMS

ELEGIES

SATIRES

LETTERS TO SEVERALL PERSONAGES

SONGS AND SONNETS

(Classification of them, 178-9)

EPITHALAMIONS, OR MARRIAGE SONGS

THE FIRST AND SECOND ANNIVERSARIES

INDEX